Sustainability Education

T0353633

ALSO AVAILABLE FROM BLOOMSBURY

Perspectives on Educational Practice Around the World, edited by Sue Hammond and
Margaret Sangster

Challenging Perceptions in Primary Education, edited by Margaret Sangster

Mastering Primary Geography, Anthony Barlow and Sarah Whitehouse

Developing Teacher Expertise, edited by Margaret Sangster

Bloomsbury Curriculum Basics: Teaching Primary Geography, Stephen Scoffham and Paula Owens

Leadership for Sustainability in Higher Education, edited by Janet Haddock-Fraser, Peter Rands
and Stephen Scoffham

Educational Leadership for a More Sustainable World, Mike Bottery

Praise for *Sustainability Education*

"*Sustainability Education* is an engaging and compelling read which deftly weaves together rich understandings from research with suggestions and ideas for practice."

Elizabeth Rushton, Lecturer in Geography Education, King's College London, UK

"This timely guide is posed to reorient thinking on sustainability education. Most importantly, young children are invited to take an active part in this journey. Authors throughout the guide display great care in their pedagogical approaches. The message of harmony, coexistence, peace, love, balance and justice is clear."

Charles Chikunda, National Program Officer – Education for Sustainable Development, UNESCO Office in Harare, Zimbabwe

"The educational system we have today was designed to suit the needs of the 19th and 20th century. Now that system is fast becoming out of date! *Sustainability Education* is a timely book outlining an education fit for the 21st century. The authors and contributors have presented a practical way forward to transform teaching in schools from job centred education to life centred and nature centred education. Every teacher concerned with the wellbeing of people and our precious planet Earth should use this publication as a handbook for regenerative learning."

Satish Kumar, Founder, Schumacher College and Editor Emeritus, Resurgence & Ecologist, UK

"The guide is an essential reading for those who engage in teaching and learning about the earth. The book is a capsule on sustainability on understanding the topic, its place in curriculum and teaching pedagogies. It discusses the current needs in transforming education to address the demands of the planet."

Radhika Iyengar, Director of Education, Center for Sustainable Development, The Earth Institute, Columbia University, USA

"The key to tackling any challenge is first to understand it, and perhaps the greatest challenge we face is climate change. So how we approach sustainability education for a younger generation is absolutely vital. This book goes beyond the important discussion of wider issues, to focus on the role of education in sustainability and navigating its complexities. It also sets out practical approaches for educators who are on the front line of helping future generations understand the challenges of the planet they are inheriting. It is an important contribution to an increasingly vital area in education."

The Right Honourable Justine Greening, Former Secretary of State for Education, England

"*Sustainability Education* is a timely and vital manual containing a wide variety of ideas to encourage, support and guide practitioners of all age groups on weaving sustainability into their teaching."

Lucy Neuberger, Classroom Teacher, International Preparatory School, Portugal

"A superb discussion of the notion of sustainability and the importance of including sustainability education in the primary curriculum, while illustrating how this can be achieved. A pleasure to read and learn from."

Margaret Mackintosh, Former Senior Lecturer on the Primary BEd. University of Plymouth, UK

"This pivotal book guides us to see sustainability education through a creative, confident and research-rich narrative. By exploring pedagogy, classroom ideas and key enquiry questions, this innovative book challenges and supports all educators towards practical, explanatory critical thinking, enabling action and understanding, vital for the futures for all learners."

Helen Martin, Headteacher, Lavington Park Federation – Graffham CE Infant and Duncton CE Junior Schools, West Sussex, UK

Sustainability Education

A Classroom Guide

**Stephen Scoffham and
Steve Rawlinson**

BLOOMSBURY ACADEMIC
LONDON • NEW YORK • OXFORD • NEW DELHI • SYDNEY

BLOOMSBURY ACADEMIC
Bloomsbury Publishing Plc
50 Bedford Square, London, WC1B 3DP, UK
1385 Broadway, New York, NY 10018, USA
29 Earlsfort Terrace, Dublin 2, Ireland

BLOOMSBURY, BLOOMSBURY ACADEMIC and the Diana logo are trademarks of
Bloomsbury Publishing Plc

First published in Great Britain 2022

Copyright © Stephen Scoffham and Steve Rawlinson and contributors, 2022

Stephen Scoffham and Steve Rawlinson and contributors have asserted their right under the
Copyright, Designs and Patents Act, 1988, to be identified as Author of this work.

For legal purposes the Acknowledgements on pp. xv–xvi constitute an extension of this
copyright page.

Cover design: Charlotte James
Cover image © Vince Cavataio/Getty Images

All rights reserved. No part of this publication may be reproduced or transmitted in
any form or by any means, electronic or mechanical, including photocopying,
recording, or any information storage or retrieval system, without prior
permission in writing from the publishers.

Bloomsbury Publishing Plc does not have any control over, or responsibility for,
any third-party websites referred to or in this book. All internet addresses given in
this book were correct at the time of going to press. The author and publisher
regret any inconvenience caused if addresses have changed or sites have
ceased to exist, but can accept no responsibility for any such changes.

A catalogue record for this book is available from the British Library.

A catalog record for this book is available from the Library of Congress.

ISBN: HB: 978-1-3502-6208-9
        PB: 978-1-3502-6207-2
        ePDF: 978-1-3502-6209-6
        eBook: 978-1-3502-6210-2

Typeset by RefineCatch Limited, Bungay, Suffolk

To find out more about our authors and books visit www.bloomsbury.com
and sign up for our newsletters.

Contents

Part IV Implementation

Figures

About the Authors

Sustainability Education: A Classroom Guide is informed by many years of working in education especially with young children and trainee teachers and draws on extensive reading and research. Both the principal authors have a long-term interest and commitment to sustainability education and practical experience of how to bring it about. Stephen Scoffham worked for many years for a charity specializing in environmental education. Steve Rawlinson, as editor of the leading journal *Primary Geography*, has done much to focus attention on innovative ways to teach children about environmental issues. We have both engaged with Higher Education over prolonged periods, served as Presidents of the UK Geographical Association, and shared our hopes and enthusiasm with an entire generation of future educators. We decided to collaborate on this book because we believe it is vital to explore how to respond to the global environmental crisis and to find ways to empower students, teachers and children for their future lives (Figure 0.1).

Steve Rawlinson

I attended a small village primary school in Buckinghamshire, UK, where the daily journey to school became an adventure, and nature rambles were a regular event. Receiving an ecology book as a prize was another of the foundations that fuelled my interest in the world about me. I took for granted the countryside which I spent much of my time exploring on bike and on foot, but which now I appreciate with greater understanding and humility.

A physical geographer by training, my teaching experience encompassed the primary, secondary and university sectors culminating in twenty-one years as a teacher educator. My life-long passion for being and working outdoors ensured those entering the profession were fully equipped with the skills and knowledge to safely take children outside to explore, understand and care for their world. The innumerable benefits of fieldwork have guided my approach to environmental education; the focusing of inquisitive young minds in the real world, alongside their enthusiasm and optimism, will largely determine the route to sustainability they take. I am enjoying sharing the adventure with them.

Stephen Scoffham

My interest in the environment is difficult to pin down but was undoubtedly nurtured by opportunities to interact with my surroundings in my youth. As a child brought up in the leafy suburbs of the English Home Counties in the second half of the twentieth century, I was lucky enough to have good access to the countryside and the freedom to explore it unaccompanied. Later I travelled outside Europe, obtained a degree in philosophy, trained as a primary school teacher, and began to engage with the literature around environmental issues and global inequalities.

These different influences led to my interest in using the urban environment as a teaching resource, resulted in my first book (Scoffham 1980) and led to my future career as an atlas consultant and educational author. However, it was only when I became involved in Higher Education that I began to understand that the way we relate to ourselves is every bit as much a part of sustainability as how we connect to the world around us. This is a journey that I am still pursuing.

Figure 0.1 Steve Rawlinson (left) and Stephen Scoffham (right). *Photo: Tan Yoke Eng.*

Contributors

Ben Ballin is a Primary Geography Consultant and an experienced teacher, writer and trainer on global sustainability issues. He is a fellow of the National Association for Environmental Education (UK), a member of the editorial board for the journal, *Primary Geography*, and author of the TTS *Upper Primary Teaching Atlas* (2019).

Patty Born is Assistant Professor of Environmental and STEM Education at Hamline University, St Paul, Minnesota, USA where she oversees an MA programme in environmental education that concentrates on nature-based early learning. Prior to this, she worked with young children in both traditional classroom and non-formal learning settings. Patty has written four books for educators, on topics ranging from STEM in the outdoors to child–animal relations. Her research interests include climate justice and multispecies relations.

Richard Hatwood is a Primary School Headteacher from North Wales, UK prior to which he was Inclusion Officer of a Local Authority. Richard has long held an interest in sustainability education as well as teaching, learning and leading primary geography. When not teaching, Richard is an avid traveller and presents continued professional development for teachers as well as being a member of the Geographical Association *Primary Geography* Editorial Board.

Elena Lengthorn is Senior Lecturer in Teacher Education at the University of Worcester, UK, teaching both primary and secondary teacher trainees. As a former Eco-Schools Co-ordinator, Elena's PhD research focuses on ESD, from embedding the UN Sustainable Development Goals in postgraduate secondary programmes, to the delivery of a flood education programme and the creation of activities on 'Education in Climate Emergency'. She is passionate about empowering educators, their pupils and wider society, to collectively face the enormous sustainability challenges of our time.

Paula Owens is an Independent Education Consultant and Senior Visiting Research Fellow at Canterbury Christ Church University, UK. With years of experience as a primary teacher and deputy head, Paula now creates teaching resources, researches children's maps as part of the *Meaningful Maps* team, and works with, and in, schools developing primary geography and sustainability awareness. Her recent publications focus on map skills (2020), subject leadership (2019) and geography and sustainability (2017).

Steve Rawlinson is a Primary Geography Specialist who, having worked in a variety of educational settings, joined the Initial Teacher Education team at Northumbria University, UK. He has a special interest in fieldwork, sustainability and environmental education which he is always willing to share. In 2015 he was elected President of the Geographical Association. He is currently a Fellow of the Royal Geographical Society, Chair of the *Primary Geography* Editorial Board and Co-convenor of the annual Charney Manor Primary Geography Research Conference.

Ingrid Schudel moved into education having completed an undergraduate science degree. She has a Masters and PhD from Rhodes University, [insert country] where she is now Associate Professor. Ingrid teaches on undergraduate and in-service teacher education courses, focusing on transformative environmental learning, curriculum and education technology. She has also supervised masters and doctoral studies in environmental learning. Her research context is science and social science education, and ranges from early primary to Higher Education.

Stephen Scoffham is Teacher Educator and Visiting Reader in Sustainability and Education at Canterbury Christ Church University, UK. He has written widely on primary school geography, is a school atlas author/consultant and was President of the Geographical Association (2018–19). Stephen's research interests focus on the educational dimensions of sustainability, creativity, cartography and international understanding. His two most recent books are *Leadership for Sustainability in Higher Education* (2018) and *Prioritizing Sustainability Education* (2020).

Hilde Tørnby is Associate Professor at Oslo Metropolitan University, Norway. She has extensive experience of teaching at all levels in Norwegian schools as well as teaching undergraduate and graduate students. Her fields of research are children's and young adult literature, literature didactics, critical thinking, practical-aesthetic methodology, and aesthetics and art within educational contexts. Her recent publications are *Picturebooks in the Classroom* (2019) and *Visual Literacy* (2020). She is also a painter and has exhibited her art nationally and internationally.

Sharon Witt and **Helen Clarke** are Independent Scholars who have both worked as teachers within primary schools and as academic tutors within Initial Teacher Education. Their work engages with playful, experiential approaches to sustainability and place responsive learning. They are currently exploring innovative practices that consider the potential of a relational approach to natural encounters through signature 'pedagogies of attention'. Their research interests include curriculum making, teacher professional development, science, geography and sustainability education. You can follow their work @Attention2place.

Yocheved Yorkovsky is Lecturer at Gordon College of Education, Haifa, Israel. She is a graduate of the Faculty of Chemistry and holds a postdoctoral degree in Medical Science from the Technion Institute of Technology in Israel. She was formerly head of the science department at Gordon and presently chair of the Green Campus Council and chair of the Health Committee. She is involved in promoting education for sustainability in the college and in the community.

Natasha Ziebell is Senior Lecturer and Coordinator of the Master of Teaching Primary programme at the University of Melbourne, Australia. She has designed and implemented initial teacher education and professional learning programmes for teachers. Her research focuses on curricular alignment and authorship, with a particular focus on the intended, enacted and assessed curriculum. Natasha began her career as a teacher in early childhood settings and primary schools.

Acknowledgments

This book has long roots which stretch back deep into my career. At times, as I was writing, I found I was rehearsing ideas which I had expressed in different ways some thirty or so years ago. Mostly, though, I was trying to understand the scale and complexity of current environmental problems, what they mean for education, and why key indicators such as carbon dioxide levels, resource consumption, biodiversity loss and global inequality continue to move in the wrong direction despite all the efforts to the contrary.

Many people have helped sharpen my thinking and shared ideas with me along this journey. I am deeply indebted to the sustainability team and close colleagues at Canterbury Christ Church University for numerous stimulating, often impromptu, conversations about the issues of the day. These have been a joy and inspiration. The UK primary geography education research community has been another source of strength, encouragement and insight without which this book would never have been written. Belonging to these and other professional communities has been crucial to its development.

While it would be invidious to single out particular individuals, I would like to offer special thanks to Alan Bainbridge, Jonathan Barnes, Nicola Kemp, Adriana Consorte-McCrea, Paula Owens, Alan Pagden, Peter Rands, Peter Vujakovic and Terry Whyte, all of whom I have worked with on research articles or aspects of curriculum development. Margaret Roberts offered invaluable help with networking and international links; Stan Ginn brought fresh perspectives to early drafts of the script; Margaret Mackintosh was unstinting in her detailed comments on the final text. Many other people responded with great generosity to requests for help and information. John Hills, especially, was endlessly patient and skilful in devising the illustrations and diagrams which appear in the following pages. Meanwhile, Alison Baker at Bloomsbury Academic nurtured the book at every stage of its development with wisdom, good humour and careful judgement.

Writing a book can be a gruelling process. I am indebted to my wife, Tan Yoke Eng, for her tolerance, support and critical engagement, and for bringing a business perspective to many of the key arguments as the chapters took shape. The children and students with whom I have worked also influenced the text in profound but often imperceptible ways. But, of course, the colleagues and friends from around the UK and other parts of the world who have shared teaching ideas have been crucial in bringing this book to life.

Stephen Scoffham
Email contact address: stephen.scoffham51@gmail.com

Being asked to contribute to this book was an incredible honour and is something I will always treasure as a kind of pinnacle in my academic career. I could not have contemplated accepting Stephen's invitation were it not for a number of important influences on my thinking and in my life. First, without the input of all the students and children I have taught, I would have had very little to contribute – over many years your enthusiasm, interest and challenging questions encouraged me to explore and understand what sustainability means from *your* perspective.

I must thank all my colleagues in education for sharing their ideas, making me think about my own understandings and for showing me what is possible. I am totally indebted to my geography and *Wildthink* 'buddies' – Helen Clarke, Mel Norman, Paula Owens, Sharon Witt and Tessa Willy – who, through their work and many late-night conversations, long walks and (more recently) Zoom meetings, have opened my eyes to so many new and intriguing aspects of 'being' in our world. I would have never have even considered writing this book without their gentle introductions to different ways of thinking and knowledgeable inputs to my continuing education – a process I am so pleased continues.

My family deserve special thanks. You have put up with holidays that inevitably turned into field trips and with my numerous disappearances into the study or the wild outdoors with the muttered excuse that I needed 'to think'. Your patience and support have been steadfast and invaluable. Nothing would have been written without you being there making our home.

And lastly, I want to thank my wonderful parents, for all their love and encouragement and teaching me to always 'strive to be the best you can be'. They would have been so proud to see this – the Rawlinson family name on the cover of a book.

Steve Rawlinson
Email contact addresses: stevergeography@gmail.com

Dedication

This book is dedicated to the community which has developed around the annual UK Charney Manor Primary Geography Research Conferences. The friendship that has blossomed between us during the writing process, which has been so fruitful, enjoyable and affirmative, is one of the many happy outcomes of this venture. We intend to use any royalties we receive to support the continuation of that unique conference in the years to come.

Introduction

Sustainability is a modern idea. Although the concept of living within ecological limits can be traced back several millennia at least, the terms 'sustainable' and 'sustainability' only date from the second half of the twentieth century. The need to coin these words arose from the realization that growth and economic progress were damaging the global environment and that the Earth was an enclosed system with finite resources. As the world recovered and changed after the Second World War, so the relationship between people and the planet began to alter. The extraordinary increase in human numbers fuelled ever greater demand for goods and resources, especially fossil fuels. At the same time, the atom bomb, detonated in anger in 1945, made it apparent that for the first time in history humanity had the power to dramatically alter the balance of life on Earth with potentially devastating consequences. Air travel and subsequent space probes further confirmed the enormous power of science and technology. Such godlike abilities heralded an era of opportunities, but also new responsibilities and anxieties.

The early notions of sustainability tended to gloss over these complexities. In essence, sustainability can be summed up as 'living within one's means'. Although this definition sounds delightfully simple and easy to grasp, it conceals the fact that sustainability involves a moral dimension. Individual needs overlap and people live in communities which require them to relate to each other and their environment. Should there be any limits to personal consumption and greed or can those who have the power simply appropriate resources (whether plentiful or scarce) for their own benefit? Questions of intergenerational equity and the extent to which nature should be regarded as having a value in its own right also lie hidden beneath the surface of sustainability thinking. Caring about nature in all its diversity is also fundamental. Those who don't care about the environment, or who profess to have no interest in the future of the planet and its inhabitants, can sideline the whole debate.

The fact that sustainability incorporates a sense of moral responsibility plays out in different ways. Those who advocate sustainability sometimes see the world in absolute terms and, as a result, tend to become overenthusiastic about environmental issues and their own vision of the future. There is only a thin line between enthusiasm and proselytizing, and environmentalists are often accused of preaching and seeking to impose their views on others. This has the unfortunate effect of compartmentalizing sustainability as a minority interest or as something which appeals to extremists – a point of view which is exacerbated by environmental campaigns which quite often end up involving some form of confrontational action.

Political debate and strong passions are a necessary part of any democratic society. However, it is important – indeed vital – that sustainability should not be seen purely in party political terms as this risks polarization and undermines an endeavour which requires a common commitment. One particularly worrying development concerns the rise of the post-truth culture in modern politics which seeks to cherry-pick and distort evidence to promote a particular ideology. The facts about the global environmental crisis are now so well established as to be beyond all reasonable doubt. It follows that those who persist in seeking to undermine the credibility of the data are either simply malicious or retreating into a make-believe world which is bound to implode sooner or later.

One of the other points to note is that the environmental crisis has arisen largely due to the pressures that have been put on the planet since the Industrial Revolution. Economic development has brought enormous benefits but has come at a cost. With the benefit of hindsight, we now know that the demand for resources and the pollution that results from burning fossil fuels have destabilized global systems and are seriously undermining biodiversity (WWF 2020). Westernized countries are largely responsible for this predicament and have a particular duty to address it. Unless meaningful action is taken now, it is increasingly clear that the well-being of future generations will be seriously compromised. Finding new ways to encapsulate what it means to 'live well' (not just superficially but in the deepest sense of the word) lies hidden at the heart of the apparently simple idea of sustainability and it can be approached from many different directions, as Jonathan Porritt (2013) outlines.

This book considers this dilemma from an educational perspective. It explores the complexities and contradictions of sustainability education, arguing that it involves much more than simply learning about the world around us. How we think about ourselves and the narratives which underpin our mindset are every bit as important. We are very much aware of the scale and complexity of the challenges that lie ahead, but rather than being daunted we focus on ways to move forward. There is a fine line between enlarging children's understanding of the issues and overwhelming them with the facts, but as both teachers and educators we appreciate the importance of motivation in learning. In line with the Earth Charter (2000) we aim to present sustainability education in a spirit of hope and seek to promote the 'joyful celebration of life'.

Sustainability Education: A Classroom Guide is predicated on the journey that both the principal and contributing authors have taken in their careers in education and the insights they have gleaned from their experience. We recognize that it is culturally and geographically situated. Most of the references come from publications produced in the UK or USA, and they present arguments based on Western perspectives and Western ways of thinking. However, as well as inviting contributions from the UK, we have commissioned chapters from friends and colleagues in Australia, Israel, Norway, South Africa and the United States. In addition, we hope the book will stimulate debate from other parts of the world about how sustainability education is put into practice and we welcome contributions of practical activities for inclusion in the companion website. The conviction that education matters and that it can make a significant contribution to sustainability thinking and the shift towards more ecological ways of living unites us all.

Using this book

Teachers and students in training along with all those who engage with the education of children from school governors to policymakers will find plenty of practical suggestions in the following pages. Opportunities for activities both within and beyond the classroom are highlighted throughout, indicating how pupils can engage both critically and creatively with different sustainability topics. All of these are referenced both to key concepts and to the United Nations Sustainable Development Goals. Meanwhile, the in-text questions invite readers to reflect on a wide range of philosophical and pedagogical issues. In this way theoretical understanding about sustainability is combined with practical guidance on how to communicate it to pupils.

Exploring Sustainability: A Classroom Guide is divided into four parts:

Part One explores the notion of sustainability and some of the issues that surround it;
Part Two considers the purpose of education and the place of sustainability education within the curriculum;
Part Three focuses on teaching ideas and relevant background knowledge;
Part Four provides guidance on implementing sustainability education.

At the end of the book there is a glossary with succinct explanations of some of the main concepts and ideas that relate to sustainability and sustainability education. The companion website provides details of supporting resources and suggestions for further reading. The site includes images as well as text and is updated on a regular basis. The overall aim is to explore the current ecological crisis and the beliefs and narratives that underpin contemporary society with respect to children's education. We would like to stress it is not our intention to offer a fully worked curriculum for sustainability education. Rather we offer a range of structured activities and supporting rationale which indicate how sustainability might be introduced into existing programmes and frameworks (Figure 0.2).

We also recognize that education happens in both formal and informal settings. We concentrate especially on formal settings as the vast majority of children attend schools which are funded and directed by central governments. Teachers who work in these contexts have to negotiate multiple constraints, and finding ways to integrate sustainability within current practices is a challenge which this book seeks to address directly. But we are also alive to innovations and experimentation which may occur in informal settings and private schools. Learning is an unruly process which cannot be restricted to specific institutional contexts.

Writing a book on sustainability education inevitably raises questions about terminology. We have used the term 'primary education' to refer to the education of children especially those aged 5–11. However, the activities that we present cover a wider age span and are a suitable for ages 3–14. Not only will this help to cater for pupils of different abilities, it will also make it easier to plan for continuity and progression.

Acronyms are another issue. The terms 'environmental education' (EE), 'education for sustainability' (EfS), 'education for sustainable development' (ESD) and 'environment and sustainability education'

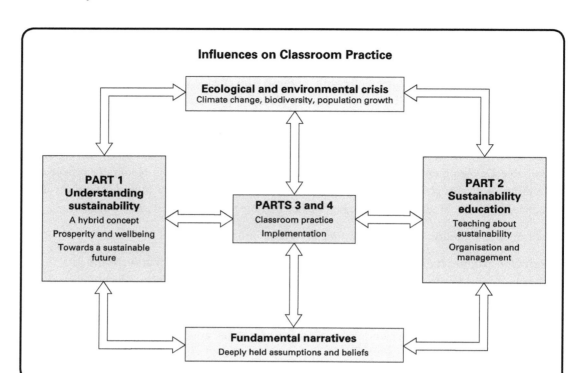

Figure 0.2 Sustainability education synthesizes many different influences and perspectives.

(ESE) will be familiar to some readers. What unites these terms is that they all refer to educational practices which seek to develop children's understanding of sustainability issues. In this book we use 'sustainability education' as an overarching term which embraces these other headings. However, just as there are worries that sustainability is a word that has complex meanings and is open to misinterpretation, so 'sustainability education' is an imperfect compromise and acts as a holding title which simply serves the needs of the moment.

References

Earth Charter (2001) available at https://earthcharter.org/library/the-earth-charter-text/.

Porritt, J. (2013) *The World We Made*, London: Phaidon.

Scoffham, S. (1980) *Using the School Surroundings*, London: Ward Lock Educational.

WWF (2020) *Living Planet Report 2020 – Bending the Curve of Biodiversity Loss*, Almond, R. E. A., Grooten, M., and Petersen, T. (eds), Gland, Switzerland: WWF, available at https://c402277.ssl.cf1.rackcdn.com/publications/1371/files/original/ENGLISH-FULL.pdf?1599693362.

Part I

Exploring Sustainability

Sustainability is an evolving concept with multiple interpretations. One of the implications is that it can be hijacked to serve established interests or simplified to the point where it becomes completely diffused. Understanding how the idea of sustainability has developed helps to uncover its deeper meaning and potential. Social welfare, global equity and economic well-being are now all seen as linked to sustainability. Recognizing and making connections is also fundamental to understanding its complexity.

This section looks at sustainability from various angles. It explores how natural systems interact, it reflects on how people relate to their surroundings, and it considers how we are linked to the past in envisioning and building the future. Searching for a path towards a more sustainable living involves reappraising current practices and forging new stories about ourselves and our place in the world. This is an endeavour which has special relevance for young people who are disproportionately affected by global sustainability challenges and have their lives stretching out before them.

1

Sustainability: A Hybrid Concept

Summary

Sustainability is a complex idea that has developed over the last fifty years. It can be traced back to seminal texts from the 1960s and 70s and was boosted by the Apollo space programme which drew attention to a global perspective. This chapter considers different definitions of sustainability, introduces the notion of planetary boundaries, and reflects on the relationship between people and nature. It concludes by considering how thought patterns from ancient Greece and China still influence ideas today.

The early exploration of space and the race to land a person on the surface of the Moon was one of the most dramatic scientific and technical achievements of the second half of the twentieth century. It culminated in 1969 with the successful mission by the Apollo 11 spacecraft which was broadcast live on television to rapt audiences around the world. The images of the Earth which the early astronauts sent back at that time captured the public imagination. Two photographs stand out in particular. 'Earthrise' taken by Bill Anders showed the Earth, which seems so huge to us, appearing in the far distance over the lunar horizon as no more than a tiny ball. A few years later, the image of the Earth taken by the crew of the Apollo 17 spacecraft proved equally compelling. Known as the 'Blue Marble', it showed the Earth as a delicate blue and white globe floating apparently magically in the vast expanse and deep darkness of space (Figure 1.1).

What made both these photographs so powerful was the way that they captured the extraordinary fragility, isolation and incontestable beauty of the planet that we inhabit. Among the most widely distributed images in the history of photography, they were adopted as a symbol by the environmental movement and did much to support the growth of global consciousness. For the first time ever, people were able to see the world from the distance of space. This offered an external perspective on human affairs and served as a stark reminder that the Earth is humanity's only home. 'We came all this way to explore the Moon, and the most important thing is that we discovered the Earth,' commented astronaut Bill Anders. Meanwhile, Soviet cosmonaut Alexei Leonov declared, 'The Earth was small, light blue and so touchingly alone, our home that must be defended like a holy relic.'

The idea that 'by going to the moon we discovered the Earth' hints at one of the key features of sustainability thinking. Journeys of discovery and exploration often involve a process of

Figure 1.1 This photograph of the Earth from the Moon is one of a number of images which helped to kickstart the global environmental movement. *Photo: NASA Images at the Internet. Archive, Wikimedia Commons.*

self-exploration. While this is easier to understand on an individual level, this relationship also permeates larger groups, and indeed entire societies and cultures. The lunar astronauts certainly appear to have found their experiences extraordinarily powerful. The comments that they made express a deep sense of awe, humility and reverence. 'Seeing this has to change a man,' announced James B. Irwin. '[The Earth] looked so fragile, so delicate, that if you touched it with a finger it would crumble and fall apart.' Such thoughts are not restricted to astronauts. People of all ages have moments when they suddenly become aware of the immensity of time or the vastness of space. These offer an interesting way for teachers to introduce children to some of the key ideas in sustainability education.

Can you think of any experiences in your life which have evoked a sense of awe and wonder, albeit on a small scale? Why were they so powerful?

Growing environmental awareness

The image of the Earth travelling silently and effortlessly through space spawned a powerful metaphor. Environmentalists responded to the spirit of the times by talking about the Earth as a 'spaceship'. While this metaphor captured the sense of wholeness and isolation which was represented in the lunar photographs, it also spawned a misleading assumption. It implied that the Earth was like a machine which functioned mechanically and could be controlled using an operating manual (if only one could be discovered). The idea of the spaceship also positioned people as outsiders watching terrestrial affairs from afar, just as the astronauts themselves had done, rather than as participants in the community of life. As we shall see later, ecological thinking takes a different stance. It represents the Earth is a dynamic, self-organizing system rather than a static entity and it stresses that people are part of nature and utterly dependent upon it.

The growth in global consciousness which arose from the Moon landings lent support to the environment movement. This had been gathering momentum for some time but was given a significant boost by the publication of Rachel Carson's groundbreaking book, *Silent Spring* (1962). Carson highlighted the potentially harmful effects of pesticides, including DDT, which were being sprayed on the land in vast quantities at that time in an attempt to increase crop yields by controlling insect populations. Not only did she alert readers to the inherent risks to wildlife, she also set out a wider argument about the proper relationship between people and nature and the interconnectedness of all living things. A few years later, the biologist Paul Ehrlich turned his attention to human affairs and the possible consequences and dangers of population growth in *The Population Bomb* (1968). Meanwhile, Donella Meadows and her colleagues at the Club of Rome focused their attention on economic issues and the risk of exhausting natural resources in their aptly named book, *The Limits to Growth* (1972). All three texts were criticized as alarmist at the time, but they represented new ways of thinking based on fundamental principles which attracted considerable interest and which have proved remarkably prescient. Indeed, as the impact of climate change and the devastating loss of biodiversity have become ever more apparent, they have taken on renewed significance.

In parallel with these developments a radical new theory about life on Earth was being developed by the scientist James Lovelock. Drawing on concepts such as self-organization, emergent properties and chaotic events, Lovelock argued that, over many millions of years, primitive plants modified the Earth's atmosphere and created the conditions in which more complicated organisms could develop. His hypothesis, known as Gaia theory after the Earth goddess of Greek mythology, originally provoked fierce opposition but gained increasing acceptance when Lynn Margulis identified the mechanisms linking organic and inorganic matter during the 1970s. What makes Gaia theory particularly important (Lovelock 2000) is that it explains how natural systems interact on a global scale to maintain a delicate and ever-changing balance which has enabled life on Earth to evolve over millions of years. Dick Vane-Wright (2009) argues that, along with Darwin's theory of evolution and the Copernican revolution, it offers a major new way of thinking about the planet. It also casts a light on contemporary problems. By rapidly releasing vast quantities of fossil carbon that took millions of years to sequester, human activity has now become a 'force of nature' which threatens to destabilize the entire planetary system on which we depend.

Gaia theory suggests living organisms such as plants and animals co-operate rather than compete. Can you think of examples of this?

Figure 1.2 A knowledge of the globe and world map underpins children's understanding of environmental issues. *Photo: Geographical Association.*

Sustainability emerges as a concept

Further developments occurred in the 1980s with the publication of two high-profile reports. The first was an independent report on development issues chaired by Willy Brandt, the former Chancellor of West Germany (Brandt 1980). This drew attention to the need to address the disparities between a cluster of powerful 'developed' industrialized countries (the North) and a much larger group of developing countries (the South). Significantly, these disparities more or less mirrored the pattern established in previous centuries in which colonies (mostly in the tropics) provided crops and goods for their European rulers. Today, the inequalities and injustices of the colonial era still remain deeply embedded in the world economy. A few years later, the Brundtland Report (WCED 1987), named after the Norwegian premier Jo Brundtland and commissioned by the United Nations, extended the argument about economic inequality. In particular, it identified the enormous poverty of the South, coupled with the non-sustainable patterns of consumption and production in the North, as a prime cause of global environmental problems. This paved the way for the use of a new term, 'sustainability', that brought social welfare, economic activity and environmental considerations together in a single idea.

The Brundtland Report argued for greater fairness and justice in global affairs, both between different nations in the present and between different generations in the future. Famously, it called for sustainable development that 'would meet the needs of the present without compromising the ability of future generations to meet their own needs' (WCED 1987: 2.1). This has now become a classic definition that is widely quoted in policy statements and other documents around the world. In the business community it has provided the foundations for the notion of the triple bottom line – people, planet and profit – which is widely used for reporting purposes. Within education, there are various acronyms such as ESD (Education for Sustainable Development) which incorporate 'sustainable development' in their title. And it is, of course, the focus for the United Nations Sustainable Development Goals (SDGs).

There are a number of other points to note about the Brundtland Report. Crucially, in calling for greater equity and fairness, it placed sustainability firmly on an ethical footing. It declares, for example, that poverty is 'an evil' (1.27) that people across the developing world 'have legitimate aspirations for an improved quality of life' (2.4) and that there are ethical reasons for conserving 'wild beings' (1.53). Recognizing that sustainability is predicated on values is fundamental to understanding what it actually involves. But the report also contained very significant ambiguities and weaknesses. It begged the question about what sustainable development might look like in practice and it left the notion of 'needs' open to debate. How, for example, are needs to be decided, how far do they extend into the future, and who has the authority to determine them? Furthermore, the report accommodated national interests by recommending that sustainability could be achieved by and through economic growth. Unfortunately, the tension between living within limits and increasing resource consumption has never been resolved. This has led some critics such as Michael Bonnett (2013) to argue that sustainable development is little more than a political slogan which brings together two incompatible ideas in a catchy phrase. Are we, he asks, simply trading in ambiguities?

Why do you think people keep talking about sustainable development if it is an ambiguous idea?

Different responses

Drawing on these different strands, sustainability has slowly risen up the agenda of governments around the world in recent decades. The United Nations (UN) Conference on Sustainability and Development (the Earth Summit) held in Rio de Janeiro in 1992 was a particularly important landmark which attracted over a hundred heads of state and was the biggest event of its kind ever held. This led to the formulation of an agenda for the next century (Agenda 21) and a visionary statement for the future (the Earth Charter). Major international conferences held in Kyoto (1997), and subsequently in Copenhagen (2009), Paris (2015) and Glasgow (2021), have attempted to build on these achievements and resulted in numerous international agreements and accords – there have been literally hundreds. At the same time, the UN has sought to stimulate action to protect the natural environment and welfare of people around the world by negotiating a set of agreed goals with targets to be achieved within a given time frame. The Millennium Development Goals (2000–15) and the Sustainable Development Goals (2015–30) are the results of these endeavours, and both have had a certain amount of impact.

However, despite these endeavours and ever-growing evidence of environmental catastrophe, many governments have failed to meet their pledges and aspirations, and the pace of political action remains painfully slow. This is partly because different nations have different needs. For example, the island nations in the Pacific Ocean and elsewhere are at risk of disappearing as sea levels rise. Meanwhile, countries like India and China, which are industrializing rapidly, depend heavily on coal to fuel their economic growth. Generally, developing countries around the world are suffering disproportionately from emissions that have emanated from the industrialized West and need financial help to change their practices. Issues of global justice and equity are thus entwinned with questions about technological innovation and social aspirations, resulting in complicated and often ineffective negotiations.

Young people are justifiably angry. Greta Thunberg, leader of the School Strike for Climate movement, has been unequivocal in her criticism of world leaders. She addressed the UN Climate Summit in New York in 2019 with these bitter words:

> You have stolen my dreams and my childhood with your empty words . . . We are in the beginning of a mass extinction, and all you can talk about is money and fairy tales of eternal economic growth. For more than 30 years, the science has been crystal clear. How dare you continue to look away and come here saying that you're doing enough, when the politics and solutions needed are still nowhere in sight?
> Thunberg 2019

Just as in politics, the pace of change in education has been painfully slow, notwithstanding the determined attempts by groups of committed teachers to instigate reform. Sustainability, the most urgent issue of our time, is hardly mentioned in the formal curricula of most 'developed' nations, and in some jurisdictions may well not feature at all at primary level. The students who founded the Zero Hour youth movement for climate change in Seattle, USA, report that young people are considerably more aware of environmental issues than their educators. Individual members of the group say that they felt that their teachers did not know how to nurture their passion for the environment, that climate change was never part of their formal teaching, and they talk about the 'legacy of inaction' that will result from their schooling (Artis et al. 2020: 28). It appears these are not isolated experiences. Sustainability fits uncomfortably into an academic framework constructed around traditional disciplines and is often difficult to encapsulate meaningfully in current classroom practice and initial teacher education programmes.

How have you learnt about sustainability (if at all) in the different phases of your education?

Defining sustainability

One way to make better sense of sustainability is to recognize that it is a hybrid concept with a number of different dimensions. Since the Brundtland Report, it has been widely acknowledged that finding ways to live within planetary means involves addressing not just environmental concerns, but taking account of social and economic issues as well. The way these three dimensions – environmental, social and economic – interact can be illustrated diagrammatically in a number of ways. They are often shown metaphorically as the columns or pillars which provide the structural support for the roof of a classical temple (Figure 1.3). Other representations portray them as overlapping circles in a Venn diagram or as concentric rings on a dartboard. The question that arises from all these representations is whether the different dimensions have equal importance or whether they have a hierarchical relationship. Ultimately, all life depends on the environment which suggests it should take pride of place, but on an everyday level economic concerns tend to dominate. There are also problems in focusing on just three dimensions – power, politics, culture, religion and multiple other factors also contribute to a sustainability mindset.

Sustainability can also be seen in terms of links and connections. Capra and Luisi (2015), for example, argue that sustainability, whether of ecosystems or human societies, involves a web of connections across a living community. This means that reciprocal and dynamic interactions

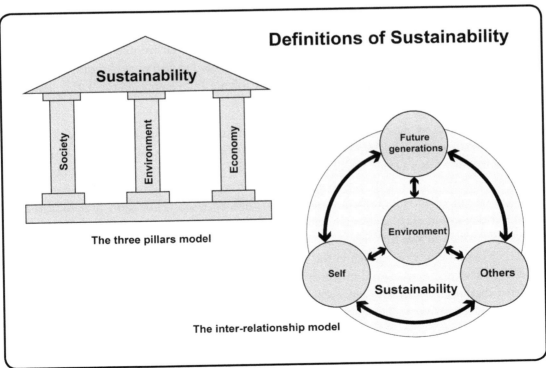

Figure 1.3 Two different ways of representing sustainability. The three pillars model is simple to understand but the relational model is better at showing interactions.

between a range of different forces play a pivotal role. Human beings are one of these forces, and how we respond to different situations and the way we assess them depends on our self-understanding, self-awareness and the values that we hold. Recognizing this subjective element shifts the focus away from the outsider view encapsulated in the notion of 'spaceship Earth' and it positions human beings as part of the natural world along with, and not separate from, all other creatures. It also suggests that we need to respect and co-operate with others.

The working definition of sustainability which arises from such considerations and which is used in this book can be summed in the following form of words:

> Sustainability involves reconnecting
> (a) to yourself,
> (b) to other people and
> (c) to the environment, at a range of scales from the local to the global.

The idea of 'reconnecting' is important. It serves not as nostalgia for the past but as a reminder that modern life, especially in industrialized economies, risks becoming disconnected from its roots. The guiding sense of purpose and meaning which we seek in our lives urgently needs to be acknowledged but is all too easily squeezed out by more visible matrixes and targets. This definition also recognizes that sustainability operates at both an individual and a community level. The solutions to current problems may well lie in making changes in the way that we behave which reflect an ethic of Earth care and which are predicated on universal values such as justice, equality and peace. This is a fundamentally hopeful perspective with considerable implications for education. Most importantly, it suggests that, while knowledge of environmental issues provides a bedrock for understanding at a foundational level, schools need to find ways to create spaces where pupils can explore both their inner selves and their role in, and responsibility for, the planet that supports them.

In school contexts, it may not be necessary or appropriate for pupils to compare different definitions of sustainability. However, it is important for teachers and educators to recognize that sustainability has multiple facets and that it is open to interpretation. Sustainability involves much more than simply learning about the natural environment or climate change. In fact, although we talk of an environment crisis, the environment itself is not really the problem at all. Whatever disruption may lie ahead, nature will eventually find a balance. However, the decisions that people make and how they respond to the events around them are likely to make a fundamental difference to our ability to flourish in the years to come. Scientists warn that we are in danger of expelling ourselves from a world in which we have been able to flourish for the last 10,000 years and that disrupting natural systems will lead to a much more hostile environment. Read and Alexander (2019: 5) are not alone in concluding that in its present form 'our civilization is finished'. Whether or not we accept this blunt conclusion, it certainly seems that vision, wisdom and self-knowledge will be crucial in seeking a way forward. These qualities, which are fundamentally embedded in educational endeavour, offer a hopeful way of negotiating the uncertainties that lie ahead.

What gives you hope that people will take decisions that will ensure our civilization will survive?

Planetary boundaries

Since the turn of the century a new way of thinking about sustainability has been developed that uses the notion of planetary boundaries. Drawing on concepts from ecology, such as carrying capacity, feedback and resilience, an international group of scientists led by Johan Rockström and Will Steffen of the Stockholm Resilience Centre have identified nine planetary support systems which are essential for survival, and they have attempted to assess the points at which they could become dangerously destabilized. Their research indicates that three boundaries – climate change, biodiversity loss and soil pollution (nitrogen and phosphorus loading) – have already been breached, while others, such as ocean acidification and land use change, are fast approaching their critical threshold (Figure 1.4). The idea that human activity has to operate within certain limits concentrates attention on the 'ecological budget' and is a stark reminder of the scale of the current crisis. It is a warning which has been echoed by many other scientists.

Rockström and Klum (2015) make the point that, because the Earth is a complex, self-regulating system in which everything is connected to everything else, disruption can have unexpected consequences. So far 90 per cent of greenhouse gas emissions have been absorbed by the oceans and more than 50 per cent of carbon dioxide emissions have been soaked up by natural ecosystems. There is a danger that, at some unspecified point in the future, these negative feedbacks which maintain the status quo will turn positive, triggering runaway events. Until now, the remarkable resilience of Earth's systems has lulled us into a false sense of security. Thinking in terms of planetary boundaries and safe operating spaces focuses directly on the emergency which lies ahead and offers what Ronald Clift and colleagues (2017) call a 'global dashboard' for vital Earth systems.

The notion of planetary boundaries focuses on bio-physical processes but takes little or no account of social factors. However, economist Kate Raworth (2017) has found a way to apply the idea of limits not only to the natural environment but also to human welfare. She uses the metaphor of a ring doughnut as a visual device to encapsulate her ideas. In Raworth's model, the outer edge of the doughnut is bounded by ecological overshoot (breached natural boundaries) and the inner edge by social deprivation (breached welfare limits). The area inside the ring represents a sweet spot which Raworth describes as a 'safe and just place for humanity'. This model reconceptualises sustainable development and offers a vision, grounded in economics, of how to live within planetary boundaries without constraining human well-being. The fact that the ring doughnut looks like a lifebuoy reinforces this message. It's time that we reached out to save ourselves!

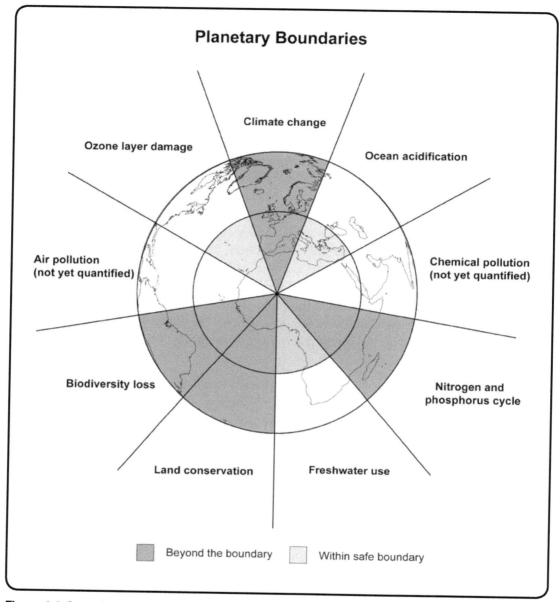

Planetary Boundaries

Figure 1.4 Some key planetary boundaries have already been breached, risking irreversible change, while others are only just within the safe boundary. *After Rockström and Klum 2015 and Raworth 2017.*

Try to devise your own doughnut diagram with notes to explain ecological overshoot and social deprivation. How does your version compare with the ones that are available on the Internet?

People and nature

In many ways, sustainability and sustainable development hinge around the relationship between people and nature. Understanding this relationship is something which has exercised people for thousands of years, and it is explored in religion and sacred texts around the world. Interestingly, there is considerable agreement across different traditions. For Hindus, for example, protecting the environment is seen as an important expression of dharma – the principle that makes life and the universe possible. Buddhists, meanwhile, are enjoined to adopt a simple life which respects plants and creatures as well as balance and peace in nature. In a similar vein, the biblical Book of Genesis (a sacred text for Christians, Jews and Muslims) tells how God gave man 'dominion' over all living things (1:26). This is generally interpreted as giving people responsibility to look after and care for the world. The modern environmental conservation movement can thus be traced back to early beginnings.

When did you first realize that you had a responsibility towards the environment? Were there any specific events which triggered this?

The question which arises is the extent to which human beings are separate from or part of nature. The fact that we depend on the Earth for our physical survival is incontrovertible. Despite all the trappings of modern life, we are utterly dependent on the Earth for all basic physical needs, such as food, fresh air, clean water and shelter. But we also depend on the natural world for our mental health and well-being. For example, artists, musicians, poets, architects and others have drawn creative inspiration from nature throughout the centuries, and many mathematicians and scientists have devoted all their energies to studying it. The symbolic representation of nature is also encoded in our culture and language. Some see nature as a source of mystery and existential meaning. Environmentalist Stephen Kellert (2012: xiii–xiv) goes further. 'The more we draw from its nourishing waters,' he declares, 'the more we sustain the human, body, mind and spirit.' Nature is our 'magic well' and the 'source of who we are and can become as individuals and societies.'

Yet, we know that everything that we do impacts the environment in one way or another. To meet their needs people have cleared the land and extracted natural resources from the Earth for thousands of years. When human numbers remained relatively low, these activities only had local or regional impact. Since the Industrial Revolution, however, human numbers have mushroomed and human activity has increased exponentially. The last seventy years have seen the most dramatic changes as both industrial production and the globalization of trade have gathered pace. Since the mid-1950s every environmental indicator from soil and habitat loss to air pollution and weather disasters has shown similar worrying trends. The relentless exploitation of both animate and inanimate resources and the pollution resulting from it are now starting to bring about planetary changes. In the past people were not particularly aware of what was happening but it is now clear that the impact is potentially catastrophic. As the World Wide Fund for Nature (WWF 2018: 8) concludes, 'We are the first generation that has a clear picture of the value of nature and our impact on it. We may be the last that can take action to reverse this trend.' Sustainability involves recalibrating the relationship between people and nature. The search for solutions goes far beyond superficial adjustments and digs deep into the human psyche.

We live at a moment in history when people are dazzled by the power of technology and put extraordinary faith in their ability to change the world. People dominate nature on many different levels from the modification of food crops to the use of insecticides, fertilizers and antibiotics. Scientific discoveries have brought great benefits but they have come at a cost and have helped to stoke the idea that human beings are somehow separate from other forms of life. Human exceptionalism is deeply engrained in modern thought (see Chapter 3). It is implicit in the notion of stewardship which sets people apart from the rest of creation. It contributes to the thinking that favours grandiose engineering projects as a way of fixing environmental problems. And it is reflected in the very name that geologists have given to the current epoch (the Anthropocene) in which people are now regarded as a force of geological significance.

There are those from all walks of life including science and economics who think that humanity has overreached itself and that we should show greater humility. When faith leader Oren Lyons complained to a United Nations Conference in 1977 that he saw 'no delegation of the four-footed' and 'no seat for the eagles', he was making a significant point. Who speaks for the dispossessed and what are the legal rights of plants and animals? Putting this question another way, is nature in all its diversity and abundance simply a resource to be exploited by whoever has the power to do so, or does it have intrinsic value? The affinity which young children have for animals and other creatures is well known. In education there is now a debate as to whether the time has come to replace the idea of stewardship with its implied notion of control and human superiority with the gentler form of learning which respects non-human others. This shifts the focus away from people as outsiders who observe the Earth (the spaceship approach) to a learning and meaning-making relationship with nature. Donna Haraway's (2016) ideas about companion species and her suggestion that we need to 'stay with the trouble' neatly sums up our entanglement with nature. As she puts it, 'No species acts alone.'

Different ways of thinking

The idea that we are somehow part of, but also separate from, nature links into different cultural traditions. In a fascinating study of cognitive history, Jeremy Lent (2017) offers an analysis of the root metaphors which different civilizations use to make meaning of the world, and he dwells at some length on the contrast between ancient Greek and ancient Chinese thought. Lent argues that Greek philosophers and mathematicians specialized in generalizing and developed patterns of thought based on systematic reasoning. For example, Pythagoras envisaged an orderly, symmetrical world and developed the use of empiricism to test and prove a theory, Aristotle invented the formal syllogism (drawing conclusions from two or more propositions), while Plato argued that the body and soul were separate and regarded desire as being in conflict with reason. By contrast, the ancient

Chinese developed a different way of seeing the world. They posited an all-pervasive energy source called *qi* (pronounced 'chee'), which exhibits a never-ending interplay of polarities known as *yin* and *yang*. Rather than being in antagonism, *yin* and *yang* are harmonious opposites in that each pole contains the seed of the other and cannot exist in isolation. By focusing on the associations between things, Chinese philosophy thus emphasized context and connections.

Ancient Greek and Chinese modes of thought have persisted over millennia and they still affect how many people think today. To give just one example, Lent refers to a simple experiment in which Chinese and American children were presented with pictures of a cow, a chicken and a patch of grass, and asked to say which two went together. Most of the American children, focusing on categorization, grouped the cow and the chicken together, saying they were both animals. The Chinese children, emphasizing relationships, said that, because cows eat grass, it was the chicken that was the odd one out. Another way to express the difference between Eastern and Western thought patterns is to think of how two travellers might navigate across an unfamiliar landscape. One might use a map and a compass (the Greek approach based on universal laws); the other might steer by landmarks (the Chinese contextual approach). Both travellers would find their route but they would have very different understanding of the environment they had travelled through (Lent 2017: 206 and 213).

The emphasis on logic, categories and universal truths which derives from the Greeks provides a powerful way of understanding mechanisms and processes and underpins the Western scientific tradition. The more contextual and holistic approach developed by the Chinese emphasizes harmony and balance in a world that is continually changing. The tendency of the Greeks to universalize and the Chinese to contextualize also results in different conceptions of human nature. The Greeks saw reason as the faculty unique to human beings, whereas the Chinese saw morality as the key quality that differentiated humans from other animals. From the Chinese perspective, attempting to dominate nature makes little sense as it disrupts the harmony which is essential to the cosmic order. The more general point is that ideas which are currently considered as universal and drive today's global society are actually culturally relative. Recognizing that sustainability can be framed through different modes of thought highlights the opportunity for new approaches.

Can you think of any examples from your own experience where people from different backgrounds have interpreted the same situation in different ways?

Conclusion

Sustainability is a hybrid concept which describes a vast endeavour – the search for a way that humanity can continue to thrive and prosper on a finite planet. Rooted in ecology and environmental activism and predicated on values, it encompasses social, economic and personal dimensions. Sustainability operates on different levels and requires a global perspective as well as self-understanding. The ambiguities and contradictions which are embedded in the concept make it difficult to communicate and easy to subvert. Furthermore, its meaning continues to change along with the context and our understanding of the challenges that lie ahead. In many respects, sustainability is best regarded as a mindset which helps us to attribute meaning to the world and our place within it. This suggests that it acts as a signifier which cannot be neatly defined. Despite these problems, sustainability is a term which captures an absolutely essential idea. Living within planetary means is the key issue facing us today. Some of the ways this might be addressed, both within and beyond education, are considered in the next chapter.

References

Artis, S., Cohen, A. M., Juguzny, I., and Kieras, K. (2020) 'This is Zero Hour' in Armon, J., Scoffham, S. and Armon, C. (eds), *Prioritizing Sustainability Education*, London: Routledge.

Bonnet, M. (2013) 'Sustainable Development, Environmental Education and the Significance of Being in Place', *The Curriculum Journal* 24:2, 250–71, DOI: 10.1080/09585176.2013.792672.

Brandt, W. (1980) *North-South: A Programme for Survival*, London: The Brandt Commission, Pan Books.

Capra, F., and Luisi, P. (2015) *The Systems View of Life: A Unifying Vision*, Cambridge: Cambridge University Press.

Carson, R. (1962) *Silent Spring*, New York: Fawcett Crest.

Clift, R., Sim, S., King, H., Chenoweth, J., Christie, I., Clavreul, J., Mueller, C., Posthuma, L., Boulay, A.-M., Chaplin-Kramer, R., et al. (2017) 'The Challenges of Applying Planetary Boundaries as a Basis for Strategic Decision-Making in Companies with Global Supply Chains', *Sustainability* 9:2, 279, https://doi.org/10.3390/su9020279.

Ehrlich, P. (1968) *The Population Bomb*, New York: Buccaneer Books.

Kellert, S. R. (2012) *Birthright: People and Nature in the Modern World*, New Haven and London: Yale University Press.

Haraway, D. (2016) *Staying with the Trouble: Making Kin in the Chtulucene*, Durham, NC: Duke University Press.

Lent, J. (2017) *The Patterning Instinct: A Cultural History of Humanity's Search for Meaning*, Amherst, NY: Prometheus Books.

Lovelock, J. (2000) *Gaia: A New Look at Life on Earth*, Oxford: Oxford University Press.

Meadows, D. H., Meadows, D. L., Randers, J. and Behrens, W. W. III (1972) *The Limits to Growth*, New York: Universe Books.

Raworth, K. (2017) *Doughnut Economics: Seven Ways to Think Like a 21st-Century Economist*, London: Random House.

Read, R., and Alexander, S. (2019) *This Civilization is Finished*, Melbourne: Simplicity Institute.

Rockström, J., and Klum, M. (2015) *Big World Small Planet*, Stockholm: Max Ström Publishing.

Thunberg, G. (2019) Speech to the United Nations Climate Action Summit, New York, 23rd September, available at https://www.nbcnews.com/news/world/read-greta-thunberg-s-full-speech-united-nations-climate-action-n1057861.

Vane-Wright, R. J. (2009) 'Planetary Awareness, World Views and the Conservation of Biodiversity' in Kellert, S. R., and Speth, J. (eds), *The Coming Transition*, New Haven: Yale School of Forestry and Environmental Studies.

WCED World Commission for Environment and Development (1987) *Our Common Future*, Oxford: Oxford University Press.

WWF (2018) *Living Planet Report 2018: Aiming Higher*, Grooten, M., and Almond, R. E. A. (eds), Gland, Switzerland: WWF, available at https://www.worldwildlife.org/publications/living-planet-report-2018.

2

Sustainability, Prosperity and Well-being

Summary

Sustainability is a multifaceted challenge which requires multiple solutions. How we respond to it will depend on our perspective and the context at the time. Modern Western industrial societies are underpinned at a deep level by a belief in progress and economic growth. By contrast, ancient hunter-gatherer societies tended to see the world as a dynamic whole in which everything was connected. It is argued in this chapter that the environment crisis means that the current economic model, while it has brought huge benefits, is no longer viable. Our future prosperity and well-being will require a broader, principled and more inclusive approach.

According to legend, when Alexander the Great marched his victorious troops into the city of Gordium in Asia Minor on the journey that was to establish his empire, he encountered an unusual problem. He was shown a wagon which was believed to have belonged to the father of the celebrated King Midas but which was so firmly secured by knots that it could not be moved. Tradition had it that an oracle had proclaimed that anyone who could unravel the knots that held the wagon would become the ruler of a vast kingdom. Many had tried and many had failed. Alexander, too, decided to try his luck and wrestled with the knots but found he could make no progress. Finally, he opted for a different approach. Stepping back, he drew his sword out of its sheath and sliced the knots in two with a single stroke. Based on this story, the phrase 'cutting the Gordian knot' has come to describe a creative or decisive solution to a problem which otherwise appears insurmountable (Figure 2.1).

The challenge of sustainable living is indeed a seemingly intractable problem but, unfortunately, slicing through it with a single stroke is not an option. Interconnections and relationships are inherent in natural systems and they interact in complex and unexpected ways. Attempting to search for one-stop solutions which will 'fix' problems such as climate change or biodiversity loss is to misread the nature of the challenge. While it is tempting to think that there must be an answer, when multiple factors and emergent properties are involved, a different approach is required.

Figure 2.1 When it comes to speculating or solving problems, children have a propensity to come up with fresh or unusual perspectives. *Photo: Geographical Association*

Furthermore, the law of unexpected consequences means that any attempt to impose a universal solution is liable to have damaging implications. H. L. Mencken pointed this out in a succinct and memorable aphorism: 'To every complex problem, there exists a solution which is neat, simple and wrong.'

The wider point is that the way a problem is framed will indicate certain types of solutions and exclude other possibilities. Some problems are well defined and can be seen as linear processes with a clear beginning, middle and end. Others are more ambiguous and involve multiple links and connections. In their study of social policy issues, Rittel and Webber (1973) contrasted 'tame' problems which are linear, with 'wicked' problems which are ill-defined and ambiguous. This distinction is particularly relevant when it comes to environmental issues which, because they are interrelated and constantly changing, have wicked characteristics. Some of the other features of wicked problems is that they tend to have multiple causes, are context dependent and require a range of strategies none of which can be shown to be better than another. A further dimension is that they are difficult to understand until a solution emerges but the solution itself changes the nature of the problem and leads to other impacts. Ultimately, it may be more constructive to think of environmental issues as wicked problems rather than seeking hard and fast solutions.

Can you think of actions which you or others have taken that have had unexpected consequences? Are you aware of any environmental examples?

Indigenous knowledge and understanding

When it comes to searching for ways to respond to the current environmental crisis, the example of indigenous cultures has attracted considerable interest and attention. The remnants of traditional hunter-gatherer societies which still survive in isolated pockets around the world provide a fascinating insight into different ways of thinking. Jeremy Lent (2017) explains, that the basic idea which underlies hunter-gatherer perceptions of the world is the belief that everything, whether it is animate or inanimate, is integrated in a dynamic whole. This brings together not only humans and their ancestors but also trees, rocks, rivers and more ephemeral entities like spirits into a unified vision. The interconnectedness of aspects of life that we tend to keep separate, or even discount as irrelevant, is demonstrated particularly clearly in the Australian Aboriginal concept of the Dreamtime. This postulates that the world was brought into being by creative entities called Dreamings who criss-crossed the landscape leaving traces of their activities, continually changing their shape from animal to human and back again as they went. The idea of the Dreamtime thus weaves the human, natural and spirituals worlds together in a unified whole. It also integrates time, as Aboriginals see the Dreamtime as a beginning which never ends, which means it is a continuum that links together the past, present and future. This world view, so dramatically different from modern sensibilities, has taken on renewed significance given the current environmental crisis. And it opens up possibilities for new ways of thinking and meaning-making in which nothing exists in isolation.

Similar ideas are also found among the Sami people who have inhabited northern Scandinavia for thousands of years. Tim Frandy, an academic who is a member of the American Sami community, reflects on his cultural identity and beliefs in the following words:

> This world is one my family has long known … Our lives are still structured and shaped by the seasons and the weather, by maple runs and fish spawns, by wild berries and late frosts, by deer activity and bird migrations, . . . by the places we understand as important and sacred. The forest and waters are how we think, how we communicate, and who we are, in ways too profound and complex to fully elucidate here.
>
> Frandy 2018:2

It would be naive to think that the ideas which underpin traditional societies where small numbers of people lived close to the land can be transposed and applied directly to postmodern industrial contexts. Nor were hunter-gatherer ideas about themselves and their surroundings uniform or static. However, many of the systems which indigenous communities devised to protect the environment were both sophisticated and effective. They made use of concepts such as seasons, sanctuary areas and habitat protection to help ensure that people lived in harmony with their surroundings. The idea of balance and harmony also applied to social relations as hunter-gatherer societies were for the most part strongly egalitarian. They employed systems of wealth redistribution which minimized the profitability of overharvesting, and they were structured in such a way to prevent powerful males taking too much control. Decision-making considered future implications as well as immediate needs. The North American Iroquois, for example, are noted for their 'seventh generation' principle which takes account of the needs of children far into the future and served as a practical moral guide to responsible and respectful living.

Are there any ways in which you think intergenerational equity (or the lack of it) is a problem in your life?

Hunter-gatherer societies were far from perfect and it is all too easy to construct an image of a golden past in which people lived in harmony with nature and each other. The harsh reality is that life expectancy was short, there was little support for those who were injured or diseased, and infants were particularly vulnerable to premature death. The early hunter-gatherers also appear to have taken what they could from the environment with devastating effects. The arrival of humans in Australia from the Indonesian archipelago around 45,000 years ago, for example, coincides with a wave of mass extinctions of large animals. This was followed by an even larger ecological disaster in the New World, which again corresponds with human migration as temperatures warmed at the end of the last Ice Age. Yuval Harari (2015) concludes that a mixture of technology and co-operative skills ushered in an era in which humans decimated the megafauna in previously uninhabited parts of the world. Speculating about how people who respected nature and the spirit natural world could wreak such damage, Lent points out that extinction is a gradual process which would have been imperceptible from one generation to the next, particularly when there was no way of seeing the overview. However, this counter-story, the story of destruction, could be seen as a warning to people today and it adds further weight to the urgency of conserving the plant and animal life that still survives.

Do you think some cultures have ideas and values which are 'better' than others? What are their respective strengths and weaknesses?

Different frames of reference

Learning about hunter-gatherer belief systems illustrates how it is possible for people to attribute very different meanings to the same events. How we behave, how we conduct our lives and what we think matters depends to a very large extent on the beliefs and assumptions we have about the world and our place within it. These ideas, which are deeply felt and which underlie many of the choices that we make, are culturally encoded and so well embedded that they often remain unquestioned and unacknowledged. In his work on transformational learning, Jack Mezirow (1985) drew attention to the importance of the 'lenses' or 'frames of reference' that we use when we interpret new experiences. He argued that disorientating dilemmas can sensitize individuals to meaning-making structures, resulting in changes that have lasting impact. A key point is that seeing something in a new way is irreversible in the sense that once it has been viewed from that perspective it cannot be undone.

Stepping outside our established frames of reference can be traumatic but Mezirow argues that disorientating dilemmas sensitize us to our meaning-making structures and can have a transformational impact. As with Gestalt images which are open to different interpretations (Figure 2.2(a)), so the patterns that we see around us are subject to our mindset at the time. How we respond to events is also heavily influenced by the context and the influence of preceding events. This is graphically illustrated by the Ebbinghaus Illusion. In Figure 2.2(b) the black dot in the centre is exactly the same in both diagrams but appears to be a different size due to the impact of the grey circles around it. While these examples are drawn from studies in perceptual psychology, they both provide useful metaphors. Sharing these images with children and conducting experiments into how colours appear to change when set against different backgrounds will also help to alert them to way our perceptions change with circumstances.

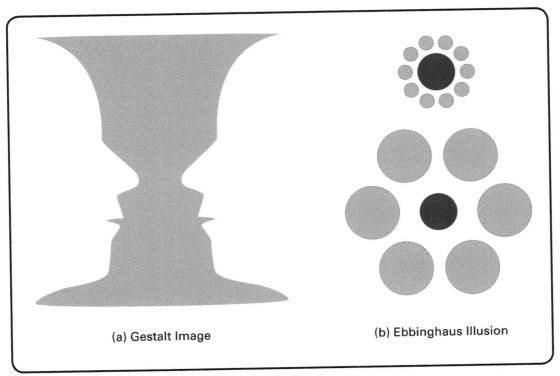

(a) Gestalt Image   (b) Ebbinghaus Illusion

Figure 2.2 Our perception varies according to the focus that we take and the surrounding context.

Progress, growth and prosperity

What then are the assumptions, or frames of reference, which underlie Western industrial societies and thus extend to the global community as a whole? With respect to economic activity, a number of ideas stand out as being particularly significant in shaping our expectations and mindset. Technological progress, economic growth and financial prosperity are three key notions which are widely accepted and serve to guide activity at all levels of society. In recent decades these ideas have taken on new significance as the neoliberal ideology of the free market, deregulation and minimal government intervention have come to dominate public policy. George Monbiot (2016) argues that the result has been to emphasize the role of competition in human relations and that citizens have been redefined as consumers. One of the other consequences is that individualism has been elevated to new levels.

Progress

The idea of progress, the idea that the future will be better than the past, is deeply rooted in modern thinking. It was given a huge boost by the Industrial Revolution which began in western Europe in the late eighteenth century and has now extended around the world. Inventions such as the steam engine, electricity, air travel, modern medicine and the Internet have transformed living conditions. Not only do people have more material goods and better housing but they are also living longer. Life expectancy in the UK, for example, is now more than twice what it is was in the 1850s, while in China (where industrialization came much later) life expectancy has doubled since the 1950s. This is an extraordinary achievement and it has been accompanied by a massive increase in human numbers. While current estimates suggest that world population may stabilize by the end of the century (UN 2021), there is now speculation that biological engineering and artificial intelligence could be starting to change the laws of life itself. In time this might extend life considerably beyond its biological limits and may even begin to set humanity free from the spectre of mortality (Harari 2015). Progress is intoxicating, but it needs to be understood in context – we have to ask what it is that we are progressing towards.

What are the arguments for and against using our technological expertise to strive towards immortality?

Economic growth

Progress is often associated with economic growth. There has been an extraordinary burgeoning of economic activity over recent years. Not only are more and more goods being produced but there has also been a huge increase in the volume of international trade. The value of world exports is now three times what it was in 2000 and several hundred times more than at the end of the Second

World War. The unique period of exponential growth which we are currently witnessing is known as the Great Acceleration and it is evident in almost every sector of the economy. Just one statistic sums up the enormous scale of the changes. More cement was consumed in China in just three years (2011–13) than was used in the United States in the entire twentieth century (Swanson 2015). The world economy is geared towards expansion, and politicians depend on economic growth for their electoral success. The problem is that this level of activity is putting unsustainable stress on Earth systems.

It is tempting to believe that science and technology will be able to solve future problems just as they have in the past and that progress will continue unabated. Change is one of the defining features of our times and the frontiers of knowledge are constantly being pushed back. The World Wide Web and mobile phones, for example, date from around the turn of the century. Medical procedures, which we now regard as commonplace, such as heart and kidney transplants, have only become possible within living memory. New discoveries and innovations will undoubtedly be important in the years ahead, but much will depend on how they are used and perceived.

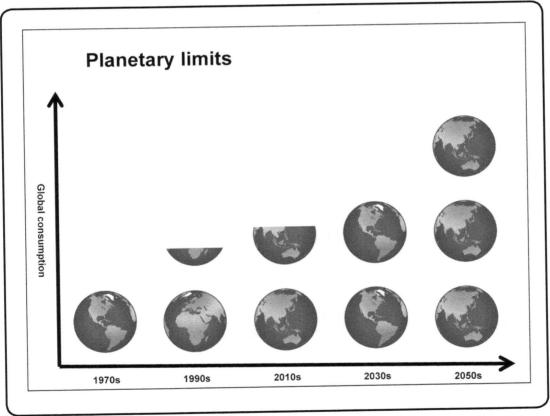

Figure 2.3 Since the 1970s the world economy has exceeded the capacity of the planet and the trend is ever upwards. *Source: Global Footprint Network.*

Technologies that are tied to commercial gain rather than social and environmental benefit are likely to increase, rather to mitigate, the demands that we make on the natural environment. Somewhat paradoxically, technological innovation leads to lower production costs which stimulates consumption and increases the use of resources. This inverse relationship, which is known as the Jevons paradox, suggests that changing how we relate to nature is going to be more important than waiting for breakthroughs which have not yet been achieved.

The key point is that growth cannot be maintained indefinitely. As the economist Tim Jackson (2017) explains, simple logic means that in the end industrial activity is bound to be limited by economic and resource constraints. For example, if the global economy continues to expand even at the seemingly modest rate of 2 or 3 per cent a year, it would be around twenty times bigger at the end of the century than it is today. This is manifestly impossible; we are already consuming more resources and creating more pollution each year than the Earth can sustain (Figure 2.3). Another respected economist, Herman Daly (2008), argues that from a purely utilitarian perspective there comes a point when development involves sacrificing more natural capital than the wealth that can be added by exploiting it. This raises the question of whether the current economic system is structurally faulty and needs to be redesigned around different priorities. Ideas such as biomimicry, regenerative design and integrated business reporting are suggested as offering interesting ways forward (see Glossary).

> Is a commitment to unending economic growth a classic example of addiction –
> clinging to short-term rewards regardless of long-term costs? How do you think this
> cycle might be broken?

Prosperity

At the current time, the benefits of prosperity are very unevenly distributed. While some people enjoy riches that were previously unimaginable, many others (around 3 billion or well over a third of the world's population) continue to live in poverty and do not have enough to eat. Comparisons between countries indicate that once a certain level of income has been achieved, the benefits of further increases rapidly tail off. For example, although the average income in Costa Rica is around a third of that of the United States, life expectancy is almost the same in both countries (CIA 2021). Jackson asks whether we can find a way of living well but consuming less or, to put it in a catchy phrase, 'have more fun with less stuff'. He believes we can. In rich countries, acquiring more and more consumer goods is much more about raising social status than increasing happiness. At the moment we are in the tragic position of destroying our ecological base to produce goods that we do not actually require in order to maintain a system that no longer serves our needs. In a graphic metaphor, Samuel Alexander reflects that the global economy resembles 'a snake eating its own tail' because it is seemingly unaware that it is consuming its own life support system (Read and Alexander 2019: 45).

Prosperity can be seen in many different ways. The mindset which currently dominates global economic activity focuses especially on profit, consumerism and short-term financial returns. A broader vision of what it means to be prosperous would shift the focus away from growth towards more sustainable ways of living. It would take into account the quality of people's lives, the resilience of communities, and our individual and collective sense of meaning and purpose. It would also place greater emphasis on equality and social justice. Interestingly. Wilkinson and Pickett (2018) have presented compelling evidence that, whatever their status, people in very unequal societies are generally likely to suffer from a wider range of health and social problems compared to those in countries where income disparities are lower. And, in a brave attempt to generate new thinking, legislation in Wales now recognizes that prosperity involves both the 'proportionate' use of natural resources and respecting the 'limits of the global environment' (The Well-being of Future Generations (Wales) Act 2015).

Can you think of ways of having 'more fun with less stuff', as Tim Jackson suggests?

Measuring value

Thinking about prosperity raises questions about what we value. Imagine, for example, a venerable oak tree which has been standing in open countryside for several hundred years. A tree like this can be valued in many different ways. Ramblers might linger in the shade that it gives, birds and animals will find shelter in the branches, the roots will protect the ground in heavy rain, and the leaves will rot down each year to enrich the soil. Our oak tree could be a source of inspiration for artists, musicians and poets, while scientists might focus on the way the leaves take carbon out of the atmosphere. For indigenous communities, trees are a valuable source of medicine and contemplation; for builders, the wood is a valuable construction material. Depending on their 'frame of reference', people will attribute value to this tree in different ways. It may also be seen as having an intrinsic value – a value in its own right – which has nothing whatsoever to do with utility. This is a value that is fundamentally irreducible, as the pioneer ecologist Aldo Leopold pointed out when he scornfully declared that the person who asks about the use of a plant or animal was expressing the 'last word in ignorance' (1993: 147).

The problem with financial accounting is that it struggles to attribute monetary value to all these different dimensions. Indeed, the dominant systems in use today attribute very little value to a tree when it is growing in the ground but put a considerable price on it once it has been cut down and is waiting to be turned into products. This leads to the extraordinary situation where an entire wood, forest, or even a major biome like the Amazon rainforest, has little value until it is used in some way or another. In economic terms, virgin forests, oceans and the atmosphere are mostly regarded as externalities which at best provide 'eco-system services'. They are unregulated resources which everyone can use according to their own self-interest. In a graphic turn of phrase, Garret Hardin (1968) termed this the 'tragedy of the commons'.

There are now increasing calls to reform the economic system so that it focuses not only on utilitarian value but intrinsic and social value as well. Contemporary conceptions of economic growth are based on the assumption that humanity will be able to break free of the biosphere in the long run. This is misguided and potentially disastrous. For example, Satish Kumar (2009: 30) argues that 'real wealth is good land, productive soils, rivers, animals, vibrant communities and human creativity'. Redefining what we mean by prosperity is essential if we are to preserve the ecological base on which life depends. What we need now, as the Dasgupta Review (2021) of economics and biodiversity argues, is an inclusive measure of wealth which will establish whether or not development is truly sustainable. We have to develop, in Dasgupta's words, a 'grammar for understanding our engagement with Nature' (2021: 12). There is nothing particularly new or surprising about this conclusion but it is heartening to see it expressed in a mainstream government report. Furthermore, enlightened self-interest suggests that taking early action on environmental problems will significantly outweigh the costs of ignoring them. The Stern Review of the Economics of Climate Change (2006) made this point very clearly the best part of two decades ago.

These considerations may seem a long way away from the realities of classroom teaching but children, just like adults, have clear views about what they value and the things which contribute to their well-being. In one school in the suburbs of London, pupils aged 9–11 worked in groups to talk about the things that helped them to flourish. These are some of the things that they listed:

- When we are valued
- When we learn new things
- When we stand up for what we believe in
- When we realize our potential
- When we care
- When we are creative and imaginative
- When we connect to nature
- When we have time to think, reflect, pray

In another project, children from different parts of the UK were asked to draw maps and write about those aspects of their local area that they regarded as meaningful (Owens et al. 2020). Unsurprisingly, family and friends scored highly but it was also apparent that, even if they seemed ordinary to outsiders, children valued the surroundings where they lived. Almost universally, they spoke highly of their school, and their intense interest and feelings for the natural world, along with the importance of friendship and physical activity, shone through in their responses. These findings are not only significant in their own right, they indicate that finding out about the places which pupils find meaningful can help teachers develop their thinking about their place in the world.

What are the things that you value most? Try drawing a map or picture of a place that is special to you. Would other people see it in the same way? Would there be any difficulties undertaking this activity with your own class?

My area is important to me because it's got lots of beautiful animals and nature. I put my school because it's special to me and I go there every day and I enjoy playing with my friends.

Cassey   Age 9

Figure 2.4 School, friends and the natural world are what makes the locality special for this 9-year-old girl. *Source: Meaningful Maps Project.*

Developing a new mindset

Economic systems are not immutable: they are made by people and represent a particular set of values and power relationships at a given time. It follows, as we have already seen, that notions of prosperity will vary between different cultures. Similarly, what we think of as progress will depend on our underlying beliefs and assumptions, and our ideas about what we are progressing towards. The current environment emergency is a wake-up call that has alerted us to new realities and forced us to question our priorities. We now know we have to live within planetary limits and need to respond to unprecedented environmental challenges. Imagination, creativity and integrity will all be at a premium as we investigate different ways forward.

The responsibility for action and wise decision-making rests with us all. It is incumbent on us to behave responsibly in our private life and not to squander Earth's precious resources. This is a matter of personal integrity and it is something which some people take very seriously. But we also find ourselves in an ambiguous position. When social norms are out of balance with ecological imperatives, individuals can only deviate to a certain extent before they start to incur considerable penalties. Moreover, if sustainable living involves making personal sacrifices, it not only becomes unattractive to most people but is unlikely to gain widespread support. A broader view of our self-interest which takes into account the well-being of future generations and the welfare of the natural world, and which commands widespread social support, holds out the possibility of a different approach. Prosperity is much more than just making money, and if making money ends up literally costing the Earth, it is a totally futile quest.

Can you think of ways in which sustainability might be achieved without involving 'sacrifices' being made?

Sustainability is sometimes characterized as a minority interest that appeals only to those who care about plants and animals – the tree huggers and creepy-crawly brigade. Campaigns and protest movements, while undertaken for the best of motives, can also be limiting in that they may only appeal to certain groups and leave others feeling threatened or excluded. The climate change protest group, Extinction Rebellion, has demonstrated how this can happen. Seeing the whole of humanity as deeply entangled and dependent on nature changes the agenda. Furthermore, it may be time to question whether labelling activities, ideas and policies as 'green' is counterproductive. Communicating the wider meaning and complexities of sustainability – making it clear that it matters to us all – requires a new language and an inclusive mindset. How this might be brought about is an open question but schools certainly have a crucially important part to play. They provide a safe and neutral setting for building knowledge and understanding of issues, nurturing critical and creative thinking and exploring deep questions about values and meaning. We need to do our best to ensure that primary school children, who have an acknowledged curiosity and wonder for the natural world, have the knowledge, resilience and understanding to make wise decisions as they move towards an ever more uncertain future.

Are terms such as 'sustainability' and the 'green agenda' still useful or can you think of something more meaningful and inclusive?

Conclusion

Sustainability is a multifaceted and interconnected challenge which is not amenable to simple solutions. The beliefs and practices of other cultures, particularly indigenous societies, help to cast this challenge in a new light and reveal the assumptions which guide our current behaviour. Three key notions – a belief in progress, a commitment to growth and a focus on material prosperity – underpin contemporary economic Western thinking. However, these ideas fail to take account of the intrinsic value of nature, and need to be recalibrated if we are to live within planetary limits. A broader view of our self-interest which takes into account the well-being of future generations and the welfare of the natural world, and which commands widespread support, holds out the possibility of a different approach. It is important that this vision is inclusive rather than sectarian and that it is seen in terms of benefits and not sacrifices. How this vision might be developed and communicated is considered in the next chapter.

References

Daly, H. E. (2008) 'A Steady State Economy', *The Ecologist*, available at https://theecologist.org/2008/apr/01/steady-state-economy.

Dasgupta, P. (2021) *The Economics of Biodiversity: The Dasgupta Review, Abridged Version*, London: HM Treasury, available at https://assets.publishing.service.gov.uk/government/uploads/system/uploads/attachment_data/file/957292/Dasgupta_Review_-_Abridged_Version.pdf.

Frandy, T. (2018) 'Indigenizing Sustainabilities, Sustaining Indigeneities: Decolonization, Sustainability, and Education', *Journal of Sustainability Education* 18, available at http://www.journalofsustainabilityeducation.org/.

Harari. Y. N. (2015) *Sapiens: A Brief History of Humankind*, London: Vintage.

Jackson, T. (2017) *Prosperity Without Growth* (2nd edn), London: Routledge.

Kumar, S. (2009) 'Grounded Economic Awareness' in Stibbe, A. (ed.), *The Handbook of Sustainability Literacy*, Totnes: Green Books.

Lent, J. (2017) *The Patterning Instinct*, New York: Prometheus Books.

Leopold, L. B. (1993) (ed.) *Round River: From the Journals of Aldo Leopold*, Oxford: Oxford University Press.

Mezirow. J. (1985) 'A Critical Theory of Self-Directed Learning', *New Directions for Adult and Continuing Education* 25: 17–30.

Monbiot, G (2016) 'Neo-liberalism – The Ideology at the Root of All our Problems', *The Guardian*, 15 April 2016.

Owens, P., Scoffham, S., Vujakovic, P., and Bass A. (2020) 'Meaningful Maps', *Primary Geography* 102: 15–17.

Read, R., and Alexander, S. (2018) *This Civilization is Finished*, Melbourne: Simplicity Institute.

Rockström, J. (2020) 'Ten years to transform the future of humanity – or destabilize the planet', TED talk available at https://www.ted.com/talks/johan_rockstrom_10_years_to_transform_the_future_of_humanity_or_destabilize_the_planet?language=en#t-44.

Rittel, H. W. J., and Webber, M. M. (1973) 'Dilemmas in General Theory of Planning', *Policy Sciences* 4:2, 155–69.

United Nations (2021) *Population*, available at https://www.un.org/en/sections/issues-depth/population/.

Stern, N. (2006) *The Economics of Climate Change: The Stern Review*, London: HM Treasury, available at https://webarchive.nationalarchives.gov.uk/+/http:/www.hmtreasury.gov.uk/media/4/3/executive_summary.pdf.

Swanson, A. (2015) 'How China used more cement in 3 years than the U.S. did in the entire 20th Century', *The Washington Post*, 24 March 2015, available at https://www.washingtonpost.com/news/wonk/wp/2015/03/24/how-china-used-more-cement-in-3-years-than-the-u-s-did-in-the-entire-20th-century/.

Wilkinson, R., and Pickett, J. (2018) *The Inner Level*, London: Penguin.

3

Towards a More Sustainable Future

Summary

We can respond to the environment crisis by adapting present practices, opting for much more fundamental change or trying to ignore it altogether. This chapter begins by noting that, despite repeated warnings from scientists, factual information about the state of the planet has had remarkably little impact on public opinion. It is suggested that there is an urgent need to develop new narratives which will set out a compelling vision for the future. A number of major international initiatives which could offer a way forward are highlighted. The chapter concludes by contending that education has an important part to play as we navigate towards a more sustainable future.

Easter Island lies nearly 4,000 kilometres off the coast of South America. It is surrounded by the waters of the Pacific Ocean and is one of the most remote places on Earth. Yet despite its isolation, there is evidence that Easter Island once supported a flourishing culture. There are literally hundreds of huge stone statues, often arranged in lines, which archaeologists believe people erected in honour of their ancestors. It would have taken considerable skill to carve these monuments and extensive organization to put them up. However, at some point in the past this practice was abandoned, the statues began to fall over and the population fell into abject poverty (Figure 3.1). There are different theories about what caused this disastrous change in fortunes. One suggestion is that, as the population increased, trees and other resources were overexploited and fighting broke out between different groups. An alternative explanation is that disease and raids by European colonists destroyed the culture. Whatever happened at Easter Island, this story is a salutary reminder that societies are vulnerable to collapse. And it provides a metaphor for what could happen in a finite world where people fail to respect natural limits.

The current environment emergency is a wake-up call that has alerted us to new realities and forced us to question our priorities. We now know we need to live within planetary limits and have

Figure 3.1 The stone statues on Easter Island symbolize the collapse of an historic culture.
Photo: Richard Hatwood.

to respond to challenges which humanity has never confronted before. Macy and Johnstone (2012) identify three possible scenarios:

1 The 'Business as Usual' approach which assumes that economic growth is essential for prosperity and trusts that technology will fix problems as they arise;
2 The 'Great Unravelling' which takes a pessimistic view and emphasizes how looming ecological and social disasters will eventually overwhelm us;
3 The 'Great Turning' which sees the possibility of transitioning from an industrial society based on economic growth to a life-sustaining society committed to the restoration and recovery of the Earth.

Understanding what each of these different scenarios might mean in practice is no easy matter. Nor is it likely that humanity will follow a single course. The unpredictability of the future means that we should always be aware of the risk of radically unexpected 'black swan' events, such as the sudden outbreak of Covid-19 in 2019 (see glossary). Nevertheless, there are many who believe that we are at a critical moment in Earth's history and that the decisions that we take in the next few decades will have ramifications far into the future (Sterling 2019; Rockström 2020). The challenge is to see that we do what we can in the coming decade to reduce carbon emissions, reverse biodiversity loss and tackle other negative environmental trends while we still have the chance.

Which of the three scenarios outlined by Macy and Johnson do you think is most likely to happen and why?

Dangers ahead

Scientists have been warning about the impact of human activity on the natural environment since at least the 1960s and campaign groups have done their best to draw attention to the perils ahead. Simply conveying the facts has, however, proved surprisingly ineffective and may even have been counterproductive. Nobody wants to hear unwelcome news, and highlighting dangers can sometimes trigger denial and disavowal rather than constructive action. Indeed, as George Marshall (2014) reports, even people who have suffered terrible damage from unusual weather events may suppress discussing any possible links to climate change, preferring instead to focus on how they have coped with adversity. Furthermore, because the future is always uncertain, predicting disasters can easily turn out to be untrue or exaggerated. This makes it that much easier to discount or question scientific evidence, even when it is very securely grounded. Climate change deniers thrive on these ambiguities.

Human behaviour is complex. Most of us obtain information from people that we trust, drawing either on friendship and professional networks or on the opinions expressed by public figures. Moreover, we are apt to cherry-pick information which conforms with our pre-existing views (confirmation bias) and have an innate desire for social conformity. This means we prefer belonging to groups rather than being out on a limb and we feel comfortable when we are surrounded by like-minded people. The extraordinary power of social media to create and amplify social groups through virtual communication shows the strength of this desire. Our propensity to form shared opinions may have been useful in evolutionary terms but it also means that attitudes can become entrenched and that factual information may be discounted as irrelevant. The misinformation surrounding the Covid-19 vaccination programme has shown how easily facts can become distorted.

Understanding how people acquire their attitudes and recognizing how they can be modified is crucial to effective communication about environmental issues and the sustainability debate. This is a complex endeavour as it involves a mixture of psychological and social factors. In a fascinating study, Kollmuss and Agyeman (2012) found that only a small fraction of pro-environmental behaviours can be directly linked to factual knowledge – social factors and personal circumstances were more important in at least 80 per cent of cases. Other researchers have confirmed that knowledge and understanding do not always lead to behaviour change, or indeed any change at all (Moss et al. 2016; Markinowski and Reid 2019). Recognizing that our behaviour is contextualized and embedded in sociopolitical and personal circumstances suggests that appealing to the emotions and generating peer pressure is liable to have more impact than objective arguments. Reflecting on their careers as environmental scientists,

Rockström and Klum (2016: 10) observe: 'How naïve it was to assume that just because the facts were on the table, people would make the right decisions. That wasn't the way the world worked.'

What instances can you think of where people hold strong opinions which fly in the face of the facts? Can you think of ways in which their opinions might be changed?

Environmental problems have a number of features which make them especially hard to communicate. To begin with, they are often rather ambiguous and involve complex interrelationships. Also, they play out in unexpected ways, can never really be resolved, and need to be understood over long periods of time. In his review of climate change psychology, Marshall (2015) observes that we are hardwired to respond to immediate risks where there is an obvious enemy but not nearly so well equipped to deal with intangible and distant dangers. One of the other consequences of learning about hazards, whether actual or perceived, is that we may end up feeling threatened. These are exactly the circumstances which are liable to evoke denial responses and disavowal

Figure 3.2 Young children have a natural curiosity and fascination for the world around them.
Photo: Cathy Martin.

strategies. Marshall (2015: 2) concludes that climate change, more than any other issue, 'shows our extraordinary and innate talent for seeing only what we want to see and disregarding what we would prefer not to know'. Unfortunately, these same psychological mechanisms tend to be triggered by most other environmental problems as well.

Similar considerations apply in a classroom context. There is a very real danger of frightening children as they find out about the damage human activity is doing to the planet. Children don't come to school to be scared and making them worried is liable to leave them feeling powerless and depressed. It is thus incumbent on teachers to introduce environmental issues in a measured and positive way and to provide a safe and secure environment where pupils can come to terms with the emotional implications of what they are learning. In psychoanalytical terms, teachers need to hold their pupils' anxiety as they enlarge their perceptions. At the current moment, when many children are aware from a very young age that wildlife is in danger and that the climate is changing, introducing them to the facts is essential. The challenge is to keep a balance between cognitive awareness and emotional and spiritual responses.

Myths and narratives

If presenting the facts about environmental issues is not enough and can even be counterproductive, what are the alternatives? Marshall (2015: 157) argues, in a succinct but powerful turn of phrase, that climate change is a 'wicked problem in search of a narrative'. In other words, he sees it as a problem which needs to be explored through stories that develop our understanding, rather than facts which are simply alarming and often decontextualized. This approach has the potential to engage people imaginatively and help them to make sense of dilemmas which they would otherwise find disorientating and disabling. When combined with a sense of vision and purpose, it is also an extremely effective way of binding people together in a shared endeavour. As George Monbiot (2017: 6) puts it, the challenge today is to produce a restorative political story that is 'faithful to the facts, faithful to our values and faithful to the narrative patterns to which we respond'.

Stories operate on many different levels. They can entertain; they can express our fears and worries; they can encapsulate our hopes for the future. Stories are also incredibly powerful because they can enable people who have never met to collaborate in a common cause. This is an argument that is made by Harari (2015), who contends that the medieval church and the modern nation state are both examples of institutions that have been united by a common idea presented through myths and/or stories. When it comes to sustainability and environmental issues, stories of gloom and doom have remarkably little appeal and are likely to leave us feeling powerless in the face of overwhelming odds. Hopeful stories, on the other hand, serve as a rallying point for action and, by tapping into our emotional responses, leave us feeling empowered. That's why the great speeches of politicians, religious leaders and others are passed down from one generation to another. Amanda Gorman (2021), the US youth poet laureate, achieves a similar feat in her rap poem 'Earthrise', which succeeds in presenting unpalatable facts about environmental problems in an upbeat and engaging manner.

Can you think of any texts, poems, raps or protest songs which have inspired you to think differently? Can you explain how some images (a photograph, drawing or artwork) may have similarly altered your views?

Finding a hopeful sustainability story – a new and compelling vision which is true to our own lives and to current realities which can be told in many ways – is going to be crucial in shifting perceptions and creating new mindsets. We are in trouble now, theologian Thomas Berry explains, because we have come to see the world only as a collection of objects to be used. One of the consequences is that we no longer think of animals as our companions within a single community of existence and have 'devitalized' (2006: 18) the planet. How we see ourselves in relation to the natural world is a recurring theme in any discussion about sustainability and it raises questions (a) about human exceptionalism and (b) about human nature.

Human exceptionalism

People are clearly different from other creatures, not least because they have developed highly sophisticated symbolic communication systems such as language and found ways to use technology to achieve powers far beyond their physical strength. However, on a biological level, human beings are part of the chain of creation which links people directly to other organisms. Our closest living animal relatives include chimpanzees, gorillas and orangutans, and we are part of a larger family called 'the great apes'. In a world which is dazzled by technology and progress, it is easy to lose sight of our evolutionary heritage and the fact that we depend on the environment for our survival. Human exceptionalism elevates people and suggests we have somehow left our past behind. The idea that we are destined for greatness flatters our egos but is also highly corrosive. It validates grand engineering projects that modify the physical world on a huge scale, it justifies the environmental devastation caused by industrial agriculture, and it suggests there that are potentially no limits to human achievements. The balance between people and nature is lost in the process.

Exceptionalism permeates our thinking in unexpected ways. Nowadays many children take part in school projects which focus on different ways of 'saving the planet'. These projects can result in much worthwhile work but they also inadvertently reinforce a particular mindset. The charming picture book, *George Saves the World by Lunchtime* (Readman 2006), highlights this problem. The slightly tongue-in-cheek text describes how, by adopting certain pro-environmental behaviours, George becomes a 'world-saving super hero' in the space of just a few hours. Encouraging readers to recycle and reuse materials, as George does, is altogether laudable but the deeper point is that the world will always survive and doesn't need to be saved; it's people who need to be saved from themselves.

Do you think it is realistic to place the responsibility for sustainable living on individuals? What has to change in society for it to become the norm?

Human nature

It is often claimed that human beings are naturally greedy and self-seeking. Just as in the animal kingdom only the fittest survive, it is argued that competition is an integral part of human nature and that self-preservation is a key motivational force. To put it crudely, if we strive for success we will rise to the top, but we have to compete to get there. While there may be some truth in this viewpoint, it is incomplete and ultimately misleading. To begin with, it is now recognized that co-operation and interrelationships are fundamental principles governing the natural world, which are perhaps even more important than competition and independence (Capra and Luisi, 2014; Sheldrake 2020). Also,

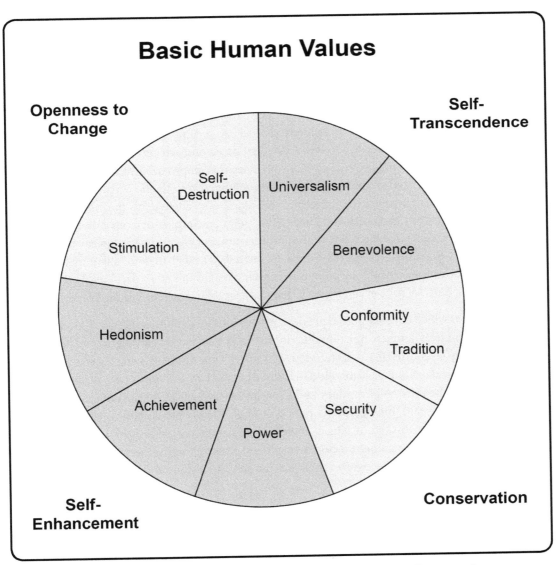

Figure 3.3 The theory of human values developed by Shallom Schwartz illustrates how our behaviour may be motivated by conflicting goals. *After Schwartz (1992).*

human beings are imbued with many different qualities which operate in tandem. Values to do with survival and personal enjoyment need to be seen alongside altruism, co-operation and empathy for others. Psychologist Shallom Schwartz (2012) concludes from extensive cross-cultural surveys that values can be arranged into four main types which operate in two opposing dimensions: openness to change versus conservation, and self-enhancement versus self-transcendence (Figure 3.3). We prioritize different values according to our social and cultural context, our personal beliefs and our circumstances at the time. The complexity of human nature is evident in other ways. Rather than contrasting selfishness with altruism, Lent (2017) argues that it is the capacity for symbolic thought communicated through language which distinguishes human beings from other creatures.

> How can we equip children with strategies to find a way forward in situations where values conflict?

The assumptions about human nature and human exceptionalism which are deeply embedded in modern society have been thrown into sharp relief by the environment crisis. Tim Jackson (2017: 131) argues that modern capitalism is underpinned by a simple yet 'ferociously destructive' misconception of human nature which sees individual greed and self-interest as the engine which will bring benefits to the whole of society. Not only does this emphasize just one aspect of human nature at the expense of all the others, it also justifies unfettered growth and consumerism which we know is no longer sustainable. This perception is aided and abetted by the notion of human exceptionalism which, as Kingsnorth and Hine (2009) point out, implies that our actions do not have consequences. They argue that the vision of the glorious future of plenty and prosperity that will arise when our mastery of nature is complete is indeed a myth. It is a story that no longer matches reality and fails to meet our needs. And they point out that what makes this story particularly dangerous is that, for the most part, we have even forgotten that it is a myth and believe it is the 'truth'.

Replacing notions which have supported previous generations for centuries and which now underpin the global community is bound to be a tumultuous process. It will involve rearranging and recalibrating our ideas at a deep level. This process is referred to as a paradigm shift, following the seminal study of scientific revolutions by Thomas Kuhn (1962). Kuhn described a paradigm as the cluster of thought patterns – shared theories, beliefs, values and procedures – which enables a community to make progress in its practice and thinking over a period of time. The key point about a paradigm is that it has many different elements, all of which interrelate and reinforce each other to create a unified interpretation of reality. A paradigm includes values and assumptions just as much as hard physical facts. A paradigm shift therefore involves multiple changes, all of which will have knock on effects.

Forging a new approach

It was argued in the previous chapter that the current world economic order (neoliberalism) is based on a limited, and increasingly unhelpful, view of what constitutes prosperity and wealth.

Neoliberalism is well established and it has all the strengths which comes from a paradigm that has developed over time and which is entrenched in political and social structures. However, as environmental problems have become more evident, there have been increasingly urgent attempts to modify neoliberal practices. Some of these are principled and well intentioned; others are more concerned with window dressing. The problem is that they all have to operate within a larger system which is designed to extract and create monetary wealth from the natural environment. This system lacks any meaningful way to account for the impact of economic activities on the resources on which it depends. It is increasingly evident that the 'business as usual' approach which has been, and continues to be, the mainstream neoliberal response to the environment crisis is no longer viable. Changing it requires a paradigm shift.

There have been many attempts to kickstart this process of wholesale change. The Earth Charter and the United Nations Global Goals are two major international initiatives which have achieved considerable resonance.

The Earth Charter

The Earth Charter (2000) was a civil society project arising from the 1992 Earth Summit in Rio de Janeiro. It was informed by extensive consultations over a six-year period and it draws on ideas and wisdom from different communities, cultural traditions and religions. The resulting document is structured around four main themes:

1 respect and care for the community of life
2 ecological integrity
3 social and economic justice
4 democracy, non-violence and peace

The Charter has a rousing text. It opens by declaring 'we stand at a critical moment in Earth's history' which holds both 'great peril and great promise' and it ends by calling for the 'awakening of a new reverence for life'. One of the key ideas in the Charter is that people need to co-operate to 'bring forth a sustainable global society' – an aim which requires governments to work together. But what is particularly significant is that the Charter is based on values, and thus provides an ethical compass towards a more caring, respectful and responsible way of living. Scott and Vare (2021) speculate that, because the Charter concerns rights, responsibilities and justice, it might come to fulfil a much-needed role as the Magna Carta of our times. However, they also question the contradictions it contains and the assumption that humanity can ever attain harmony and perfection. This raises the question of whether the quest for sustainability represents a search for some kind of utopia, and hence an enticing vision, which is never actually attainable. This is not to say that visions are not needed – simply that they need to be recognized as aspirational.

Can you think of any visions which have inspired people in the past? What issues might be encountered in turning a vision for the future into a reality?

Global Goals

There have been literally dozens of conferences, resolutions and international agreements relating to the environment over the last few decades. On an international level, the United Nations has made repeated attempts to co-ordinate action and promote sustainable living. Two programmes which take a broad overview stand out as especially significant. The Millennium Development Goals (MDGs) outlined a programme for combatting poverty, reducing hunger, enhancing social welfare and improving environmental sustainability in the period 2000–15. Building on this momentum, the Sustainable Development Goals (SDGs) extended the agenda for the next fifteen years (2015–30) and placed a stronger focus on environmental issues as well as partnerships between organizations and governments.

Both the MDGs and the SDGs have achieved almost universal support from governments around the world and were endorsed by all UN member states. They involve clear reporting mechanisms and have the advantage of bringing together social and environmental issues under a single heading. As well as being aspirational, they are grounded in what can actually be achieved. Like any international agreement, they are inevitably based on compromises and ambiguities. Despite this, they provide a broad framework for action and, in educational circles, serve as a useful reminder of the different dimensions of sustainability. Local groups, communities and institutions, including schools and universities around the world, have endorsed the SDGs and pledged to promote them.

One of the chief criticisms that has been levelled at the SDGs is that they are purely voluntary. As a result, governments can gain credit for signing up to them without any obligation to actually do anything in practice. The goals themselves are cumbersome, technocratic and difficult to communicate – there are seventeen goals with a total of 169 targets. The goals are presented as separate rather than interconnected objectives and are considered out of context. This means that the legacy of colonialism which still permeates trade and economic relations today is not taken into account. One of the key aims is to support sustainable development but there is no attempt to unpick what sustainable development might actually mean or whether development can ever actually be sustainable. Moreover, while the goals appear to give equal weight to economic, social and environmental aspects of sustainability, they are actually dominated by economics. As they stand, it is difficult not to see the SDGs as one more example of the 'business as usual' approach which fails to break through the invisible ceiling of the neoliberal paradigm. This ceiling acts as a barrier and often invalidates attempts to reform current practices across many spheres of life, including education.

If you were to write your own global goals, what would they be? Would they all have equal importance? What do you think would have to change to bring them about?

The global challenge

It is now increasingly recognized that the different environmental and social issues which seem to be discrete and self-contained are actually manifestations of a single bigger problem about how to live within planetary limits. William Rees (2021) expresses this challenge in terms of ecological overshoot and he focuses especially on the extraordinary growth in human numbers in the last two hundred years. It is estimated that after millennia of very slow growth, the world population reached 1 billion in 1800. This number more or less doubled in the nineteenth century and nearly quadrupled in the twentieth (Figure 3.4). Rees (2021) suggests that this trajectory is typical of the plague stage of a boom-bust cycle that applies to all species as they acquire food and resources to support their expansion. He argues that sooner or later essential life support systems, such as food and fresh water, will become exhausted, leaving an ever-larger population competing for dwindling supplies. This echoes the gloomy predictions made by Thomas Malthus in the eighteenth century and raises the prospect of global social and economic chaos as organized life implodes. However, human beings are significantly different from other animals and have the capacity to plan ahead and anticipate the future. In some countries human numbers are currently declining as couples delay having children, and around the world there now appears to be a dramatic drop in fertility rates. In the longer term, rather than overshoot, this could lead to population collapse.

Do you think that William Rees is right to be worried about population growth?

There are many different ways of responding to an emergency. There are those who call for immediate decisive action which mobilizes all the available physical and human resources. This response resembles a war effort and it draws its strength from the realization that we simply cannot continue on our present trajectory. The difficulty which then arises is to decide what action is actually needed – something which is highly problematic when the 'enemy' is constantly changing and appears in many guises. It also raises questions about implementation at a time when there are few appropriate global governance structures and little international political agreement. Quite simply, dramatic one-stop solutions are unlikely to be the answer to sustainability problems which are multifaceted and span many domains from the geo-physical and biological to the political, social, cultural and psychological. Climate scientist Mike Hulme (2014: 138) argues that it is all too easy to fall into the trap of regarding the Earth as a spaceship with technical problems that need to be fixed when the human dimension is at least half the story. Instead, he favours multiple 'clumsy solutions to regularly reframe problems in order to achieve merely incremental gains' as the best way to tackle the super wicked problem of sustainable living.

The challenges facing us today are unlike any which have confronted us in the past. Using the metaphor of a journey, James Speth (2008) sees humanity as having reached a fork in the road along which it has been travelling for centuries. Both the routes ahead lead into unknown territory and to dramatically different environments. However, one route ('business as usual') leads to a

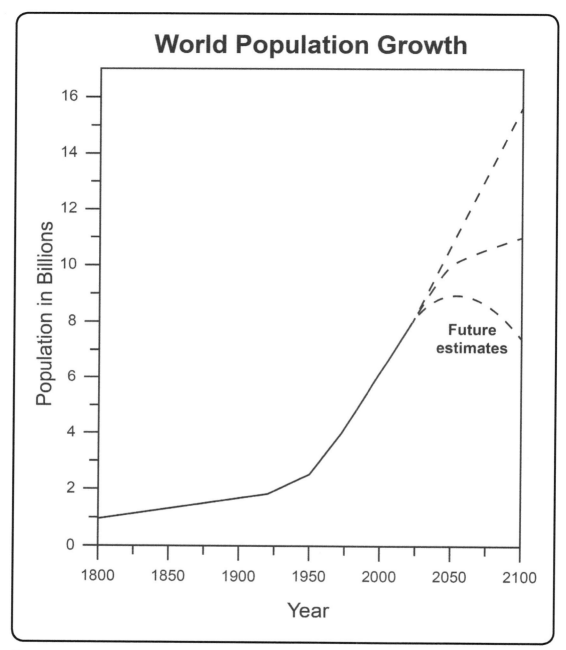

Figure 3.4 The latest estimates suggest world population will grow to around 11 billion people by the end of the century. *Source: UN World Population Report 2020.*

ruined planet. The other route (the 'Great Turning') goes over a bridge and into the future. In a 2021 report to inform public policy, Dasgupta uses remarkably similar words:

> Humanity now faces a choice: we can continue down a path where our demands on Nature far exceed its capacity to meet them on a sustainable basis; or we can take a different path, one where our engagements with Nature are not only sustainable but also enhance our collective well-being and that of our descendants.
>
> 2021, headline messages

What are the factors that will determine which path we take? Much depends on how we see ourselves, our wisdom and our vision of the future. Reimagining the world and reinventing the narratives which underpin our lives at a fundamental level will help to steer us over the bridge that leads from environmental crisis to sustainable living. There is a deep sense that the future is in our hands as never before. Just imagine, Kate Raworth (2107: 58) exclaims, if ours could be the turn-around generation that started putting humanity back on track for a globally sustainable future. Raworth, like many others, believes that education has an important role in nurturing the young people that could bring about change. Education on its own is unlikely to be the solution to current problems but it could help to initiate the thinking or paradigm shift that might bring it about.

Conclusion

Scientists and campaign groups have been warning about environmental problems for many decades to little effect. It is now recognized that simply telling people the facts has only a limited impact on our behaviour – social and psychological factors are much more important. An alternative approach is to set out a vision of the future based on ecological and sustainability principles encapsulated in compelling stories and accounts of the world. Trying to maintain our present trajectory, the 'business as usual' approach, is manifestly untenable but the transition to more sustainable ways of living will require a wholesale shift in the ideas which underpin society today. As we negotiate the troubled times that lie ahead, wisdom and humility will be at a premium. It is both salutary and inspiring to think that the leaders of tomorrow are in schools and universities today where they will be developing the ideas and abilities which will permeate their own lives and those of the people around them. Education has a vital role in nurturing the qualities that will be essential in an uncertain future.

References

Berry. T. (2006) *Evening Thoughts*, San Francisco: Sierra Club Books.

Capra, F., and Luisi, P. (2014) *The Systems View of Life: A Unifying Vision*, Cambridge: Cambridge University Press.

Dasgupta, P. (2021) *The Economics of Biodiversity: The Dasgupta Review, Abridged Version*, London: HM Treasury, available at https://assets.publishing.service.gov.uk/government/uploads/system/uploads/attachment_data/file/957292/Dasgupta_Review_-_Abridged_Version.pdf.

Earth Charter (2000) available at https://earthcharter.org/library/the-earth-charter-text/.

Gorman, A. (2021) *Earthrise*, available at https://www.youtube.com/watch?v=xwOvBv8RLmo.

Hulme, M. (2014) *Can Science Fix Climate Change?*, Cambridge: Polity Press.

Jackson, T. (2017) *Prosperity Without Growth* (2nd edn), London: Routledge.

Kingsnorth, P., and Hine, D. (2009) *Uncivilization: The Dark Mountain Manifesto*, available at https://dark-mountain.net/about/manifesto/.

Kollmuss, A., and Aygeman, J. (22002) 'Mind the Gap; why do people act environmentally and what are the barriers to pro-environmental behaviour?' *Environmental Education Research* 8:3, 241–59.

Kuhn, T. (1962) *The Structure of Scientific Revolutions*, Chicago: The University of Chicago Press.

Lent, J. (2017) *The Patterning Instinct*, New York: Prometheus Books.

Macy, J., and Johnstone, C. (2012) *Active Hope*, Novato, CA: New World Library.

Markinowski, T., and Reid, A. (2019) 'Reviews of Research on the Attitude–Behaviour Relationship and Their Implications for Future Environmental Education Research', *Environmental Education Research* 25:4, 459–71.

Marshall, G. (2015) *Don't Even Think About It*, London: Bloomsbury.

Monbiot, G. (2017) *Out of the Wreckage*, London: Verso.

Moss, A., Jensen, E., and Gusset, M. (2016) 'Probing the Link Between Biodiversity-Related Knowledge and Self-Reported Proconservation Behaviour in a Global Survey of Zoo Visitors', *Conservation Letters* 10:1, 33–40.

Raworth, K. (2017) *Doughnut Economics*, London: Random House.

Readman, J. (2006) *George Saves the World By Lunchtime*, London: Penguin.

Rees, W. (2021) 'Climate Change Isn't the Problem So What Is?', keynote lecture delivered at Tel Aviv University, 28 January 2021, available at https://www.youtube.com/watch?v=9oVTHKzC7TM&feature=youtu.be.

Rockström, J. (2020) 'Ten years to transform the future of humanity – or destabilize the planet', TED talk available at https://www.ted.com/talks/johan_rockstrom_10_years_to_transform_the_future_of_humanity_or_destabilize_the_planet?language=en#t-44.

Rockström, J., and Klum, M. (2015) *Big World, Small Planet*, Stockholm: Max Ström Publishing.

Schwartz, S. H. (1992), 'Universals in the Content and Structure of Values: Theoretical Advances and Empirical Tests in 20 Countries', *Advances in Experimental Social Psychology* 25, 1–65.

Schwartz, S. H. (2012) 'An Overview of the Schwartz Theory of Basic Values', *Online Readings in Psychology and Culture* 2:1, available at https://doi.org/10.9707/2307-0919.1116.

Scott, W., and Vare, P. (2021) *Learning, Environment and Sustainable Development*, London: Routledge.

Sheldrake, M. (2020) *Entangled Life*, London: Bodley Head.

Speth, J. G. (2008) *The Bridge at the Edge of the World*, New Haven and London: Yale University Press.

Sterling, S. (2019) 'Planetary Primacy and the Necessity of Positive Dis-Illusion', *Sustainability* 12:2, 60–6.

Part II

Sustainability Education

In many countries there are formidable barriers to introducing sustainability education in formal educational contexts. Limited support from government, the pressure on the curriculum and its implementation, and the lack of expertise and guidance for teachers are notable factors. The current focus on factual knowledge, accountability and compliance is also an unhelpful development which serves to hinder innovation and experiment.

This section explores a range of practical and theoretical challenges. Two key issues are dealing with denial and anxiety, and finding ways to talk about controversial issues in a neutral way. The value of structuring learning around concepts and principles is also stressed – there is no prescribed body of knowledge relating to sustainability education. What then does it mean to be sustainability literate and how can sustainability education be assessed? This is a question which suggests the need for a broad conception of educational purpose and success criteria.

4

Teaching About Sustainability

Summary

This chapter raises questions about the purpose of education and how it needs to be reframed in the light of the environment crisis. It also draws attention to some of the problems associated with sustainability education and suggests pedagogical strategies for dealing with them. Although sustainability education is often seen in terms of practical action, it is argued that critical reflection and analysis are equally important. Rather than being mutually exclusive, different approaches are a source of strength. Even within the constraints of current educational systems there is scope for innovations and they have the potential to refresh, and eventually replace, established practices.

Thomas Gradgrind is a notorious character from literature who will probably be familiar to quite a number of readers. He appears in the opening pages of Charles Dickens's *Hard Times* (1854), where, in the role of school proprietor, he quizzes a class of school children about their factual knowledge. 'What I want is Facts,' he roundly declares in the opening paragraph of the book. 'Teach these boys and girls nothing but Facts. Facts alone are wanted in life. Plant nothing else, root out everything else.' As the classroom scene unfolds, one unfortunate child, Sissy Jupe, is castigated for allowing sentiment or 'fancy' into her thoughts. She would paper the walls of a room with pictures of horses and have carpets with patterns of flowers on the floor of her house. You are not to have any ornament or decoration, she is told, which would contradict the facts. In Gradgrind's world, the only knowledge that counts is based on mathematical figures which are susceptible to proof and demonstration (Figure 4.1).

This representation of an English Victorian school is clearly a caricature but it draws attention to a fundamental question. What is the purpose of education and what do we want children to learn when they are at school? Educational philosophers have been asking this question for centuries and it remains as pertinent today as it ever has done. The values and aspirations of society are centred on schools because young people hold the key to the future. It is through education, in the broadest sense of the term, that a culture perpetuates itself. As a result, education is often seen as having a powerful role in bringing about social change. It is prized because it has the potential to nurture the best qualities in human nature and to create the conditions in which young people can

Figure 4.1 Thomas Gradgrind only wanted children to be taught facts. © *Illustration by Pat Tourret reproduced with kind permission of B L Kearley Art & Antiques.*

flourish. But unless education is underpinned by an appropriate set of values, it can also pave the way to social engineering and, in extreme cases, indoctrination.

Striking a balance between the transmission of knowledge and personal development is a delicate process. Gert Biesta (2015), a leading authority in the field, argues that education has multiple purposes. He points out that it always involves the acquisition of something – knowledge, skills or dispositions – and this is given formal recognition in qualifications. However, schools also communicate strong messages about desirable ways of living and how we relate to others which means they are engaged with socialization. Additionally, education in all its forms, impacts the formation of the person. Biesta calls this 'subjectification' because it operates on the level of the person or subject. These three purposes or domains – qualification, socialization and subjectification – are distinctive but cannot be separated. When we focus on just one of these domains, as Gradgrind did in his model school, things go wrong. We also need to remember that education is a practical not a theoretical endeavour. It has to balance not just educational practice, but also educational policy and educational research. This brings to the fore judgements about what we want to accomplish in each of the three domains, as well as decisions about the most appropriate ways to achieve them.

Are there any particular aspects of your own education which you felt were unbalanced? What impact did this have on you? How might such problems be addressed in future?

Reframing education

At the moment education in mainstream settings across the world is largely structured around traditional academic disciplines. Indeed, apart from the addition of ICT, the curriculum in many jurisdictions would be familiar to teachers from the nineteenth century. This is strange because the last couple of centuries have witnessed some of the biggest changes the world has ever seen. Political and social structures have been transformed, and science and technology have recalibrated the way we live our lives almost beyond recognition. Many critics have commented on the failure of schools to adjust to circumstances. Stephen Sterling (2001), for example, notes that education is preparing students for a world that no longer exists, Jon Jensen (2014) argues that we are still educating as if there was no planetary crisis, and Erik Assadourian (2017) talks about how the curriculum is maladapted to current needs.

The growing environment emergency might suggest the need to broaden the curriculum but in fact the opposite has happened. High-stakes assessment, accountability, and a managerial culture which has come to dominate education in many countries in recent years have had a limiting effect. For example, international rankings such as the PISA (Programme for International Student Assessment) tests conducted by the OECD focus on just three subjects – reading, mathematics and science. These tests for 15-years-olds are widely publicized and have a significant influence on government policy. Meanwhile, at primary level, the three Rs of reading, writing and arithmetic continue to take pride of place, just as they did in the past. As a result, the curriculum has become significantly unbalanced and limited in its ambition. In England, for example, music and the arts have only a tenuous place on the timetable, while in many schools it appears that the humanities are 'struggling to survive' (Barnes and Scoffham 2017: 298). Another aspect of contemporary education which needs to be questioned concerns the notion of achievement. Is education, Tony Eaude (2017: 348) asks, simply a frantic 'race' to accumulate information and skills, or is it the much more 'sinuous process' of helping children develop the qualities and dispositions they will need in a puzzling and uncertain world?

Are you aware of any problems or limitations in the curriculum you have to follow at the moment? Would you make any change if you had a free hand?

Schools have a duty to educate children for the future. The extent to which they can question and challenge the norms of the society of which they are a part is open to debate. However, if they lag behind the world around them, then it is difficult to see how they are living up to their responsibilities and fulfilling a leadership role. In setting out the case to systematically reframe education around Earth care principles, Assadourian makes this point particularly forcefully:

> Most schools are foregoing their responsibility to question the status quo – whether this is the dark history of colonization and genocide on which industrial civilization is founded, or the horrific ecological and societal abuses on which the consumer economy continues to be built. The current role of schools will have to change if we are to prepare students to slow down – and survive – the ecological transition ahead.
>
> Assadourian 2017: 7

Trying to anticipate what might lie ahead is fraught with difficulties. Many would agree with Dave Hicks (2014) that we are educating children for 'troubled times' and that there are great uncertainties ahead. However, there are also some aspects of our lives which have enduring qualities and which are likely to persist. Biesta (2015) identifies a number of issues which he believes will remain central concerns for both education and wider society in the years to come:

(a) Democracy – how to live together and value our differences
(b) Ecology – how to manage and sustain our lives on a planet with limited capacity
(c) Care – how to 'carry' others, particularly those who are not yet, or no longer, able to carry themselves

Do you agree with Biesta that these are central concerns? Would you identify any others?

These questions all involve moral choices and lead Biesta (2015: 8) to argue that the fundamental educational task is to arouse in pupils the desire to question whether what they desire is actually desirable for (a) their own lives, (b) the life they live with others, and (c) the life they live collectively on a vulnerable planet. He sees this as the shift from an 'ego-logical' to an 'eco-logical' perspective, and as part of what it means to live in the world in a 'grown-up' way. This task not only confronts education in general, it is central to sustainability education in particular. And it suggests the need for a deep shift or reorientation. Biesta sees this as a process of interruption and resistance in which schools provide a refuge where other ways of being (and being together) can be practised. This applies to all levels of education from early years settings upwards.

The terms in which Biesta frames the task of education chimes with the working definition of sustainability used in this book. It was argued earlier (see page 14) that sustainability involves reconnecting to yourself, each other and the environment at a range of scales. What Biesta makes particularly clear is that this is an endeavour which is predicated on an ethical base. David Orr (1994: 5) made the same point over twenty years ago when he cautioned that, without attention to

Figure 4.2 Arousing the desire to learn is a key feature of sustainability education. *Photo: iStock. com/FatCamera.*

basic principles and values, education might merely equip pupils to be 'more effective vandals of the Earth'. Sustainability issues nearly always involve values and often involve judgements about values which are incompatible and conflict with each other. A balanced approach to education which gives proper scope to subjectification or personhood suggests how values, rather than being externally imposed, can be aroused or drawn out as pupils engage critically and creatively with learning over a period of time.

Primary school teachers have many different opportunities, despite the constraints of the formal curriculum, to construct situations that excite children's curiosity and which will prompt them to reflect deeply on their experiences and beliefs (Figure 4.2). Practical activities can be particularly powerful motivators, but, as Barnes (2017: 10) explains, these do not have to be high-profile, resource-heavy events that take weeks of planning. An engaging story, an interesting visitor or a trip to the school pond or local side streets all have the potential to grasp learners' attention at an emotional, sensory, social and intellectual level. Even within the classroom there will be many situations, often completely unplanned, which invite discussion and critical reflection. One of the skills of teaching is to seize opportunities as they arise. They are much more likely to occur when pupils feel confident in their relationship with their teacher and sufficiently secure to ask questions which could leave them looking exposed. The ethos of the school and classroom also makes a big difference.

Have you ever found that pupils sometimes 'take over' a lesson in a way you didn't expect? How did that make you feel? What were the positive and negative consequences?

Overcoming barriers and obstacles

Sustainability education touches upon sensitive and contested areas. It is sometimes argued that these are too complex for young children to understand and thus better left until they are older. The science behind climate change, for example, is highly technical and, even if its impacts are clearly visible, the causes can be hard to comprehend. Scoffham (2015) reports on the range of ideas about climate change in a sample class of English 9-year-olds, which reveals their confusion. 'It's something in Antarctica,' one child declared. 'The Earth gets really hot and starts to crack,' said another. 'It's when you close the door and all the heat goes out,' said a third. However, these misconceptions are certainly not a reason to ignore an issue which is impacting on people's lives all over the globe. By the time they come to school, most children will be well aware of the unfolding global crisis. They will have seen videos and images of endangered wildlife, bush fires, storm damage and other disasters. Learning about what is causing these problems can help to empower them and allay their fears. Environmental issues need to be addressed rather than ignored, even if they are controversial. For teachers to turn inwards and pretend that nothing is wrong would, as Hicks (2014: 23) puts it, be 'an educational crime'.

Engaging with environmental issues raises questions about activism and what is legitimate within an educational context. How, for example, should teachers position themselves with respect to campaigns and protests relating to sustainability and the current environment emergency? The climate change strikes inspired by Greta Thunberg are a case in point. Some schools and teachers aligned themselves with the protests but others, including UK government ministers, expressed concerns that pupils were missing out on lessons. The wider perception that such events might challenge the status quo and lead in unexpected directions leaves teachers in an ambiguous position. Although there is little or no reference to direct action in most formal school curricula, Howard Jones and colleagues (2021) found from a study of secondary school teachers in England that there was considerable support for forms of learning about climate change that pushed boundaries, even if it was intentionally disruptive. An additional point is that an in-depth understanding of environmental issues will almost inevitably involve critiquing existing power structures and relationships. This means that there is inevitably a political dimension to addressing issues around sustainability education which cannot be easily ignored, especially with the older pupils. Teachers will always have to tread a delicate line between supporting and challenging social values.

What role do you think teachers should take with respect to encouraging or supporting climate change action?

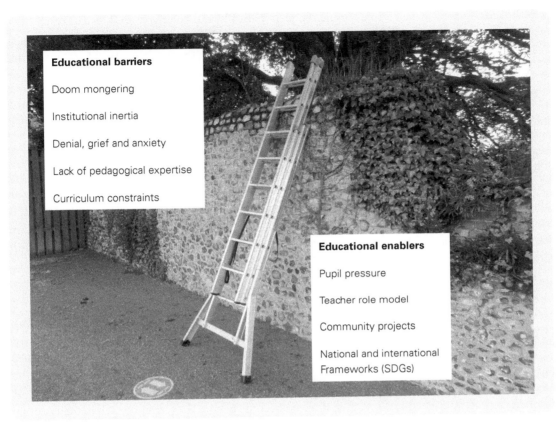

Figure 4.3 Some of the obstacles and opportunities to sustainability education. *Photo: John Hills.*

There are a number of other considerations to take into account when teaching children about environmental issues. These include (a) doom-mongering, (b) denial, (c) grief, (d) hope, (e) spiritual awareness. Being aware of the issues that may arise and having practical strategies to deal with them are part of building a pedagogy for sustainability education (Figure 4.3). There is no set formula, rather a broad recognition that what children are learning can impact their sense of identity and well-being, and therefore sustainability education needs to be approached with care.

Doom-mongering

The facts and figures behind the current crisis make grim reading. One consequence is that it is all too easy to become overzealous in presenting ever more startling information, and for pupils to become overwhelmed by what they are learning. Striking a balance isn't always easy but needs to be kept firmly in mind. Scott and Vare (2021) point out that, in the past, ESD (Education for Sustainable Development) was often the province of very committed teachers who were prone to proselytizing, and this is often still the case. Preaching about sustainability is liable to be counterproductive in any context and is particularly inappropriate in educational settings where pupils need to be encouraged to examine the facts critically and creatively so they can reach their own conclusions. If education simply becomes a process of inculcating predetermined values, it ceases to be education and becomes indoctrination instead. There is no place for curriculum 'green-washing' in a democratic society.

Denial

Learning about the damage that human activity is causing to the planet which we treasure is potentially traumatic. Realizing that we are all implicated in environmental exploitation on multiple levels and that our current prosperity depends on unsustainable practices is particularly painful. This means that teaching about climate change and other environmental problems is potentially a safeguarding issue as it impinges on pupils' mental health. It can also elicit denial responses. Naomi Klein summarizes a number of the different well-known strategies that people invoke in difficult situations:

> We look for a split second and then we look away. Or we look but then turn it into a joke . . . Or we look but tell ourselves comforting stories about how humans are clever and will come up with a technological miracle . . . Or we look but try to be hyper-rational . . . Or we look but tell ourselves we are too busy to care about something so distant and abstract.
>
> Klein 2014:3

Primary school children, just as much as adults, are liable to invoke denial strategies of this kind. Similarly, initial teacher education students often become particularly inventive when they attempt to undermine the evidence about the scale and the urgency of environmental problems.

Are there ways of positively addressing denial strategies?

Grief and anxiety

While factual knowledge is a necessary part of sustainability education, how pupils respond to what they are learning may be equally or even more important. Macy and Johnstone (2012) acknowledge that many of us today are living double lives. One part of our brain operates on the default assumption that things are fine (the 'business as usual' approach), while another part knows that they are not. When we feel dread about what may lie ahead, outrage about what is happening to the environment, or sadness about what has been lost, we have to do something with our feelings. If we bring our fears out into the open, they lose their power to haunt us. Outrage, alarm, grief, guilt, dread and despair are normal, healthy responses to a world in trauma but they do not need to paralyse us (Figure 4.4). Grieving has a therapeutic role in helping us to acknowledge loss and it shows that we care. There are many ways that teachers can help children come to terms with environmental degradation and gain strength from their emotional distress. For example, Alexander (2010) in his seminal report on English primary education noted how pessimism about

A Letter to the Future

OK is the first Icelandic glacier to lose its status as a glacier.

In the next two hundred years all our glaciers are expected to follow the same path.

This monument is to acknowledge that we know what is happening and what needs to be done.

Only you will know if we did it.

August 2019
415ppm CO_2

Figure 4.4 Angry street protests in New York City and a funeral plaque for an extinct glacier in Iceland are two ways people have responded to climate change. *Photo: Alejandro Alvarez, Wikimedia Commons.*

climate change turned to hope in those schools where factual information and practical action had replaced unfocused fear.

Hope

Hope is the last stage in the grieving cycle that begins with shock and denial and leads into anger and grief. Hope is a complex idea. It goes much deeper than wishful thinking and optimism which tend to be rather bland and lacking in purpose. Instead, hope is grounded in the problems of the present and imagines a better future which we can all help to bring about. The great Brazilian educator Paulo Freire sees hope as an ontological need – in other words, it is essential for our existence. This leads him to conclude that one of the tasks of the progressive educator is to 'unveil opportunities for hope, no matter what the obstacles might be' (2004: 3). With respect to sustainability education, Hicks also acknowledges the importance of a hopeful disposition and highlights the importance of success stories that can be a source of empowerment for pupils and teachers alike. 'No problem,' he writes, 'environmental or otherwise should be taught at any level of education without a concomitant emphasis on positive strategies for its resolution' (2006: 76). Children do not come to school to be made to feel anxious or depressed. They come to school to fulfil their potential as joyful and imaginative learners. Approaching sustainability education in a spirit of hope does more than counter the stultifying effect of gloom and despair. Such an approach has the potential, Macy and Johnstone (2012: 2) claim, to position us at the start of an 'amazing journey'. This is a journey which involves waking up to the beauty of the world and expressing our gratitude for what can still be saved in order to develop new ways of thinking for the future.

What is the difference between being hopeful and having a vision for a better future?

Spiritual awareness

Sustainability education can never be simply restricted to cognition. Not only does it involve emotional responses such as anger, anxiety, grief and hope, it also has a spiritual dimension. A sense of wholeness, an appreciation of the harmony of the universe, underpins a sustainability mindset. Many people experience moments in their lives when they feel deeply connected and at peace with the world. They may marvel at the mystery of creation or suddenly feel immensely small as they gaze at the stars. When he wrote about seeing 'a world in a grain of sand' or 'eternity in a grain of sand', the poet William Blake was alluding to something which poets and mystics have been trying to encapsulate for centuries. This might be expressed in secular terms as a sense of the sublime, or as the sacred in religion. The key point is that there are some experiences which simply cannot be put into words and elude comprehension. The theologian Rudolf Otto (1923) uses the term 'ineffable' to describe this type of awareness, and he argues that it embraces religious fear and dread as well an apprehension of our own nothingness. In today's educational environment, which is driven by targets and measurable outcomes, it is difficult to acknowledge the spiritual dimension of life. Awe and wonder cannot be quantified. Yet the psychological and mental well-being of children is increasingly recognized as part of the remit of primary schools and seen as a matter of growing concern. Sustainability education, far from unsettling children with doom-laden predictions, can nurture the psychological resources which will give them the strength to face changing circumstances.

Different settings

Sustainability education is not confined to formal education and classroom environments. Indeed, it developed outside these settings and is only now starting to come, rather haltingly, into mainstream practice. A range of initiatives which flourished in the final decades of the last century set the scene. These included peace education, development education, futures education, human rights and justice education, as well as education for sustainable development. All these different movements had a strong ethical base and they generated considerable enthusiasm among committed teachers at the time. However, they never really coalesced under a single heading or succeeded in forging an organized and systematic body of knowledge. As a result, sustainability education still flies under a number of different banners. In the UK, for example, many children learn about sustainability through eco-schools projects, forest schools, or the government-sponsored Global Learning Programme. This means they will engage with some aspects of sustainability but are unlikely to develop an overview. Furthermore, many of these projects have a strong focus on the natural environment. While they may introduce children to the principles of ecology, such projects can easily mask sustainability principles which are significantly different in their focus. Every discipline has its own unique way of seeing the world, and ecology (the study of organisms and their environment) is different from sustainability which is about how people can live with each other within planetary limits.

One of the distinctive features of sustainability education is that it is strongly associated with practical action. Since the 1970s, United Nations conferences have made it clear that environmental education goes beyond knowledge to include the development of active citizens. Recent statements continue to affirm this goal. For example, the guidance for schools issued by UNESCO (2019) opens with the following words:

> ESD empowers learners to take informed decisions and responsible actions for environmental integrity, economic viability and a just society, for present and future generations, while respecting cultural diversity. It is about life-long learning and it is an integral part of quality education.

Practical action, whether growing food, planting trees, raising money for good causes or campaigning on environmental issues, is seen by many primary school teachers as almost synonymous with sustainability education. It is no coincidence, for example, that Dolan (2021) focuses on giving multiple examples of the things that schools can do in her text on education for climate change and a post-carbon future.

What environmental activities are you aware of in primary schools? What are their proposed and actual outcomes?

Sustainability education has many manifestations. Environmental projects in and around the school can be highly motivating, and engaging with local community groups brings sustainability to life in a way that cannot be achieved in the classroom. Such activities also allow children to channel their energies in a constructive manner and can be an excellent way to build sustainability awareness across the school and the wider community. At a time when many people feel the need to 'do something' to combat environmental degradation, literally getting your hands dirty is both cathartic and affirmative. However, there is a danger that practical projects will lack critical depth unless they are accompanied by reflection and analysis. Scott and Vare (2021) see sustainability education as having two dimensions. On the one hand, it promotes positive behaviours where the need is identified and actions are agreed. On the other, it builds capacity for critical thinking and explores the contradictions that are inherent in trying to do the 'right' thing. These are not separate approaches, rather they are different sides of the same coin. Lander (2017) takes a similar approach and brings these different dimensions together under the broad heading of wisdom.

An inclusive approach

As the urgency of the environment crisis becomes increasingly apparent, the question of how best to respond becomes ever more pressing. There are those who favour direct and decisive action and believe the time for talking is over. Others are more circumspect, worry about environmental authoritarianism which polarizes debate around compliance or rejection, and see long-term behaviour change as offering a more promising route forward. These different responses play out in primary schools just as they do in wider society. Sterling (2019: 64) speculates that the current enthusiasm for environmental projects, such as tree planting, local food production and action on plastic waste, may be a reactive response as people wake up to current realities after a 'kind of collective sleepwalking'. As an alternative, he favours anticipative learning which is 'reflexive and critically self-aware and is directed at wise corrective action in the light of evidence'. A further point is that direct action within mainstream educational structures may not always be appropriate. What is important is that children are given opportunities to harness their strengths and abilities in constructive ways. Helping them to develop a sense of agency is deeply empowering and counters the helplessness experienced by those who think of themselves as victims.

Different approaches to sustainability education are not necessarily contradictory or mutually exclusive. Indeed, a variety of responses would be in line with the ecological principles of diversity and resilience and might be expected when dealing with complex and ambiguous issues. The paradox model proposed by Kemp and Scoffham (2022) provides a framework that embraces difference. Their model is structured around two axes. The horizontal resistance-alignment axis (x axis) refers to the extent to which sustainability education can be authentically developed within existing educational structures. The vertical slow-fast vertical axis (y axis) relates to the educational challenge of responding to an emergency or crisis situation (Figure 4.5). Campaigning and political action fall into the 'fast-resistance' quadrant of the diagram; desk-bound curriculum activity fits into the 'slow-alignment' quadrant. Both contribute to sustainability education, and can be pursued in tandem.

The paradox model can be applied to a range of circumstances and at different scales. The inner circle represents the individual level, with the surrounding rings corresponding to group and whole school/organization responses. The point where the x and y axes intersect is the position of maximum tension but also a vantage point where possibilities can be considered and compared. Furthermore, the framework indicates how the demand for fast action might actually be reconciled with slow responses. Equally, the desire to resist has to be understood in relation to alignment to current demands for accountability and compliance. The proposal from the Sustainable Solutions Development Network (2020) to build a 'second operating system' within existing structures makes sense in this context. Inspirational processes and practices can, over time, refresh and replace traditional structures.

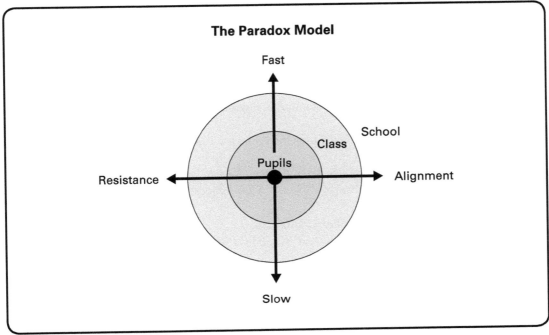

Figure 4.5 The paradox model provides a conceptual framework that unites different approaches to sustainability education. *After Kemp and Scoffham (2022).*

Conclusion

The environment crisis raises questions not only about sustainable living but also about the role and purpose of schools. At the moment education is seen in largely utilitarian terms and the curriculum is structured around traditional academic subjects which restrict the possibilities for integrated learning. Sustainability education suggests the need for a new approach underpinned by an ethic of social and environmental care. It combines practical action with critical reflection and raises far-reaching questions about what is desirable. As they introduce children to environmental issues, teachers need to be aware of the dangers of 'green-washing', on the one hand, and the risk of exciting pupils' anxieties, on the other. A focus on hope and a positive vision for the future can help to overcome obstacles and provide spiritual nourishment. Working within the constraints of current educational systems and the growing evidence of environmental catastrophe creates many tensions but it also offers exciting points for embarking on new approaches. There is an urgent need to start teaching *as if* the planet matters because it most certainly does.

References

Alexander. R. (2010) *Children, Their World, Their Education*, London: Routledge.

Assadourian, E. (2017) 'EarthEd: Rethinking Education on a Changing Planet' in *EarthEd: Rethinking Education on a Changing Planet*, Washington, DC: Island Press.

Barnes, J., and Scoffham, S. (2017) 'The Humanities in English Primary Schools: Struggling to Survive', *Education 3–13* 45:3, 298–308.

Biesta, G. (2015) 'The Duty to Resist: Redefining the Basics for Today's Schools', *Research on Steiner Education* 6: 1–11.

Dolan, A. M. (2022) *Teaching Climate Change in Primary Schools*, London: Routledge.

Eaude, T. (2017) 'Humanities in the Primary School – Philosophical Considerations', *Education 3–13* 45:3, 343–53.

Freire, P. (2004) *Pedagogy of Hope*, London: Continuum.

Hicks, D. (2006) *Lessons for the Future*, Victoria, BC, and Oxford: Trafford.

Howard-Jones, P., Sands, D., Dillon, J., and Fenton-Jones, F. (2021) 'The Views of Teachers in England on an Action-Orientated Climate Change Curriculum', *Environmental Education Research* 1–37, DOI: 10.1080/13504622.2021.1937576.

Jensen, J. (2014) 'Learning Opportunities for Sustainability in the Humanities' in Boring, W. P., and Forbes, W. (eds), *Teaching Sustainability*, Nacogdoches, TX: Stephen F. Austin State University Press.

Kemp, N., and Scoffham, S. (2022) 'The Paradox Model: Towards a Conceptual Framework for Engaging with Sustainability in Higher Education', *International Journal of Sustainability in Higher Education* 23:1.

Klein, N. (2014) *This Changes Everything*, London: Penguin.

Lander, L. (2017) 'Education for Sustainability: A Wisdom Model' in Leal Filho, W., Mifsud, M., Shiel, C., and Pretorius, R. (eds), *Handbook of Theory and Practice of Sustainability in Higher Education 3*, New York: Springer.

Macy, J., and Johnstone, C. (2012) *Active Hope*, Novato, CA: New World Library.

Orr, D. (1994) *Earth in Mind: On Education, the Environment and the Human Project*, Washington, DC: Island Press.

Otto, R. (1923) *The Idea of the Holy*, Oxford: Oxford University Press.

Scoffham, S. (2015) 'Should Children be Learning About Climate Change?' in Sangster, M. (ed.), *Challenging Perceptions in Primary Education*, London: Bloomsbury.

Scott, W., and Vare, P. (2021) *Learning, Environment and Sustainable Development*, London: Routledge.

Sterling, S. (2001) *Sustainable Education: Revisioning Learning and Change*, Dartington: Green Books.

Sterling, S. (2019), 'Planetary Primacy and the Necessity of Positive Dis-Illusion', *Sustainability: The Journal of Record* 12:2, 60–6.

Sustainable Solutions Development Network (2020) *Accelerating Education for the SDGs in Universities*, available at https://resources.unsdsn.org/accelerating-education-for-the-sdgs-in-universities-a-guide-for-universities-colleges-and-tertiary-and-higher-education-institutions?mc_cid=57cd628037&mc_eid=726fdf3cb.

UNESCO (2019) *What is Education for Sustainable Development?*, available at https://en.unesco.org/themes/education-sustainable-development/what-is-esd.

5

Curriculum Organization and Management

Summary

Sustainability education draws together and synthesizes ideas from different subject areas to create a distinctive way of thinking. It fits uneasily into current curriculum structures but has the potential to act as a catalyst for change. This chapter sets out the principles and concepts which underpin sustainability education in the primary school years. It also considers some of the issues surrounding progression and assessment, and the importance of interactive teaching methods. This leads into a discussion about different ways of understanding sustainability literacy. The importance of connecting to ourselves, other people and the environment serves as a unifying thread.

Satish Kumar is a former monk, peace campaigner and environment activist who has been quietly advocating for change for the past fifty years. One of the founders of Schumacher College in Devon, UK, he argues that children need to learn through their whole bodies and through all their senses. 'We need to move away from just a "brain experience",' he declares. 'I would like to make education more holistic. Knowledge without experience is only half the story' (2021: 18).

The debate about how to educate children has a long history. The seventeenth-century English philosopher, John Locke (1693), set out a curriculum that included French and Latin along with Arithmetic, Geography, Chronology, History and Geometry. Meanwhile, the eighteenth-century French thinker, Jean-Jacques Rousseau, argued that children should be allowed to develop naturally without constraints. There is no shortage of opinions about educational matters and they have a strong political dimension. The curriculum is contentious because it reflects social values and involves making hard choices about what to include and what to leave out. It also begs the question of whether learning is actually a step-by-step process and whether all pupils follow the same learning trajectory. However, there is often a gap between what is explicitly stated in a programme of study and the way it is interpreted and delivered in the classroom, so any attempt to exercise control is bound to be an imperfect process. Much depends on the skills of the teacher and the influence of the hidden curriculum, because unwritten rules and expectations can have a big impact on how children approach their learning.

Cross-curricular approaches

One area of contention which affects primary schools in particular concerns the extent to which the curriculum should focus on traditional academic disciplines. Generally speaking, cross-curricular or trans-disciplinary learning is favoured in early years settings, while older pupils are expected to focus on single subjects in order to develop greater depth and more specialist knowledge. The middle years of childhood (ages 7 to 11) are a transition period in which both approaches are adopted. However, they sit rather uneasily alongside each other – those who argue for the integrity of their subject are opposed to those who prefer not to divide learning into rigid categories. Sustainability education is a newcomer to this contested terrain and straddles both approaches. It draws on different subject areas in order to explore contemporary issues but also seeks to combine them to create a synthesized understanding. As a result, sustainability education embraces integrated perspectives which go beyond single subject teaching and has a rather ambiguous place in the established curriculum.

There are a number of different ways of structuring cross-curricular or trans-disciplinary approaches which are especially relevant to sustainability education. In a theme-based approach, pupils explore a place, artefact, process or issue related to sustainability using the perspectives of several different subject disciplines. For example, applying the language, skills and attitudes of science, geography and English to an area of marsh or woodland near the school or the water cycle or forms of transport would allow pupils to explore sustainability more deeply. An alternative is a synthesis approach which starts from a powerful learning experience that engages pupils both socially and emotionally. This can promote new learning in two or more different subject areas whose approaches are subsequently integrated as part of an original presentation, performance or exhibition on a sustainability theme. Direct engagement with a local issue such as air pollution, plastic waste or habitat destruction are all examples of powerful learning experiences which engage children emotionally, drive them to want to find out more and raise questions about what they value. In

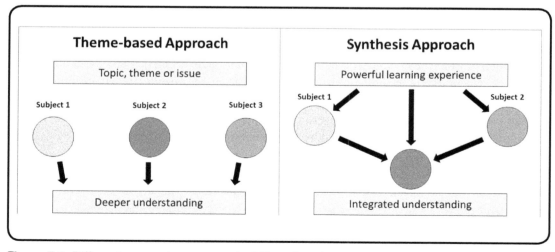

Figure 5.1 Different approaches to sustainability education: (a) theme-based, (b) synthesis.

practice, these two approaches or models are liable to become blurred – which one you adopt and how they develop will depend on your circumstances and educational objectives (Figure 5.1).

What do you think are the advantages and drawbacks of both approaches?

At a classroom level it seems likely that the forms of knowledge and understanding, which will prove useful as the twenty-first century matures, will be fundamentally interdisciplinary. Barnes (2015: 21) draws attention both to the unprecedented rate of social and technological change, and to the increasing expectation that schools will promote children's physical and mental health. He argues that cross-curricular themes and groupings 'more properly address our changing times and uncertain future' and sets out the case for a curriculum that emphasizes global interrelationships and understanding. Coming from an ecological perspective, Capra and Luisi (2014: 12) reach a broadly similar conclusion. They maintain that, because 'all phenomena are ultimately connected and embedded in the cyclical processes of nature', an holistic perspective is essential to understanding the world and our place within it. Fortunately, we can think holistically and adopt integrated approaches to learning without losing the knowledge and understanding that stands at the heart of subject disciplines. However, there is a powerful case for a curriculum that better reflects the unity of lived experiences and for pedagogies that are informed by research and analysis into how children learn. By highlighting current needs and different responses to them, sustainability education thus has the potential to foreground principles and concepts that over time could prompt far-reaching curriculum reform.

Areas of study

At the moment, many primary schools are introducing children to specific sustainability topics. For example, climate change, plastic pollution and the Amazon rainforest are widely studied; so, too, are biodiversity loss and natural disasters. However, these topics are often selected on an ad hoc basis in response to current affairs and depend to a large extent on the enthusiasm of committed teachers to carry them forward. What tends to be lacking is a curriculum which sets out a balanced range of study areas and which identifies unifying concepts and principles. Progression and assessment are also neglected areas, and are especially challenging given the ambiguities that permeate sustainability thinking. The teaching suggestions and activities outlined in this book have been devised with these considerations in mind and seek to provide an organizational framework for sustainability education which will help to move it more securely into mainstream practice.

Twelve areas of study covering different aspects of the relationship between people and the natural world are featured in subsequent chapters. These emphasize social and environmental issues and highlight important contemporary concerns. Each study area is then broken down into topics with age-related teaching ideas. The first few study areas focus on the physical setting: the final ones are geared much more strongly towards personal and interpersonal understanding. All the study areas are keyed into the United Nations Sustainable Development Goals (SDGs) which, despite their imperfections, provide an agreed framework that has gained widespread acceptance. It would have been impossible to reference the curriculum from more than one or two jurisdictions anyway, so having this common reference point has the advantages of reaching out to schools and teachers who may be working in a wide range of contexts and to different curriculum specifications.

One of the challenges of teaching about sustainability concerns the extent and depth of the knowledge required. Environmental problems often draw on several subject areas and even apparently simple issues can quickly become quite technical and complex, so it is easy for the teacher to feel ill-informed and tempted to avoid tackling them altogether. This would be a mistake. It is important to recognize and understand that primary school teachers are responsible for many different subjects and cannot be equally knowledgeable about them all. Sara Parkin (2010: 10) has a reassuring dictum which applies in these circumstances. She argues that with respect to sustainability what matters is 'having *sufficient* knowledge and understanding to make a *good enough* choice or decision'. Parkin makes the point that with *good enough* insight you should be able to work out when you need to know more and whether you can go ahead with reasonable confidence. As she puts it, *enough* is often *sufficient*. Expressing the same idea a slightly different way, robust subject knowledge doesn't necessarily have to be comprehensive. What matters more is having the confidence and ability to offer an adequate explanation at an appropriate level.

How do you feel about 'learning with the children'? Do you think it provides a sound learning experience for both parties?

A further point is that sustainability education involves much more than just factual knowledge. It was argued in the previous chapter that it engages pupils on an emotional and spiritual level, and cultivates fundamental dispositions such as values, beliefs and judgement that only develop over long periods of time. A synoptic vision, the ability to see the big picture, as well as attention to detail, is part of a sustainability mindset, so it is sometimes helpful to check whether a particular topic or area of study contains a balance of perspectives. Learning about the natural environment is an obvious starting point, but social and economic affairs also need to be taken into account as they can be crucially important. Terms such as 'wonder' and 'engagement' point the way to a focus on creativity and imagination. These different elements can be associated with the four points of the compass as illustrated in the diagram below (Figure 5.2). This makes them easy to remember and helps to provide a sense of direction in investigations that may vary from the local to the global.

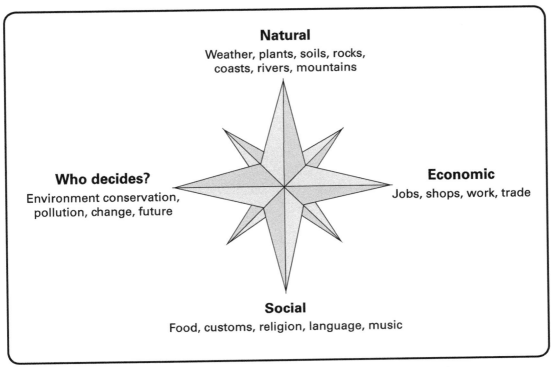

Figure 5.2 A balanced sustainability study will encompass a range of perspectives.

Pedagogy

Perhaps one of the most enduring legacies of the environmental movements of the late twentieth century is that they forged pedagogies based on active and co-operative learning. The techniques that they pioneered were a timely reminder that *how* children learn is every bit as important as thinking about *what* they should learn. This was one of the conclusions highlighted by Robin Alexander (2010) in his seminal report into English primary education. Furthermore, as Satish Kumar (2021) points out, children approach learning in many different ways. Rather than focusing on the traditional three Rs (reading, writing and arithmetic), Kumar argues schools would do well to pay greater attention to the three Hs (head, heart and hands). After all, learning about the future of the world is fundamental to sustainability education and it comes from the heart as well as the head.

Findings from neuroscience research confirm the importance of affective engagement in learning. Immordino-Yang and Damasio (2007), for example, draw on empirical evidence to conclude that rational thought depends on emotional triggers, and Fischer (2009) stresses the importance of active experience in sculpting neural connections. More recent studies (Immordino-Yang et al. 2018) confirm that opportunities to engage actively and safely with rich and meaningful environments, along with supportive social relationships and exposure to a wide range of ideas, have a significant impact on brain development. Sustainability education has inherited this tradition and is widely seen as involving 'participatory teaching and learning methods' (UNESCO 2017: 53). The importance of activity is summed up by one trainee teacher who noted in her journal, 'Sustainability and climate change cannot be tackled through school textbooks alone. Our students must experience sustainable behaviours for themselves through hands-on learning' (Dolan 2020: 224).

Have you any experience of bringing participatory learning into the classroom? What was the effect on pupils and the way you planned future sessions?

The pedagogies that are associated with sustainability education match those employed by creative and imaginative teachers. In their research into creative teaching, Cremin et al. (2009) found that such teachers adopted a wide variety of approaches. No single method could be singled out for its value or effectiveness, rather creativity was promoted by a mixture and combination of styles. Over thirty pupil-initiated activities were noted (Figure 5.3). One teacher commented, 'The more ways you have of conveying information, the better.' Another observed that mixing different styles involved 'adopting to changing circumstances but staying true to the learning objectives'. The research emphasized the benefits of providing children with multiple entry points for learning and allowing them to take control of their work. It also highlighted the value of linking ideas together, connecting pupils' lives to the curriculum, asking questions, working collaboratively and encouraging independence and responsibility. Such approaches, when set alongside the personal qualities of the teacher and the ethos of the school, created a powerful cocktail of ingredients that nurtured pupils and made learning more interesting, exciting and effective.

Enquiry/investigation	Role play	Internet and library research
Construction	Reflective writing	Fieldwork
Demonstration	Using picture books	Discovery
Conversation	Devising stories	Photographs and videos
Explanation	Poetry and riddles	Making maps and diagrams
Simulations	Role play and drama	Making models
Debate	Dance and music	Quizzes
Reverse/open questioning	Making games	Competition
Problem solving	Playing games	Tests
Time for reflection	Edible and visual aids	Class league tables

Figure 5.3 Teaching techniques and activities used by creative teachers. *(After Cremin et al. 2009)*

Principles and concepts

Whatever form it may take, sustainability education needs to be underpinned by general concepts and principles. As well as providing guidance when it comes to selecting content, these overarching ideas provide a structure which helps to reveal the deeper meaning and significance of specific topics and activities. The table below (Figure 5.4) highlights:

(a) general principles which apply in a wide range of settings;
(b) concepts which relate more specifically to economics, society and the environment (the three dimensions of sustainability highlighted in the SDGs);
(c) personal qualities which are integral to sustainability education.

Unifying ideas

General Principles
Balance Care Connections Cycles Harmony Peace Resilience Systems

Economic concepts	Social concepts	Ecological concepts
Capital	Citizenship	Conservation
Development	Community	Diversity
Growth	Democracy	Habitat
Innovation	Equality	Interdependence
Progress	Health	Place
Prosperity	Inclusion	Pollution
Resources	Power	Resilience
Technology	Social justice	Tipping points

Personal Qualities
Creativity Criticality Curiosity Empathy Humility Integrity Vision Wonder

Figure 5.4 Sustainability education is underpinned by multiple principles and concepts, and favours pedagogies that nurture children's environmental awareness.

Which general principles do you think are the most important? Can you devise a diagram to show how they interrelate?

Sustainability education is an emerging area of study and the ideas presented here are not intended to be definitive or prescriptive and are liable to change over time. However, they do illustrate its distinctive characteristics:

- The general principles are particularly important when it comes to recognizing patterns and the links between different topics and areas of study.
- The economic, social and environmental concepts highlight the ideas which relate to particular aspects of sustainability.
- The personal qualities focus on the intellectual tools, beliefs and values that pupils will draw on and develop through their work.

Although these principles, concepts and qualities are presented in separate columns, they are all interrelated. The overlap between sustainability and ecology is particularly striking and it reflects the way that sustainability has grown out of a concern for nature and the environment. However, ecology is about understanding the laws of nature whereas sustainability is about finding ways to live within environmental limits and focuses especially on human behaviour. It follows that using a solely ecological paradigm to underpin sustainability education will be inappropriate because it adopts a different perspective and seeks to do different things.

Progression and assessment

What might progression in sustainability education look like and how can it be assessed? This is a complex question which can be answered in a number of ways. On a general level, the depth of thinking and understanding about a specific issue is a useful indicator of a child's progress. Achievement may also be evidenced through a pupil's ability to weigh different arguments, to think critically and creatively about a problem which they have investigated, and to reach balanced judgements in situations where there are conflicting viewpoints. This is an ability which develops gradually with age. It is also important to remember that sustainability education is every bit as concerned with ways of living as with subject knowledge, so assessment needs to take spiritual and emotional learning into account. Bringing together the different dimensions of sustainability education (head, hands and heart) suggests a route towards deep and lasting educational impact. This can only be achieved over long periods of time and is not amenable to quick fixes. It is also hard to assess. One practical strategy is to compile a portrait of pupil achievement that focuses on three different dimensions: (a) knowledge and understanding, (b) fieldwork and investigations, (c) critical thinking and reflection. These categories recognize the multifaceted dimensions of sustainability education and acknowledge its various manifestations including its local and global dimensions (Figure 5.5).

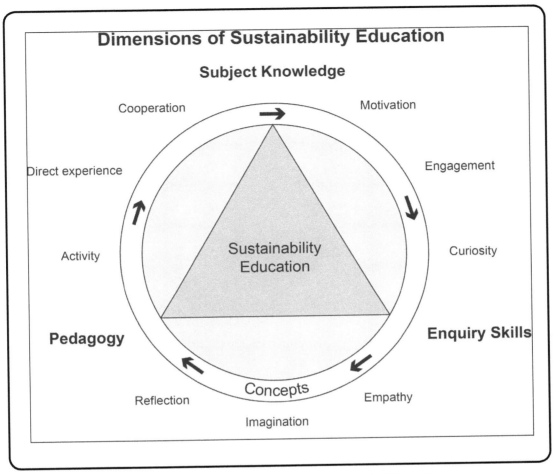

Figure 5.5 Concepts provide a structure for progression in sustainability education bringing knowledge, enquiry and pedagogy together in powerful ways, and deepening understanding of complex issues.

In what other ways do you think progression might be usefully indicated in sustainability education?

Progression in sustainability education also needs to be informed by a generic understanding of child development. The focus on tactile exploration and physical movement in the very early years gives way in infants to role play, make believe and experimentation. As children grow older their self-identity becomes stronger and they develop the ability for symbolic thought. In terms of environmental education, David Sobel (2008) contends that a deep sense of connectedness with nature, yet also the feeling of being unique and separate from it, is one of the 'core gifts of middle

Figure 5.6 Pupils from a London school taking photographs for a portrait of their local area.
Photo: Gemma Anidi.

childhood' (15). He sees a sense of agency as the foundation for responsible action and he advocates small world play where children can create miniature environments to explore abstract ideas in a concrete way. The problem with a lot of education, he contends, is that it gets 'too big, or too abstract, too fast' (46). And he makes a plea to keep environmental tragedies out of the classroom until children reach at least the age of 9.

By the time they have completed their primary education at age 11, pupils should have achieved a certain level of sustainability literacy. While it is tempting to enumerate this in terms of competencies, it may well be better to adopt a more open and less prescriptive stance. Competencies and measurable outputs align with a technocratic mindset and tend to reflect production-line thinking. Furthermore, as Biesta (2016: 4) argues, education is an inherently 'weak' process which is 'slow, difficult and frustrating' and can never be guaranteed. Rather than focusing on the production of predetermined learning outcomes in a small number of subjects, it should be seen as opening up safe spaces where students can encounter their freedom to make informed choices and opportunities to consider how they want to live their lives. In other words, learning needs to be drawn out of pupils by skilful teachers in carefully crafted situations and cannot be prescribed. Furthermore, because sustainability thinking requires an holistic view, it resists being atomized. If it is broken down into components, there is a danger that its essential quality will be lost (Figure 5.4).

Perhaps this is also the place to note that learning, in sustainability just as in other domains, is not simply a matter of individual achievement. It is often a collective endeavour and the result of collaboration across a group, or co-constructed by a teacher and pupil working together. The notion of 'scaffolding' that was pioneered by Lev Vygotsky and Jerome Bruner, and the idea of the 'community of practice' developed by Etienne Wenger (1998), help to explain how people of all ages work together rather than in isolation. Indeed, even when we have an idea which we think is original, it often arises in the context of a wider discussion and has much more extensive roots than we consciously acknowledge. The concept of 'distributed intelligence' (Gardner 1982) points to how people spark ideas off each other and move forward in their thinking as part of a creative bubble. The implications for assessment are that the credit for individual progress needs to be tempered by an understanding of the context in which it happened. Moreover, because the pedagogies and practices of sustainability education are orientated towards co-operation and collaboration, group assessment has particular relevance. Conversely, the ethos of competition which is so deeply rooted in contemporary education may need to be reframed in the light of the priorities which we are now confronting.

Do you think that some tasks are better suited to individual rather than group work? How might group work be assessed?

Whole school approaches

Whatever the external constraints, teachers have considerable scope to exercise their professional judgement within their classrooms, particularly with respect to the way that they interact with pupils. In favourable circumstances they may be able to make sustainability the keystone of everything that they do. In other situations, they may be limited to introducing environmental issues as examples and case studies. It is important to remember, though, that even if sustainability education is not explicitly mentioned in the curriculum it is often implied in one way or another. Also, teachers can hold firm to their values and beliefs despite demands for compliance and the constraints of accountability and league tables. As one of the first adults outside the family that children encounter on a regular basis, teachers are very significant role models who do much to shape both the formal and the hidden curriculum. This influence is often underestimated because it is difficult to document. In their research, Cremin et al. (2009) noted how a range of personal qualities from enthusiasm and curiosity to risk-taking, humour and fun had a major impact on the style and effectiveness of the teachers that they studied. But they also acknowledged the impact of school leadership and the importance of school ethos. Whole school approaches in which all staff collaborate on agreed objectives and subscribe to a common vision of education are liable to be particularly effective in allowing sustainability education to flourish.

What barriers to introducing sustainability have you encountered? How might these be overcome?

Conclusion

Sustainability education cuts across traditional subject boundaries and has an ambiguous place in the curriculum in many jurisdictions. In the absence of an established knowledge base, children's achievements need to be understood in terms of the propensities they develop rather than competencies they can exhibit. Whatever form it takes, sustainability education gains in coherence when it is underpinned by general principles and concepts. Progression is not easy to quantify but can be evidenced through investigations, critical thinking and reflection just as meaningfully as through knowledge and understanding. It also involves a spiritual and emotional dimension. While learning is seen in terms of individual achievement, it often arises from group and collaborative endeavour. Whatever circumstances they are working in, teachers have significant opportunities to nurture sustainability thinking through active and participative learning. Whole school approaches in which all staff collaborate on agreed objectives and subscribe to a common vision of education are liable to be particularly effective.

Ultimately, thinking about the organization and management of sustainability education challenges us to articulate what we are seeking to achieve. Reflecting on the purpose of education, David Orr (2020) emphasizes the importance of making connections. Connections operate on a number of different levels. We make connections to ourselves and our inner being, to the people around us, and to the physical environment and places that we know. We also make connections to the past through our individual and collective memories, and to the future through our hopes and expectations. Sustainability education is about reframing the way we see ourselves and our place in the world. Two deceptively simple questions go straight to the heart of this endeavour: What kind of person do I want to be? What kind of society do I want to live in? Keeping these questions firmly in mind will serve as a lodestone as we proceed into a future that will be unlike anything that has gone before.

References

Alexander, R. (2010) *Children, Their World, Their Education*, London: Routledge.

Barnes, J. (2015) *Cross-Curricular Learning 3–14* (3rd edn), London: Sage.

Biesta, G. (2016) *The Beautiful Risk of Education*, London: Routledge.

Capra, F., and Luisi, L. (2014) *The Systems View of Life: A Unifying Vision*, Cambridge: Cambridge University Press.

Cremin, T., Barnes, J., and Scoffham, S. (2009) *Creative Teaching for Tomorrow: Fostering a Creative State of Mind*, Deal: Future Creative.

Dolan, A. (2020) *Powerful Primary Geography*, London: Routledge.

Fischer, M. B. E. (2009) 'Building a Scientific Groundwork for Learning and Teaching' in Christodoulou et al. (eds), *Usable Knowledge*.

Freire, P. (1970, 2007) *Pedagogy of the Oppressed*, New York: Continuum.

Gardner, H. (1993) *Frames of Mind: The Theory of Multiple Intelligences*, London: Fontana.

Immordino-Yang, M., and Damasio, A. (2007) 'We Feel Therefore We Learn: The Relevance of Affective and Social Neuroscience to Education', *Mind, Brain and Education* 1: 3–10.

Immordino-Yang, M., Dorling-Hammond, L., and Krone, C. (2018) *The Brain Basis for Integrated Social, Emotional and Academic Development*, Washington, DC: Aspen Institute, available at https://www.aspeninstitute.org/wp-content/uploads/2018/09/Aspen_research_FINAL_web.pdf.

Kumar, S. (2021) 'The Primary Geography Interview', *Primary Geography* 106: 16–18.

Locke, J. (1693, 1970) *Some Thoughts Concerning Education*, London: Scholar Press.

Parkin, S. (2010) *The Positive Deviant: Sustainability Leadership in a Perverse World*, London: Routledge.

Sobel, D. (2008) *Childhood and Nature: Design Principles for Educators*, Portland, MA: Stenhouse Publishers.

UNESCO (2017) *Education for Sustainable Development: Learning Goals*, available at https://unesdoc.unesco.org/ark:/48223/pf0000247444.

Wenger, E. (1998) *Communities of Practice: Learning, Meaning and Identity*, New York: Cambridge University Press.

Part III

Areas of Study

The chapters in this section focus on classroom practice. There are twelve areas of study covering different aspects of the relationship between people and the natural world. These emphasize social and environmental issues, and highlight important contemporary concerns. The first few study areas focus on the physical setting; the final ones are geared much more strongly towards personal and interpersonal understanding. All the study areas are keyed into the United Nations Sustainable Development Goals (SDGs).

Each study area is divided into discrete topics containing age-related teaching activities. Rather than comprehensive schemes of work or lesson plans, these are intended to indicate approaches and provide ideas that could be developed further within any setting. There is a certain amount of overlap between the topics, which offers opportunities for consolidation and re-enforcement. Each topic concludes with a fieldwork and investigation activity, thus emphasizing the way that sustainability education involves practical engagement and action.

6

Earth in Space

Stephen Scoffham

The Earth is the only known place in the universe where people can live. It supports a huge variety of life which has evolved over immense periods of time and it is home for 7.8 billion people. Clean air, clean water, food and shelter are vital for the survival not only of human beings but also for all the other creatures with whom we share this remarkable planet. This area of study sets the scene by focusing on some of the key features which make the Earth so distinctive and how they might be conserved to ensure the Earth remains habitable for all forms of life in the future.

It is believed that Earth was formed some 4,600 million years ago from the debris of a massive galactic explosion. The swirling mass of rock, dust and gas that was left behind slowly coalesced as different elements collided with each other. Dense material sank to form the core, while lighter material created the crust. As the third planet from the Sun, the Earth was the right distance away for life to develop and thrive. Much closer and it would have been too hot: much further away and it would have been too cold. Earth's location, in what has been termed 'the Goldilocks zone' (after the girl in the fairy tale who discovered porridge that was 'just right'), was particularly fortuitous. This meant that water was present on the surface in liquid form, rather than freezing or evaporating, and therefore available for the evolution of plants and creatures (Figure 6.1).

Learning about the larger architecture of planetary history is one way of putting human existence into perspective. We know that the Earth is currently about a third of the way through its life cycle and that in due course it will fall back into the Sun before being regenerated again. The impossibility of comprehending the scale of the universe, the vast extent of time and the mystery of life itself has evoked a sense of wonder throughout human history. It also challenges notions of human exceptionalism and suggests that we need to approach the Earth with humility and reverence. Thinking about our place in the universe is one way to fire pupils' imagination and stimulate the creative thinking that is fundamental to sustainability education. As Macy and Johnstone (2012) remind us, only those who love the world and are fascinated by it will want to care for it.

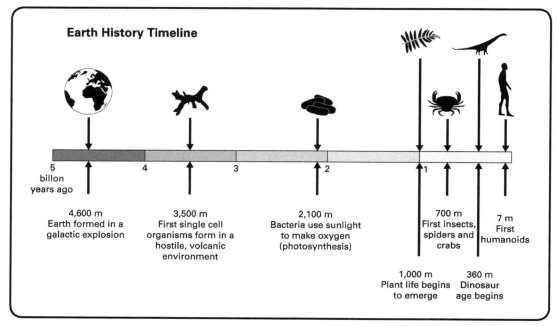

Figure 6.1 In terms of Earth history, human life is an entirely new phenomenon.

Reflection and discussion

- What do you think is most remarkable about planet Earth?
- If scientists discover other habitable planets, will this change our ideas about the need for sustainable living?
- If the Earth will eventually fall back into the Sun, extinguishing all life, does this make everything we do meaningless?

THE EARTH (AGE 3–7)

What is the main focus of this topic?

The Earth is a remarkable planet that we need to treasure.

Key ideas	Subject links	SDG links
Awe and wonder	Geography	SDG 14 Life below water
Cycles	Music	SDG 15 Life on land
Systems (solar system)	Religious Education	
	Science	

Background knowledge

Our surroundings may seem static, but the Earth is actually hurtling through space along with the rest of the solar system at roughly 67,000 miles per hour. It is also spinning as it orbits the Sun. At the same time, conditions on the Earth's surface are constantly changing. Different combinations of heat and moisture create an endless variety of weather patterns which are then modulated by the seasons. Even the rocks beneath our feet are on the move, thanks to the forces of plate tectonics. The fact that the Earth is a dynamic, living planet is one of the features which makes it so remarkable.

The Earth has just one moon. It is believed the Moon was created early in Earth history by a massive collision with another planet about the size of Mars. The impact knocked the Earth sideways, tilting the axis by 23.5 degrees, thus giving rise to the seasons. The Moon has been important to the evolution of life in other ways as, along with the Sun, its gravitational pull generates ocean tides. As the largest visible celestial objects, both the Sun and the Moon have a foundational role in human mythology and creation stories. Setting the psychological dimension alongside an understanding of the physical processes gives this topic particular traction with young minds.

Interesting facts

- The name 'Earth' is linked to a Norse myth and derives from an old Anglo-Saxon word 'erda' meaning ground or soil.
- The Earth isn't a perfect sphere – it is squashed a little bit flatter at the poles.
- The Sun is over a million times larger than the Earth.

Misconceptions and research

Young children are fascinated by the Earth and the Moon, and they ask many spontaneous questions about it (Scoffham 2013). One key issue concerns the shape of the Earth. Our eyes tell us that it is flat but photographs from space show that it is round. Young children try to reconcile this puzzle in a number of ways. For example, they may argue that there are two Earths – the one they experience and the one seen by astronauts – or that they live on the flat interface between two spheres. While the scientific conception may be true, there is a sense in which it turns people into outside observers. In a perceptive essay, Ingold (2013) reminds us that the idea of the ground beneath our feet and the heavens above our heads is a fundamental conception that children have to renounce as their learning develops.

Teaching ideas

Key vocabulary

astronaut	orbit	sun
galaxy	planet	universe
moon	space	

Getting started

Introduce the children to the idea that the Earth is one of eight planets that orbit the Sun. See if they know the names of the planets. Are the planets all the same, and which ones are closest and furthest away? Remind pupils that the Moon orbits the Earth and that the Sun is a star similar to the others that appear in the night sky.

Earthrise | *key idea: awe and wonder*

Project an image of the Earth from space onto the interactive whiteboard. The Earthrise image taken from lunar orbit by the Apollo 8 mission astronauts is a particularly good starting point as it captures the smallness and vulnerability of our planet. Edgar Mitchell described the Earth as 'a sparkling blue and white jewel, laced with slowly swirling veils of white in a thick sea of black mystery'. What words would the children use to describe it? Make a class list and discuss. Which ones are favourites?

Creation myths | *key idea: cycles*

How did the Earth begin? There are numerous creation myths from different cultures and religions which you can share with the children. The Australian aborigines are famous for their ideas about Dreamtime, Hindu texts feature a primeval cosmic being (Purusha), and the account of creation in the Book of Genesis is a key reference point for Christians, Jews and Muslims. Meanwhile, Buddhists believe the world is constantly being recreated so it has neither a beginning nor an end. Explore these different ideas, using picture books or videos to illustrate them.

The planets | *key idea: system*

Sing a song about the planets with the children. There are numerous examples to choose from available on YouTube. This is a good way of introducing pupils not only to the sequence but also to the differences between the planets. After singing one of the planet songs, they will enjoy drawing a picture to go with it. Illustrate the comparative size of the planets using balls of different sizes.

The Moon | *key idea: awe and wonder*

Read the children *Kitten's First Moon* by Kevin Henkes (website 6.1). What mistake did kitten make? Ask the children if they have ever been surprised by, or marvelled at, the Moon in any way? Have they ever seen a crescent moon in the evening sky, or a full moon which appears to be yellow or orange as it rises over the horizon? Can they see a face in the Moon? What makes the Moon so magical?

Investigations and fieldwork | *key idea: system*

Help the children to gain a practical idea of the size of the solar system. One child should stand in the centre of the playground to represent the Sun, perhaps standing on a chair holding a sun symbol. Other children should be selected to represent the planets. Working to a scale such as one pace to 50 million kilometres, they will need to position themselves as follows: Mercury 1, Venus 2, Earth 3, Mars 5, Jupiter 14, Saturn 28, Uranus 52 and Neptune 90 paces away. How does this make them feel? How long do they think it would take to travel to different planets? Which ones would they most like to visit?

Sustainability discussion | *key idea: care*

Why should we care about how we treat the Earth?

Answers might include:

(a) because it's the only home we are ever likely to have;
(b) so others can enjoy it in the future; and
(c) because it's a beautiful and wonderful planet which needs to be treasured in its own right.

AIR, LAND AND SEA (AGE 5–11)

What is the main focus of this topic?

Air, land and sea interact to provide the physical setting for life on the Earth's surface.

Key ideas	Subject links	SDG links
Diversity	English (descriptive writing)	SDG 14 Life below water
Habitat	Geography	SDG 15 Life on land
Interaction	Mathematics	
Interdependence	Religious Education	
Oneness/unity	Science	

Background knowledge

The atmosphere, and therefore the air we breathe, is made up of lots of different gases. The most important in terms of volume are nitrogen (78 per cent) and oxygen (21 per cent). The atmosphere protects us from particles and debris in space which burn up as they fall towards the surface. A thin layer of ozone in the upper atmosphere is particularly important as it filters out dangerous ultraviolet radiation from the Sun. Meanwhile, carbon dioxide, although it only constitutes a very small percentage of atmospheric gases, plays a crucial role in trapping heat and keeping the Earth warmer than it would otherwise be, enabling life to flourish. Much of the Earth's surface (71 per cent) is covered by seas and oceans. These waters are home to a rich variety of life, especially the top 100 metres where most plants and creatures are found. There are seven great blocks of land – the continents – and thousands of islands which vary in size from Greenland to tiny uninhabited rocky outcrops. This topic is about the three main components of the Earth's surface. It is also a chance to begin exploring long-term cycles and to see how different forces interact.

Interesting facts

- The average depth of the ocean is 3,600 metres, while the land is only 840 metres high.
- Europe and America are moving apart at the same speed as a human finger nail grows.
- Ten thousand years ago, Britain was joined to the mainland of Europe.

Misconceptions and research

Young children often believe that the physical landscape has been created by people. This idea, known as 'artificialism', was first highlighted by Piaget (1929) nearly a century ago and continues to be supported by more recent research. Mackintosh (2004), for example, reports than even children aged 10 and 11 hold anthropocentric ideas about rivers, although their misconceptions are gradually superseded as children grow older.

Teaching ideas

Key vocabulary

atmosphere	meteor	ozone
continent	ocean	volcano

Getting started

Using an inflatable globe (or a world map) as a teaching aid, talk with the children about the Earth's surface. Is there more sea than land? Is it possible to hold the globe so that they can only see the ocean? Is there land or water at the North and South Pole? Given that most of the atmosphere is within 10 kilometres of the surface (and that it disappears entirely above 100 kilometres), can they envisage how thin it would be on the globe you are using? Explain that sustainability involves seeing the 'big picture' and the ways things link up.

Survival needs | *key idea: interdependence*

We depend on clean air, clean water and healthy soil for our survival. To make this point, challenge the children to see if any of them can hold their breath for more than 30 seconds. Now, as a class, discuss what happens when air becomes polluted, when water is poisoned and when soil is contaminated. Ask the children to make drawings of some of their ideas for a class display. An overlapping Venn diagram with a drawing of children (and other creatures) at its centre is one possible format.

All about the atmosphere | *key idea: interaction*

Ask the children to take a clean sheet of paper and draw lines, dividing it into four sections. They should then write the following statements in each of the areas and draw a picture to go with it:

The atmosphere protects us from meteors.
The ozone in the atmosphere reduces the danger of sunburn.
The wind carries heat from one place to another.
The atmosphere holds lots of water which sometimes forms into clouds.

Talk about any connections they can see between the four sections.

Seas and oceans quiz | *key idea: biodiversity*

Ask the children to work in pairs or threes to write down half a dozen facts they know or can find out about the seas and oceans and the life it contains. Now invite them to share what they know with another group and to devise eight questions for a quiz. Stress that each question needs to have a simple, clear answer. Play the quiz, perhaps in a subsequent lesson, and reflect on the questions. How many of them related to sustainability in some way?

The continents | *key idea: habitat*

Get the children to look at an atlas to identify the seven continents and compare their shape and location. Now ask them to draw a block graph comparing the size of the continents using this data:

Asia 30%; Africa 20%; North America 16%; South America 12%; Antarctica 9%; Europe 7%; Australasia 6%. Discuss how each continent is different environmentally. For example, South America has the world's largest rainforest, while Antarctica, being covered in ice, helps keep the Earth cool.

Investigations and fieldwork | *key idea: interaction*

Have the children to draw a picture or map of an imaginary island. Talk about what they might include such as mountains, rivers, lakes, forests, glaciers, caves, cliffs and so on. They could make up little drawings to show each feature and devise suitable names for them. Get them to write a short piece explaining how it provides a suitable environment for people, plants and creatures. To complete the activity, encourage the pupils to decide where they would live on their island and where it might be located globally. For a more tactile experience, build an island model using junk or Lego.

Sustainability discussion | *key idea: care*

The planet we live on is often called Mother Earth. Discuss with the children why the Earth is seen as a mother in so many cultures. In what ways does the Earth nurture us?

Answers might include:

    (a) through providing natural resources for shelter;
    (b) by providing plants and creatures for us to eat; and
    (c) by giving us clean air to breathe, water to drink and food to eat.

LIFE ON EARTH (AGE 7–14)

What is the main focus of this topic?

Life evolved on Earth as a complex network over many millions of years – people are newcomers to the planet.

Key ideas	Subject links	SDG links
Biodiversity	Design/technology	SDG 14 Life below water
Change	Drama	SDG 15 Life on land
Human/nature interactions	English (creative writing)	
Systems	History	
Webs	Mathematics	
	Science	

Background knowledge

Life on Earth first developed nearly 4,000 million years ago as tiny organisms in a hostile environment with frequent volcanic eruptions. Over immense periods of time, other primitive organisms and bacteria began to appear. This eventually led to a sudden burst of life around 540 million years ago known as the Cambrian explosion. Fishes, crabs and spiders were some of the first creatures to evolve – the dinosaur age began 200 million years ago. In evolutionary terms humanoids are complete newcomers dating back just 4 million years, and modern humans are much more recent. Although life has developed slowly, it hasn't developed at an even pace and there have been repeated catastrophes in which nearly all life has been rendered extinct. The event which wiped out the dinosaurs 65 million years ago is perhaps the best-known example. Importantly, each mass extinction has led to even greater diversity in its aftermath. This topic touches on a number of principles which are fundamental to both sustainability and ecology. Two ideas stand out especially. First, all life is connected. Secondly, life on Earth has evolved complex networks and interconnections. These create robust systems with sufficient resilience to withstand disruption.

Interesting facts

- There are believed to be 15–30 million plant and animal species in the world but less than 2 million have so far been identified by scientists.
- The weight of all the ants on Earth is roughly equal to the weight of all the humans.
- World population has increased more than seven-fold since 1800.

Misconceptions and research

The notion of geological time is hard for both children and adults to comprehend, and it is easy to get confused with very large numbers. One way round this is to concentrate on sequencing, putting events in the order in which they occurred. Another approach is to look for examples of gradual change in and around the school – the way that metal rusts and paint slowly peels off wooden surfaces is a good starting point.

Teaching ideas

Key vocabulary

ecology	extinction	network
evolution	fossil	organism

Getting started

Introduce the children to the history of life on Earth by imagining how it might be compressed into a period of just 24 hours. There are a number of videos that do this. The key point is that while the simplest forms of life start to begin after about four hours, complex life doesn't emerge till the evening and humans only appear just a couple of minutes before midnight. And all of human history has happened in the last few seconds.

Life on Earth timeline | *key idea: change*

Set up a timeline along the bottom of a display board dating from the present day to 600 million years ago. The children can research when different creatures and plants first emerged, then make a careful drawing of one that they find interesting. Arrange the drawings on the timeline as a class display taking care to see that the scale is accurate. Talk about how organisms have become more complex with the passing of time.

Fossils | *key idea: biodiversity*

Scientists know about life in the past through the fossil record. Find out how fossils were formed (website 6.2). The story of Mary Anning, who discovered fossils of previously unknown creatures in the UK, is another way of animating this topic. Look at images of fossils and get the children to make their own fossil pictures of a variety of different creatures using potato- and junk-printing techniques. Extend the work by setting up a table where children can display their own fossils. What is it that makes them so fascinating?

Life support capsule | *key idea: systems*

Talk about what people would need in order to establish a space station on another planet. Among other things they would have to have shelter, food, water, toilets, heating, and places to exercise, play and relax. They might also want to travel to other galaxies and communicate across great distances. Invite the children to draw up designs for their own space station in either a single dome or multiple capsules. Can they imagine what it would be like to live there?

Investigations and fieldwork | *key idea: interaction*

Challenge the children to make up a poem or story about why people need to share the Earth with all living things, perhaps supported by diagrams and posters. You might read them a story or a poem which will prompt their thinking. This will form the basis for a drama which they could perform to parents or other pupils.

Sustainability discussion

What are the environmental implications of the growth in human numbers?

Answers might focus on:

(a) need for food and water;
(b) loss of space for animals;
(c) use of energy and natural resources;
(d) pollution problems; and
(e) discoveries in health, science and technology.

Introduce the notion of 'spaceship Earth'. Like any spaceship, Earth is equipped with life support systems, but if these are damaged, they can be difficult to repair and there is a danger that the craft and its crew will become marooned. Do the children think this might happen to us?

Websites

Website 6.1 Kitten's First Moon
https://www.youtube.com/watch?v=Ul1jtwcOJXM.
Website 6.2 Fossils
https://www.youtube.com/watch?v=87E8bQrX4Wg&t=35s

References

Capra, F. (1997) *The Web of Life*, London: Flamingo.
Ingold, T. (2011) *Being Alive: Essays on Movement, Knowledge and Description*, London: Routledge.
Macy, J., and Johnstone, C. (2012) *Active Hope*, Novato, CA: New World Library.
Mackintosh, M. (2004) 'Children's Understanding of Rivers' in Catling, S., and Martin, F. (eds), *Researching Primary Geography*, London: Register of Research in Primary Geography.
Piaget, J. (1928) *The Child's Conception of the World*, London: Routledge & Kegan Paul.
Scoffham, S. (2013) 'A Question of Research', *Primary Geography* 80: 16–17.

7

Life on Land

Patty Born and Stephen Scoffham

When it comes to sustainability education, many educators like to begin by teaching about the natural world. And it's no wonder: the natural world is teeming with life in all forms, from plants and mosses to insects, birds and other animals. The term 'nature' has a broad meaning. It refers to all the elements that make up the natural world: living and non-living alike. This means that it includes the inorganic world such as rocks, soils and water as well as the millions of creatures with which we share the planet. Nature is sometimes seen as cruel because it involves a fierce battle for survival and is indifferent to suffering. However, it is also seen as a source of inspiration and well-being. Either way, it provides the context for our lives.

Young children have innate curiosity about, and feelings for, animals, including those that are not immediately 'cuddly' such as fish and insects. There are so many things that young children are curious about, and, in nature, there is no shortage of teachable moments which can be meaningful and spark a sense of curiosity and wonder (Figure 7.1). Understanding how all life is interconnected changes our sense of who we are. Sustainability education thus explores what it means to be human, deepens children's sense of place, and challenges them to make choices which are responsible and socially just.

Tragically, at the present time, the natural world is threatened and thousands of plants and animal species are going extinct. This is one of the defining characteristics of the current epoch which has recently been termed 'the Anthropocene'. The geological record contains evidence of five previous mass extinctions. The best-known of these occurred 65 million years ago when the Earth was struck by a huge meteor that wiped out all large life forms including the dinosaurs. However, sufficient numbers of organisms survived each of these extinction events for life to rebuild and to return in even greater abundance. As a result of nature's resilience and diversity there were probably more than 15 million living organisms in the world by the time the first humans evolved – more than at any other time in Earth's history.

The story of how people have gradually come to dominate the world, and the impact this has had, has been told in many different ways. From the earliest times people have hunted animals and cleared land for crops but in recent decades there has been a catastrophic decline in

Figure 7.1 Drawings of mythical beast and fantastic creatures by children aged 5–10. *Drawings: Anushka and Jeevan Sharp and children from Gorilla Class, Sandgate Primary School, Folkestone, Kent, UK.*

wildlife. This collapse is largely due to a combination of events such as habitat loss, climate change, desertification, pollution, natural disasters and disease. However, human activity is now recognized as the underlying cause: overconsumption and the vast increase in human numbers are key factors. The World Wide Fund for Nature concludes that there is now 'unequivocal and alarming evidence that nature is unravelling' and that this ultimately threatens our survival (WWF 2020: 4).

Reflection and discussion

- What are your own experiences of relating to nature as a child?
- Do you feel an affinity for all plants and animals, or are there some you prefer and others that you fear? Try and explain why this is so.
- Why does biodiversity matter?

ANIMALS (AGE 3–7)

What is the main focus of the topic?

There is great diversity of animals on planet Earth.

Key ideas	Subject links	SDG links
Connections	Geography	SDG 14 Life below water
Diversity	Mathematics	SDG 15 Life on land
Webs	Science	

Background knowledge

When most people think about animals, they think about mammals and they often believe they are the most plentiful type of animal on Earth. However, less than seven thousand mammal types have been described, whereas there are over a million insect species currently known. The term 'animal' includes mammals, reptiles, amphibians, birds, reptiles, fish and insects. Classifying creatures into groups is one of the ways that people have learnt to understand them. Charles Darwin famously proposed his tree of life metaphor as part of the theory of evolution. Today, the work of taxonomists is essential for the study of biodiversity and conservation. They organize animals into groups based on their characteristics.

Animals are associated with particular qualities and attributes. Lions are seen as courageous, eagles as imperial and foxes as cunning. Heraldic and mythical beasts populate our imaginations. Young children especially are brought up on stories about animals from an early age. Monkeys, mice, elephants, pigs and chickens feature in many tales from Aesop's Fables to modern picture books. Making animal noises accompanies the first attempts of infants to make sounds as they learn to speak. As well as celebrating animals and their role in the natural world, this topic introduces children to key notions such as habitats and diversity. Even more importantly it touches on the relationship between people and nature which underpins sustainability thinking. Drawing attention to the beauty and perfection of the creatures around us highlights the richness and diversity of life.

Interesting facts

- The Antarctic blue whale is the largest of all animals and is as heavy as thirty elephants.
- There are a million ants for every human being in the world.
- Animals have been discovered in every part of the world from the depths of the oceans to the highest mountaintops.

Misconceptions and research

Although young children are usually aware of different global environments such as forests and deserts, they often struggle to say what creatures might live there. For example, research by Palmer (1998) found that only a third of 4-year-olds were able to identify creatures that live in the Arctic and even fewer were able to explain what might happen to them if the snow and ice melted. Many children thought it wouldn't matter too much. It was also suggested that they might simply hibernate.

Teaching ideas

Key vocabulary

animal	diversity	pet
bear	habitat	world

Getting started

Introduce the topic by showing the children pictures of animals from around the world. The BBC documentary films produced by David Attenborough have some extraordinary wildlife sequences, all of them beautifully filmed. There is a huge range of short clips from these films available on YouTube. 'Planet Earth: A Celebration' (website 7.1), devised during the Covid-19 pandemic, is just one example.

Pets | *key idea: care*

Talk with the children about the different pets that they keep. Why do they keep them and what do they like about them? What are their different needs – e.g. food, water, exercise, companionship and so forth? Ask the children to make a drawing of their pet and write a sentence about it. Be careful not to exclude children who don't have a pet. They could focus on an animal that they treasure or select one that interests them especially.

Somewhere safe | *key idea: co-operation*

Invite each child to think of an animal and imagine how it moves. Now get the children to make two parallel lines, facing each other so they can touch finger tips to create a 'tent' or a tunnel. The child at the end of the line should then say, '*Hello, I am a . . .*', stating the name of an animal and walk/crawl/hop through the tunnel in an appropriate manner. While they are doing this, the other children should call out '*Hello, ...! We're here to shelter and protect you!*' The child who went through the tunnel then rejoins the line until every 'animal' has had a turn. Discuss how creatures, including humans, need shelter and somewhere safe to live.

Toy display | *key idea: habitat*

Ask the children to bring a toy animal to school. Some of these will be deeply treasured so it may be best that they only come for the day! Take photographs of the toys and record their names for a class display. See if the children can make a short fact file for their toy, giving its personal name, animal type, food that it eats, and the country and environment where it might live. Can they sort the toys into groups that come from jungle, desert, oceans, polar lands? Encourage them to locate these environments on a globe, world map or atlas.

Animal quiz | *key idea: diversity*

Divide the children into groups giving each one a large sheet of paper. Now have them write down as many different kinds of animals as they can think of. Play a game. The children score a point for any animal which they have named which no one else has thought of. The aim is to have the children appreciate the great diversity of life that exists on earth.

Investigation and fieldwork | *key idea: habitat*

Go out to the school playground or a park. How many different creatures can the children find? They will probably spot quite a few small creatures such as spiders, worms, snails and birds. Help them to use specific names (e.g. green fly rather than bug) and stress they must not disturb or pick up any of the creatures as this could harm them. Back in class talk about the different places where the creatures live, reminding pupils of the safety tunnel activity. Ask them to think of ways they can ensure the animals continue to live alongside them in the school grounds. Could they plan a 'nature park' for their school?

Sustainability discussion

How are animals important in your life?

Answers might include:

- because they are companions and we'd be lonely without them;
- because they make the world more interesting; and
- because they share the world with us.

LIVING IN THE WILD (AGE 5–11)

What is the main focus of the topic?

All animals have evolved to survive in the wild.

Key ideas	Subject links	SDG links
Co-operation	Art	SDG 14 Life below water
Empathy	Drama	SDG 15 Life on land
Interaction	English (creative writing)	
Habitat	Geography	
Protection	Music	
	Science	

Background knowledge

All animals have adaptations and characteristics that make them unique. Some adaptations occur throughout a given species. For example, camouflage colouration will be present in all frogs of a particular species. There are also characteristics which can vary within species. For example, some members may be larger or stronger than the others. Adaptations and characteristics help an animal survive and thrive in its environment. Camouflage allows a creature to blend in with its surroundings, making it difficult to be seen by predators. Hibernation is a type of deep sleep which lets animals rest during harsh winter months; and co-operation is about safety in numbers and working together to survive.

Rapid climate change is now putting many animal species under considerable stress. This is particularly evident with respect to migration, in which birds travel great distances to find food and places to mate and breed. They arrive hungry and exhausted after their journey, and if weather patterns are disrupted, or they find their usual habitat destroyed, they may not be able to survive to raise the next generation. This is just one example of how complex and carefully synchronized interactions, which have evolved over many thousands of years, can be disrupted, resulting in the loss of wildlife.

Interesting facts

- Snails can sleep for three years at a time.
- Octopuses can change both the colour and the texture of their skin to match their background.
- Arctic terns travel around 30,000 kilometres each year as they migrate from the Arctic to the Antarctic and back again.

Misconceptions and research

Young children often believe their surroundings, and all the life they contain, were created by people, and they have a strongly anthropocentric view of the world. Thinking about animals and their survival needs challenges this perspective. It also evokes a sense of empathy. Trying to imagine what other creatures might feel is a valuable foundation for recognizing that other people also have diverse views.

Teaching ideas

Key vocabulary

adaptation	evolution	predator
ant colony	hibernation	protection
camouflage	mimicry	survival

Getting started

Have a class discussion about animal adaptations. For example, some animals, like tigers, have large, powerful jaws and claws, and are very strong. This helps them catch prey that can run fast. Other animals, like frogs, have camouflage that helps protect them from predators, while hedgehogs are prickly. Mimicry may be of particular interest to the children as it involves deception. Watch 'Animal Mimicry' (website 7.2) to prompt further discussion.

Create a creature | *key idea: protection*

Challenge the children to create an animal from their own imagination. Is there anything special about its eyes, ears, legs, tail or its ability to smell? What is unique about its behaviour? Does it grow particularly fast or can it survive unusual conditions? Ask the children to annotate their drawings, pointing out the special characteristics that help their creature survive. Encourage them to use terms such as 'camouflage', 'hibernation' and 'co-operation' in their descriptions. This is an excellent opportunity to develop children's vocabulary and understanding of sustainability concepts.

A day in the life of a snail | *key idea: imagination*

Snails are found in many school grounds and gardens and they often fascinate children. Get pupils to explore the local environment to see if they can find any snails. Give the pupils the chance to observe them carefully, stressing that they need to treat the snails that they find with care. Now ask the children to reflect on their experience by writing a diary entry entitled 'A day in the life of a snail'. This could record where the snail goes, what it eats, the dangers it encounters, how it manages to escape and so on. You might conclude this activity by reading the children the story of *The Snail and the Whale* by Julia Donaldson (see Chapter 17).

Ant colony | *key idea: co-operation*

Watch 'Inside the ant colony' with the class (website 7.3). What do the children think is most interesting about an ant colony? Discuss how ants find their way using pheromones. Female workers lay eggs which grow into more female workers, who care for the queen, build and defend the colony, and forage for food. Identify one student to be the queen and give small groups of children other roles: 'foragers', 'builders', 'egg-layers' and so on. Play some fun music and let the children act out their roles together (website 7.4). This activity shows that all members of a community have a certain role, and that everyone depends on one another.

Migration | *key idea: interaction*

Ask the children to make a list of some of the different birds and land animals that migrate. Now let them choose one to study in detail. Where does it spend the winter? What happens in the spring/autumn? How far does it travel? Why does it go to this new place? What hazards does their creature face during its journey? As well as making a written description, pupils could draw a map to show the migration route, and add some interesting facts and figures about their chosen creature.

Investigation and fieldwork | *key idea: habitat*

Encourage the children to devise a trail in their school or home locality on the theme of 'Nature all around us'. This should link together various points of interest such as significant trees, water features (pond, stream or lake), notable gardens, and any wasteland areas which are valuable habitats. It could also include house decorations and garden ornaments which feature plants or animals. Aim for between six and eight stops on the trail and get pupils to devise a map showing the route. Other children, suitably supervised, could try out the trail and compare it with their own.

Sustainability discussion

In what ways are human beings a threat to many animals?

Answers might include:

(a) because they are clearing the land where they live and get their food;
(b) because they are disrupting the climate, creating conditions for which they are not adapted; and
(c) because they are disrupting their life cycle which has evolved over thousands of years.

RECONNECTING WITH NATURE (AGE 7–14)

What is the main focus of the topic?

There are many connections, seen and unseen, among all things and beings on the planet.

Key ideas	Subject links	SDG links
Conservation	Science	SDG 14 Life under water
Interdependence	Geography	SDG 15 Life on land
Rewilding	English	
Webs		

Background knowledge

Nothing in nature exists in isolation. Plants and animals (including humans!) all depend on each other through a complex web of interconnections. Animals and plants also depend on non-living elements such as rocks, soils and water in order to survive and thrive. The water cycle and the erosion and creation of land forms help to make the Earth a living, dynamic system. As Capra and Luisi (2014: 12) put it, recognizing that 'all phenomena are ultimately connected and that people and societies are embedded in the cyclical processes of nature' is at the core of deep ecological awareness.

It would be easy to dwell on the negative data about the steady and catastrophic collapse of wildlife at the current time. The annual reports from the World Wide Fund for Nature provide ample evidence of the scale and significance of the crisis. This topic acknowledges the seriousness of the situation but is pitched towards actions and solutions. Pupils, even more than adults, need a sense of hope for the future if they are to understand the issues, and take the positive actions to protect their futures. Harnessing their optimism and enthusiasm is the key to ensuring they are not overwhelmed by the negative perspectives that adults sometimes dwell on.

Interesting facts

- Some ants 'farm' green fly and other little insects, protecting them so they can eat the sticky fluid that they secrete.
- Despite hunting and habitat loss, the decline in wild tiger numbers has been reversed for the first time in a century.
- Conservationists have saved gorillas from becoming extinct.

Misconceptions and research

Finding out about the dangers facing wildlife and the extent of the current catastrophe is potentially very worrying. Neurological research has established that, when learners are stressed or fearful, the amygdala releases hormones that temporarily interrupt our thoughts and activate survival responses. Over prolonged periods this can have significant effects on both physiological and cognitive functioning (Scoffham and Barnes 2011). The broaden-and-build theory proposed by Barbara Fredrickson (2000) suggests that positive emotions such as happiness and elation have the opposite effect, enhancing our thought–action repertoire and allowing us to build psychological resources. There are good reasons not to dwell too much on negative scenarios.

Teaching ideas

Key vocabulary

conservation	habitat	rewilding
food web	nature	wildlife

Getting started

Talk with the pupils about any plants and creatures they have already heard or seen today. At first their minds may be blank but they will gradually come to realize they have come across different birds (can they name any of them?), flies, bees and other insects, interacted with domestic pets, and maybe seen some farm animals. You could also remind them of all the creatures in the soil and undergrowth such as worms, slugs, snails and ladybirds, that may not have been seen but are still there. Explain that this topic is about the wildlife all around us and why is it is important.

Wildlife at risk | *key idea: conservation*

Ask the children to design icons to represent: (a) insects, (b) fish, (c) birds, (d) mammals, (e) reptiles and (f) amphibians. Now get them to research the threats and dangers to these different animal categories, writing a few sentences and adding just one statistic about each one. To develop this activity, consider why so much wildlife is at risk. What could happen in a few decades? Find out how different groups, such as Greenpeace and WWF, are working to make positive changes.

The food web | *key idea: interdependence*

Give the children rectangular pieces of card with different words that all relate to different forms of life such as 'rabbit', 'soil', 'butterfly', 'worm', 'robin', 'tree', 'flower', 'grass'. Now have them stand in a circle in a large open space such as the school hall holding up their cards so others can read them clearly. Give one child a small ball of string or yarn and ask them to throw it gently to someone else in the ring, explaining why they are connected. Repeat the process until all the children are connected. Now unravel this process and discuss how breaking each connection makes survival harder. Note that groups of fifteen are ideal for this activity.

Famous conservationists | *key idea: conservation*

Many conservation projects are strongly associated with an individual who was responsible for setting them up. The children can research the lives and achievements of different conservationists. Examples include John Muir (Yosemite National Park, USA), Wangari Maathai (Reforestation, Kenya), Octavia Hill (National Trust, UK), Dian Fossey (Gorillas, Rwanda), Jane Goodall (Chimpanzees, Tanzania), Peter Scott (World Wide Fund for Nature) and David Attenborough (broadcaster). Ask them to include photographs in their case study and some information about the project they founded. What would have happened had they not left this legacy?

Investigation and fieldwork | *key idea: rewilding*

How could your local area be enhanced for wildlife? Pupils could consider a range of options such as: (a) tree planting, (b) public and private gardens (potential wildlife havens), (c) new hedges (green corridors) and so forth. Now divide the children into groups and invite them to draw up a plan for their area using a large map to help them identify suitable sites. Stress that whatever they suggest should be practical – they need to say how their plan would be implemented. Plans could then be presented to a local councillor – doing this gives the children a sense of empowerment that their views are taken seriously.

Sustainability discussion

Why is it important to have a variety of creatures in the world?

Answers might include:

   (a) because they play an important part in maintaining the health of the planet;
   (b) because we depend on animals for food;
   (c) because they provide inspiration and joy in our lives; and
   (d) because they have just as much right to live on Earth as we do.

Websites

Website 7.1 Planet Earth: A Celebration
https://www.youtube.com/watch?v=5kizCCIhtUs
Website 7.2 Animal mimicry
https://www.youtube.com/watch?v=U1aEvHRlTxE
Website 7.3 Inside an ant colony
https://www.ted.com/talks/deborah_gordon_inside_the_ant_colony/transcript?language=en#t-92751
Website 7.4 The ants go marching
https://www.youtube.com/watch?v=Pjw2A3QU8Qg

References

Capra, F., and Luisi. L. (2014) *The Systems View of Life*, Cambridge: Cambridge University Press.
Fredrickson, B. (2000) 'The Broaden-and-Build Theory of Positive Emotions', *Philosophical Transactions of the Royal Society* 359 no. 1449: 1367–77.
Palmer, J. (1998) 'Environmental Cognition in Young Children' in Scoffham, S. (ed.), *Primary Sources*, Sheffield: Geographical Association.
Scoffham, S., and Barnes, J. (2011) 'Happiness Matters: Towards a Pedagogy of Happiness and Well-being', *The Curriculum Journal* 22:4, 535–48.

8

A Watery Planet

Sharon Witt and Helen Clarke

The Earth is a watery planet. Water is life, we are water, water is a creative force. Water covers 71 per cent of the Earth's surface and, depending on temperature, water can be found naturally in different states as a solid, liquid or vapour. Earth's water is almost everywhere: above the planet in the air and clouds; on the surface in rivers, oceans and ice; and stored deep beneath as groundwater. However, water is a complex and mysterious substance, which 'will always elude our total control, and our efforts to fully "know" it' (Neimanis 2012: 5). So, this chapter focuses on watery forms of knowledge and water-centred practices. It considers what water is like and what water does. If we think-*with* water, what kind of relations and responses come to the surface?

Children encounter water every day. Indeed, water permeates stories of life on Earth. Water supports the creatures and plants with which we share this planet and is essential to human survival. Over 60 per cent of human body weight is made up of water, and proximity to water, or 'blue space', has been found to be restorative for physical health and mental well-being. Water flows through everyday activities including agriculture, industry, transportation, energy generation, leisure and culture. In Figure 8.1, a young child from an early years setting, skilfully communicates experiences of 'wateriness'.

Water exerts positive influences in survival, participation, belonging and belief. However, too much, too little, contamination and inequalities of access can result in drought, floods, disease and migration, and cause conflicts. As more and more sources of clean, freshwater are affected by climate change, water is an increasingly fragile resource. The relationships between people and water have many implications for sustainable futures, both locally and globally. Living and learning well with water raises important questions of relationships. Water is often seen as a resource, but it is also a gift, upon which we must reflect with humility and curiosity about our future water responsibility (Haraway 2016).

Reflection and discussion

1 How is water present in your everyday life?
2 What does water do?
3 What is the magic of 'blue space'?

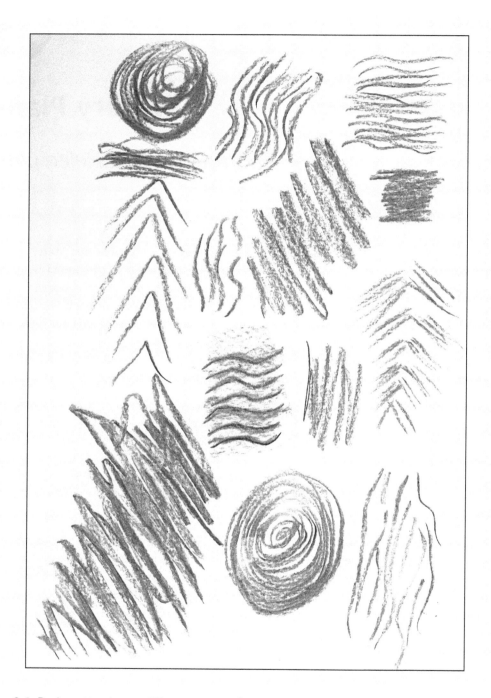

Figure 8.1 Paying attention to different types of water movement. *Photo: Sharon Witt.*

WONDERFUL WATER (AGE 3–7)

What is the main focus of this topic?

Water is a remarkable substance and is essential to life.

Key ideas	Subject links	SDG links
Care Connections Interdependence Place	Art Drama English (creative writing) Geography Music Science	SDG3 Good health and well-being SDG13 Climate action SDG 15 Life on land

Background knowledge

Water has amazing properties. It dissolves many substances which means that, as it moves, it carries the nutrients which are essential for life. Water has a high heat capacity. This helps to regulate the climate as it takes a lot of energy to raise the temperature of the seas and oceans. Water also absorbs carbon dioxide from the atmosphere which mitigates global warming up to a certain point. Water is less dense as a solid than as a liquid which is why it floats; this keeps ponds, lakes and oceans from freezing solid and allows life to continue to thrive under the icy surface. Water is tasteless, odourless and almost colourless. It spills, it pours, it flows . . .

Freshwater supports diverse ecosystems. In New Zealand, for example, the traditional concept of 'Te Mana o te Wai' refers to the integrated health and well-being of water as a continuum from the mountains to the sea, and emphasizes attitudes of respect and care. If humans are respectful about how much water they take and careful with the types of contaminants that they let go into the water, it will protect the purity of freshwater, the well-being of the environment and the health of all life, including our own.

Interesting facts

- There is more water on the Earth than any other substance.
- Water has a high surface tension, allowing some small insects to walk on its surface.
- Water 'sticks' to itself and other things and forms round droplets. This 'stickiness' helps plants to draw water from their roots up to their leaves.

Misconceptions and research

Water play extends young children's schema, as they develop understanding of the world. Horvath (2016) identifies opportunities for children to get to know water in a myriad of ways, including rolling objects (rotation); watching fish swimming (trajectory); observing the mirror-like qualities of water (orientation); gathering and grouping objects from watery environments (connection); emptying and refilling vessels (enclosure); manipulating and changing flow (transforming). How we know the world affects how we treat the world, and learning with water influences how we value this precious substance.

Teaching ideas

Key vocabulary

clean	puddle	water
drink	rain	wet
ice	wash	

Getting started

Introduce the children to 'wateriness'. Talk, model and engage in activities to encourage noticing, to observe patterns, to build vocabulary, and to use imaginations as ways of knowing. Water holds a sort of 'magic'. Think-*with* a glass of water. What has water seen? Why is water special? Why is water so important? What happens when not enough clean water is available? Think with empathy and with care.

Watching rain | *key idea: interconnections*

Water and weather are inextricably connected. Watch rain on windowpanes, trace shapes and routes of droplets with eyes and fingers. Go for a rain walk. What does rain feel like? How does it move? What patterns does it make? How does it sound? Can the children make water music or move like rain? Pause together for a rain meditation of thoughts, feelings and ideas. Make a thinking-*with* rain book (see website 8.1).

Puddle jumping | *key idea: interaction*

Water moves and changes. Find puddles in the school grounds and local area – where does water gather? Why here? Talk about puddle shapes and sizes. Notice reflections in puddles and see the world differently. Put boots on and go puddle jumping. Make splash patterns and watery sounds. Stir puddles with a stick. Throw a ball into puddles. Draw around puddles – observe and talk about changes over time.

Keeping healthy | *key ideas: health, care, community*

Water is essential for life. Celebrate 'actions that keep me healthy' – drinking, washing hands, keeping clothes and toys clean, swimming. Explore conditions for plant growth. Make the school grounds more wildlife friendly – create drinking and bathing stations for birds. Create a display and perform an assembly to involve the whole school and wider community in an ethic of care.

Investigations and fieldwork | *key ideas: place, change*

Water is all around us. Walk the school buildings, the school grounds and local area to spot water and watery places. Where does water gather? How does water move? Walk at different times of day and in different seasons and notice changes. What are watery places like? How might children describe wateriness? Gather a whirlpool of watery words as a water glossary. Fill a concertina book with rubbings, sketches, patterns and images, as a 'deep map' of awareness. Take inspiration from the work of artist James Aldridge (website 8.2).

Sustainability discussion

Why does water matter so much?

Answers might include:

(a) because water is all around us;
(b) is vital for life;
(c) there is only a finite amount of water; and
(d) water is a shared gift, not just for humans.

FRESHWATER STORIES (AGE 5–11)

What is the main focus of this topic?

Freshwater is vital to life and is finite.

Key ideas	Subject links	SDG links
Connections	Drama	SDG3 Good health and well-being
Habitats	English (creative writing)	SDG7 Affordable and clean energy
Resilience	Geography	SDG13 Climate action
	Music	SDG 15 Life on land
	Science	

Background knowledge

Freshwater is vital for all life on Earth. It can be found in glaciers, rivers, streams, canals, ponds, lakes, reservoirs, water meadows, bogs, marshes, swamps and in groundwater. Much freshwater (68 per cent) is frozen in the ice that covers Greenland, the Arctic, Antarctica and high mountain ranges. Freshwater habitats are precious. Freshwater ecosystems include fish, mammals, reptiles, birds, insects, molluscs and crustaceans. These are under threat due to a range of factors including overdevelopment, pollution, waste water discharge and climate change.

Freshwater is important every day in our homes. It is also used as a source of food, for watering crops and irrigation, for electricity generation, manufacturing and transporting goods. Accessibility to clean water remains an issue for billions of people as two out of five people do not have basic hand-washing and sanitation facilities. Only around 1 per cent of all the freshwater available is accessible for use, with 40 per cent of the global population impacted by scarcity. Freshwater habitats also face severe challenges due to pollution, and changes to the flow of rivers and lakes. The World Wide Fund for Nature (WWF 2020) warns that one third of freshwater creatures are threatened with extinction.

Interesting facts

- Three litres of water are used to manufacture a single one-litre water bottle.
- In Columbia, Caño Cristales is known as the 'River of Five Colours' because aquatic plants make the waters bright blue, red, black, yellow and green.
- As part of the water cycle, the water you drink could be the same water that dinosaurs drank 65 million years ago.

Misconceptions and research

It is often said that we need more water to grow more food. However, a great deal is wasted through inefficient irrigation methods and thirsty crops. New farm practices could ensure that scarce water resources are being used in more productive ways: more wisely to produce more food with less water. It is easy to think that dams will reduce a water crisis by creating reservoirs that store water and will not have a negative impact on the environment. However, dams fragment rivers and impact on wetlands. Water is a finite resource. Ensuring that water is managed equitably and sustainably is a priority for both the planet and people.

Teaching ideas

Key vocabulary

ecosystem	freshwater	scarcity
flood	habitat	simulation
flow	river	

Getting started

There are many freshwater features for children to identify and explore, on both a local and global scale. Diagrams, videos and models support children's knowledge and understanding of vocabulary and processes in freshwater environments. For example, follow the journey of a raindrop (website 8.3) or share a video on rivers (website 8.4). Teachers can extend children's perspectives by drawing attention to water flow and asking questions, such as 'Where is the water coming/flowing from?' 'Where is it flowing to?'

Mapping water features | *key ideas: connections, pattern*

Look at local Ordnance Survey and other maps and find the symbols for water features in the key. Go for a freshwater hunt on your map. Using Google Earth or an atlas, extend the search from local to global and consider different bodies of water on Earth. Ask the children to trace with their finger and follow a river from source to mouth. Which countries do they pass through? What landscape features do the children notice? Do the rivers flow through urban and rural areas? Look at areas of plentiful water supply and areas where water scarcity is an issue.

Freshwater habitats | *key ideas: habitats, biodiversity, webs*

Freshwater habitats support a variety of life. Discuss the features of freshwater habitats, such as rivers, bogs and lakes. Consider the flora and fauna that might be found and celebrate the biodiversity of freshwater ecosystems. Research types of freshwater creatures and create a table with three columns: classification of organism, e.g. mammal; species of animal, e.g. duck-billed platypus; and features and adaptations, e.g. strong tail for swimming. A story book such as *Pond Circle* by Betsy Franco is an inspiring introduction to food chains. You might also explore food webs and what happens when ecosystems become imbalanced.

River dance | *key ideas: awe and wonder, systems*

Rivers flow from source to mouth. Challenge children to create a river simulation in the playground including features such as source, meander, tributary, confluence, waterfall and sea to ensure use of the correct terminology. Celebrate the wonder of rivers through the creation of a dance. The soundtrack 'River Dance' (website 8.4) is a helpful stimulus. Listen to the music. Can children hear the river beginning gently at the source, cascading down the mountain until it reaches the sea? Create a word list to describe the movement of the river. The poem 'Cataract of Lodore' (website 8.5) demonstrates onomatopoeic watery words to inspire movement – e.g. flowing, bubbling, roaring, leaping. The children might begin the dance on their own, engage in some partner work and join together as the music reaches a crescendo. Plan, rehearse and perform.

Beaver engineers | *key ideas: change, conservation, vision*

Beavers have long been recognized as 'ecosystem engineers', constantly reshaping their surroundings to manage complex water systems. Programmes to protect and reintroduce beavers are a sustainable solution to the difficulties caused by flooding in some areas of human activity. Research a reintroduction project online as a case study (website 8.6). Use a beaver puppet to engage children in conversation. Script an interview with a beaver to understand their work and celebrate success stories. The Wildlife Trusts Evidence Report is a good place to start to find out about UK initiatives (website 8.7).

Investigations and fieldwork | *key idea: resilience*

Floods are on the increase due to climate change. Ask the children to enact a simulation of such an event. Research the effects and impacts of floodwater on people, fauna, flora, settlement and transport. Create a small world play scenario to enact flood events and management; consider impacts on the community. Reflect on mitigation measures and real-world applications to local and global scenarios. Further details on small world playful enquiries can be found in Witt and Clarke (2016).

Sustainability discussion

The Whanganui River on North Island, New Zealand, became the first river in the world to be recognized as a legal person in 2017, and is now known as Te Awa Tupua. The local indigenous peoples of Whanganui believe this change in status, which recognizes the river as a living being, will protect the river and surrounding area.

Consider alternative perspectives. How might things be different if we think of water as a resource, a gift, a living being?

Answers might include:

  (a) a resource – to be used, to be managed, to be exploited, to be polluted;
  (b) a gift – to be cherished, to be thankful for, to be celebrated; and
  (c) a living being – to be respected, to be in relation with, to live with reciprocity.

SALTWATER STORIES (AGE 7–14)

What is the main focus of this topic?

Marine biodiversity is critical to the health and well-being of people and planet.

Key ideas	Subject links	SDG links
Biodiversity	Art	SDG3 Good health and well-being
Change	English (creative writing)	SDG7 Affordable and clean energy
Conservation	Geography	SDG13 Climate action
	Science	

Background knowledge

All life began in the oceans, and today all life ultimately depends on the oceans. Oceans cover three quarters of the Earth's surface and contain 97 per cent of the Earth's water. Oceanographers divide the world's oceans into distinct geographic regions: Pacific, Atlantic, Indian, Arctic and Southern Oceans. Scientists know of around 240,000 ocean species and there is much more for oceanographers to explore and discover. The ocean drives global systems that make the Earth a habitable place for living beings. Drinking water, weather, climate, much of our food, and even the oxygen in the air we breathe, are all ultimately regulated here.

Ocean systems are in crisis from negative human activity. Threats to marine environments include overfishing, pollution, coastal development, shipping, invasive alien species, off-shore infrastructure, mariculture and deep-sea mining. However, given the right circumstances, marine ecosystems can recover. Oceans absorb 30 per cent of carbon dioxide produced by humans, and so buffer the impacts of climate change. Marine Protected Areas mitigate and restore the effects of marine degradation. Careful management of seas and oceans is a key feature of a sustainable future.

Interesting facts

- There are mountain ranges and deep canyons (trenches) on the ocean floor, just like those on land. Mauna Kea in Hawaii rises 10,211 metres from the sea floor making it higher than Mount Everest.
- The ocean remains a mystery. More than 80 per cent of the ocean has never been mapped, explored or even seen by humans.
- There are more historic artefacts under the sea than in all of the world's museums.

Misconceptions and research

Oceans are mysterious places. Children's understanding is often incomplete. Children may think that coasts and coastlines do not change, but these are dynamic as a result of erosion and changes in sea level. It may not seem possible that life exists in polar oceans, but both the Arctic and Southern Oceans have surprisingly rich food webs and many species are still undiscovered. It is important that children understand the complexity of global systems and their own role in maintaining balance, harmony, interconnectedness and a sustainable world.

Teaching ideas

Key vocabulary

coral reef	marine	saltwater
current	pelagic	strandline
flotsam	oceanographer	

Getting started

The open ocean (or pelagic realm) is an enormous place. Scientists divide it into five main layers or zones, which extend from the surface to extreme depths where no light penetrates (the sunlight zone, twilight zone, midnight zone, abyss and trenches). Use the BBC (2001) 'Blue Planet', or similar, video resources to introduce this topic and to inform and inspire wonder. Create vertical cross-section diagrams to share children's understanding and interpretation of these zones. Assemble text, photographs, shades of blue and artwork as collaged zones. Display as a gallery where art, science, culture and points for discussion converge.

Coral reefs | *key ideas: biodiversity, conservation*

Coral reefs are home to 25 per cent of the world's marine species, including organisms that cannot be found anywhere else on Earth. Reefs are sensitive to changes in water temperature – an increase of just one degree can cause bleaching, the loss of coral organisms. Research the ingenuity of scientists as they tackle this loss, which includes loudspeakers of reef sounds to bring fish back, construction of nursery frames to encourage new growth, and the creation of Marine Protected Areas. You might engage children with cartoon storyboards, dioramas or animations to retell and extend these stories.

Ocean journeys | *key idea: connections*

Oceans are sites for exploration and discovery. Many contemporary explorers share their travels via social media and, as they do so, they highlight issues such as marine pollution and animal behaviour. These live online blogs can be good sources of inspiration and prompts for discussion with children. As a class, follow a voyage such as the Vendée Globe Round the World Yacht Race. The online National Geographic resource 'Explorer Classroom' also connects children with researchers, scientists and storytellers.

Flotsam | *key idea: vision*

Oceans hold mystery and possibilities. Engage in speculative thinking to consider what lies beneath the surface. Share the wordless picture book *Flotsam* by David Weiner as a stimulus. This is the story of a boy who collects and examines a barnacle-encrusted underwater camera, with secrets to share. Create 'flotsam trays' for the children to investigate. Generate ideas about who the owner of the items might have been and make inferences about their stories (website 8.8).

Investigations and fieldwork | *key idea: place*

If you can, visit the coast. Undertake a strandline investigation. Create and curate a beach museum. What is washed up with the tide? What is out of place? What should not be there? What messages are carried by these items? What issues might be discussed?

Sustainability discussion

What are the environmental implications of *not* looking after marine environments? For water? For climate? For life on Earth?

Answers might focus on:

(a) marine pollution;
(b) extinction of fish, coral and other forms of life; and
(c) coastal flooding.

Websites

Website 8.1. Conversations with rain. The art gallery of Western Australia
https://artgallery.wa.gov.au/learn.artist-activation/conversations-with-rain
Website 8.2 James Aldridge
http://www.jamesaldridge-artist.co.uk
Website 8.3 Follow the journey of a raindrop
https://river-runner.samlearner.com/
Website 8.4 Riverdance: Music from the show
https://www.youtube.com/watch?v=OR4FiK-ar7w
Website 8.5 Cataract of Lodore
https://www.poetryfoundation.org/poems/57951/the-cataract-of-lodore
Website 8.6 Rewilding
https://www.rspb.org.uk/our-work/policy-insight/species/beaver-reintroduction-in-the-uk/
Website 8.7 Wildlife Trusts Report
https://www.wildlifetrusts.org/sites/default/files/2020-11/Impact%20Report%2020192020.pdf
Website 8.8 Creative ideas for using 'Flotsam'
https://www.booksfortopics.com/post/flostsam

Children's books

Franco, B., and Vitale, S. (2009) *Pond Circle*, New York: Margaret K. McElderry Books.
Wiesner, D. (2012) *Flotsam*, London: Andersen Press.

References

BBC (2001) *Blue Planet*, available at https://www.bbcearth.com/shows/blue-planet
Haraway, D. (2016) *Staying with the Trouble: Making Kin in the Chthulucene* (Experimental Futures), Durham, NC: Duke University Press.

Horvath, J. (2016) *Educating Young Children Through Natural Water*, London: Routledge.

Neimanis, A. (2017) *Bodies of Water*, London: Bloomsbury.

Wheelan, B. (1995) 'Riverdance' from Riverdance (Music from The Show), track 8, Dublin: Celtic Heartbeat.

Wildlife Trust (2017) *The River Otter Beaver Trial Science and Evidence Report*, available at https://www.exeter.ac.uk/creww/research/beavertrial/.

WWF (2020) *Living Planet Report 2020*, available at https://c402277.ssl.cf1.rackcdn.com/publications/1371/files/original/ENGLISH-FULL.pdf?1599693362.

Witt, S., & Clarke, H. (2016) 'Rescuing the earth through small world play' in Winograd, K. (ed.), *Education in Times of Environmental Crisis: Teaching Children To Be Agents of Change*, London: Routledge, 219–33.

9

Weather and Climate

Elena Lengthorn

Weather study, also known as meteorology, dates back millennia. Discussions about the process of cloud formation, rain and the seasons can be found in the Indian Upanishads from 3000 BC and Aristotle, the Greek philosopher, wrote his *Meteorology* in 350 BC. Contributions to weather study from the Middle Ages include the invention of the first standardized rain gauge by Prince Mujong of Korea in 1441, as well as the first written European account of a tropical cyclone in the Atlantic Ocean in 1494. But the science of weather prediction, of forecasting our atmospheric conditions, really took off in the nineteenth century with the emergence of a great number of new tools and processes to capture, report and predict weather. We now have highly accurate weather forecasts literally at our fingertips, on our mobile phones and household devices. Alongside and predating scientific developments, informal weather prediction methods (weather lore) have been employed for centuries, especially in rural and fishing communities, but the reliability of some of these methods is, of course, somewhat questionable.

What is the difference between weather and climate? Climate is the weather conditions prevailing in an area in general or over several decades and is calculated from hundreds of weather measurements. The UK has very varied weather conditions due to its temperate climate; other places have more predictable weather patterns. But around the world, weather and climate are changing because of the accumulation of human-induced greenhouse gases in the atmosphere that trap the sun's heat. Geological, chemical and paleontological evidence show us that climate change is nothing new as the Earth has cycled through quite a number of Ice Ages and warm periods over its long history. But what is different this time is that the changes have been triggered by human activity, and we are able to witness the loss of plant and animal life for ourselves.

The importance of weather and climate change is recognized in the United Nations SDGs and the 2015 Paris Agreement. Also, there have been literally thousands of climate emergency declarations by governments and other organizations. Teaching about weather and climate introduces young people to these developments. It provides opportunities for pupils to connect with natural systems, explore individual and collective experiences, work both empirically and

Figure 9.1 Powerful convection currents drive weather events at both a local and global scale. *Photo: Михал Орела, Wikimedia Commons.*

creatively, to be curious and fascinated by their surroundings, and to prepare for the weather and climate situations that they will face in their lives (Figure 9.1). This may sound daunting but it can also be great fun!

Reflection and discussion

- Have you had any direct experience of climate change?
- How can learning about weather and climate be made fun?

WEATHER PATTERNS (AGE 3–7)

What is the main focus of this topic?

The weather impacts our lives in lots of ways.

Key ideas	Subject links	SDG links
Celebration	Drama	SDG 13 Climate action
Interaction	English	
Pattern	Geography	
Protection	Music	
	Science	

Background knowledge

We are all familiar with the weather, regardless of our backgrounds and experience. It is part of our lives from the clothes we wear, to the activities we do, the ways we move, the foods we eat, and even our moods. The weather is measurable and meteorology allows pupils to connect their daily experiences and observations to exact measurements. Such studies can support a practical approach to learning and introduce, in an age of misinformation, the scientific method, to encourage a methodical approach to pupils' investigations. Weather events can also be dramatic and fascinating for young people, and teaching about weather patterns provides an opportunity to pique that curiosity and educate them on how best to stay safe.

The weather is the result of complex interactions between solar energy, the oceans, landscapes and Earth's movement through space. Direct overhead sun in the tropics provides an abundance of energy at the equator, causes hot, humid air to rise high in the atmosphere, and drives climate and weather patterns around the globe. As temperatures rise due to global warming it is likely that the weather will become more unpredictable and extreme, with more storms, less cold spells and more droughts, floods and heatwaves. This dynamic interface between science and sustainability makes teaching about the weather particularly relevant at the current time.

Interesting facts

- The wettest places on Earth are in north-east India with an annual rainfall of more than 11 metres.
- The highest temperature ever recorded on Earth was 56.7°C (134°F) in Death Valley, California, in 1913.
- The fastest recorded wind speed is 253mph at Barrow Island, Australia, during tropical cyclone Olivia in 1996.

Misconceptions and research

Weather experiences can be intense or unremarkable, varying from the fun of snow days and jumping in puddles, to the awe of a thunderclap or the annoyance of persistent drizzle. Some of the misconceptions to do with the weather stem from inexact use of language: 'weather' and 'climate' have different meanings; heat is not a substance but a form of energy. One of the most significant challenges is to convey the scale and interconnectedness of the weather as no weather system acts in isolation. Being aware of these complexities can help underpin teaching about weather and climate even when working with the youngest children.

Teaching ideas

Key vocabulary

chart	survey	waterproof
symbol	temperature	weather conditions

Getting started

See what types of weather the children can recall and connect to their past weather experiences, e.g. being caught in the rain, a thunderstorm, snow play, getting sunburnt. Which type of weather do they prefer? Does the weather influence how they feel? Organize a simple class vote or survey on the theme of favourite weather. What would happen if we could control the weather? Would we be able to get everyone to agree?

Weather songs | *key idea: awe and wonder*

Sing songs about the weather with the children. There are plenty to choose from and even a simple Internet search will take you to lots of different examples (website 9.1). The weather is one of the wonders of the world, but it is so commonplace that we usually take it for granted. Celebrating different types of weather and the way the weather changes is a good starting point for developing an ethic of planetary care.

Weather conditions | *key idea: interaction*

Working as a class, make a list of all the weather words the children can think of. Now identify all the words which relate to the temperature – hot, cool, mild, baking, freezing and so on. Arrange these in a sequence. Now repeat this exercise with words to do with the wind. Find out about the Beaufort scale and get the children to make their own version of (a) a wind and (b) a temperature scale, adding drawings to illustrate the different conditions. Talk about the impact of extreme weather. How does it affect people, plants and animals?

Prepared for the weather | *key idea: protection*

You will need a range of weather-related items such as an umbrella, sunglasses, scarf, gloves and sun cream for this activity. You will also need a bag containing pieces of card naming different weather conditions, e.g. wind, frost and so forth. Now choose a volunteer at random and ask them to pick an item that matches the weather conditions they have selected. Play until all of the items and conditions have been explored. Extend the activity by talking about how people protect themselves from adverse weather. Flood and hurricane warning systems give people time to take shelter. In some places in Thailand, houses are built on stilts to avoid floods. However, there is a limit to what people can do to stay safe.

Investigations and fieldwork | *key idea: pattern*

Help the children to measure and record the weather using symbols they have designed for themselves, e.g. sunshine, sun and cloud, showers, wind, rain. They will need to go outside at the same time each day and record the conditions on a chart on the classroom wall. See what pattern emerges over a given time (ten or twenty days). Talk about seasonal weather patterns in your area. Depending on the age and ability of the children, you might talk about how climate change is disrupting normal weather patterns and turn them into pretend 'weather reporters'.

Sustainability discussion

Why should we care about the weather?

Answers might include:

(a) because it affects the way we live every day, from our relationships to the food that is available to eat and our moods;
(b) because we are changing it, and we need to prepare for it and adapt to it; and
(c) because it is fascinating and inspiring.

THE WATER CYCLE (AGE 5–11)

What is the main focus of this topic?

The water cycle drives the weather and is essential for all forms of life.

Key ideas	Subject links	SDG links
Cycles	Art	SDG 6 Clean water and sanitation
Human/nature interactions	Drama	SDG 13 Climate action
Patterns	English (creative writing)	SDG 14 Life below water
	Geography	SDG 15 Life on land
	Music	
	Science	

Background knowledge

The water cycle sets out the processes and pathways by which the world's water circulates continuously, in and out of the atmosphere. Energy from the sun causes water to evaporate from the ground, trees, plants, rivers, streams, oceans. It then rises into the atmosphere where it cools and condenses into liquid droplets and falls back to the surface as hail, rain, sleet or snow. This is a constant process – no water is ever lost in this cycle. As our climate continues to warm there is increasing energy available to power the water cycle. A hotter atmosphere leads to more evaporation and warmer air has a greater capacity to carry moisture. Paradoxically, with higher temperatures and greater evaporation, there is also the potential for some areas to experience droughts of increased intensity and duration. Around the world, precipitation is increasing in higher latitudes and decreasing in areas closer to the equator. This is causing serious disruption. We rely on the water cycle for drinking, irrigation, recreation, farming and industry. Nor should we forget that all other plants and creatures rely on water, too.

Interesting facts

- Humans are mostly water! Water makes up 73 per cent of your brain!
- On average it takes 2,000 years for a raindrop which falls on the ocean to complete the water cycle.
- Each degree of warming increases the chance of global precipitation by 1–2 per cent.

Misconceptions and research

Many primary school children believe that water only evaporates into the atmosphere from the sea and oceans, and that rivers flow from the sea into the mountains rather than the other way round (May 1998). Another common misconception, that may persist even into early adulthood, is that the water cycle only includes freezing and melting processes of water (Cardek 2009). Some of these misconceptions can be dispelled fairly easily with playground experiments to demonstrate gravity moving water downhill (modelling movement from land to sea), evaporating puddles, and water percolating into soil.

Teaching ideas

Key vocabulary

atmosphere   condensation   floods
clouds   evaporation   water vapour

Getting started

Using Google Earth, a globe or an atlas, remind the children that most of the world's surface is covered by water. Now talk about where they think the rain comes from, before introducing them to one of the excellent videos that explain the water cycle (website 9.2). To conclude, ask them, more broadly, what they think might happen if the seas and oceans become warmer.

Weather music | *key idea: celebration*

We recognize weather as a never-ending source of conversation, but it is also a sustained inspiration in music creation. From weather nursery rhymes like 'Rain, Rain, Go Away', to Travis with 'Why does it always rain on me?' and Rhianna with 'Umbrella', the features of the water cycle inspire us creatively. Invite pupils to recall songs that involve the water cycle and listen to a selection, ideally drawing from different countries and traditions, great composers and musicians. There is the potential to get really creative here and invite pupils to develop their own songs and rain refrains with appropriate dances to go with them.

Clouds | *key idea: beauty, pattern*

Clouds form part of the water cycle and are endlessly attractive as they change and evolve in shape. Encourage the children to find photographs of the different cloud types on the Internet and go outside to identify the clouds. Let pupils lie on their backs and gaze up at the sky. Give them sufficient time to use their imagination to picture shapes in the clouds, create stories and use their senses to stimulate cross-curricular vocabulary. **Remind the children that, as they look upwards, they must never look at the sun directly, and tell them why.** On returning to the classroom get the children to paint their own cloudscapes, perhaps using water colours if they are available.

Breaking the cycle | *key idea: interaction*

With the help of an atlas or globe, ask the children to identify rainforest regions around the world. In these areas much of the moisture in the air evaporates from plants and trees. If too many trees are cut down, less water evaporates so there is less cloud and less rain. This may cause the trees to die back, reducing evaporation even further. Get the children to draw two diagrams showing (a) an uninterrupted water cycle and (b) how the cycle can be disrupted. Each diagram should show the impacts these changes have on people's lives and the implications in terms of sustainability.

Investigations and fieldwork | *key idea: water cycle*

Floods, an overflow of water that submerges usually dry land, are among the most common natural disasters. Have there been any floods in your area? If so, what happened? Find out about famous floods now and in the past, and challenge the children to devise a newspaper page about one of them. Their report should contain a description of what happened, a map to show the area affected and an imaginary onsite interview. It should also say what could be done to prevent further flooding in future. You might develop this activity to consider the pros and cons of different flood prevention measures. Hard engineering such as walls and banks simply pushes problems elsewhere; planting trees upstream helps to delay run-off and prevents a surge in water levels happening in the first place.

Sustainability discussion

In what ways is the water cycle essential in our lives?

Answers might include:

(a) it creates the rain which fills rivers, streams and lakes;
(b) it brings moisture to the soil so that plants and trees can grow; and
(c) if all the water stayed in the oceans, all the land would be desert.

CLIMATE CHANGE (AGE 7–14)

What is the main focus of this topic?

Climate change is a very serious threat which calls for individual, community and global co-operation.

Key ideas	Subject links	SDG links
Cycles Partnerships Technology	Citizenship English (descriptive writing) Geography Science	SDG 4 Quality education SDG 13 Climate action SDG 17 Partnerships to achieve the goals

Global climate has varied dramatically over the lifespan of our planet, but the last decade has been the hottest on record, with troubling consequences in the form of extreme weather events. These have impacted on ecosystems, agriculture and the livelihoods and movements of people, contributing to the refugee crises which have shaken governments around the world. The science is clear: the causes of global heating are anthropogenic, and the consequences are broad, immense and planet-changing. This is a global emergency and one which will affect every living organism on the planet.

Awareness of and concern about the climate crisis are growing rapidly but heightened awareness does not directly translate into action to mitigate or adapt. Teachers have an individual and collective responsibility, both morally and in terms of the UN Convention of the Rights of the Child (1990) and the UN Transforming our World Agenda (2015), to take action in education. There are some encouraging developments. In 2019 Italy's education minister announced the addition of climate change and sustainability for every grade of learning in the Italian civics' curriculum. China has incorporated environmental lessons into the nine compulsory years of education, and there is pressure for the USA to follow suit.

Interesting facts

- The concentration of carbon dioxide (CO_2) in the atmosphere is the highest it has been in human history.
- Over 30 million people were forced to move from their homes by floods and other natural disasters in 2020.
- Some low-lying countries like the South Pacific island of Tuvalu could completely disappear in the next fifty years as sea levels rise.

Misconceptions

There is a misunderstanding that the ozone layer is related to climate change, that the hole is letting in more of the sun's rays and heating the planet. This is incorrect. The ozone hole is caused by pollutants in the upper atmosphere reacting to sunlight, allowing harmful ultraviolet rays to reach the surface. Global warming is caused by a 'blanket' of carbon dioxide and other gases that prevent solar radiation escaping back into the atmosphere.

Teaching ideas

Key vocabulary

adaptation	convection	emergency
climate change	declaration	mitigation

Getting started

Invite pupils to share what they know about climate change. What do they think it is? Using their own words, get them write down a short definition. This will give you a good idea of their existing knowledge and any misconceptions. Now briefly explain that, although learning about climate change can be worrying, it is a collective concern felt by people across the world. There are things we can all do which will collectively make a difference, but no one person will solve the problem.

Convection currents | *key idea: cycles*

The notion of convection currents underpins a scientific understanding of climate change. There are some excellent videos which demonstrate this process (website 9.3). As a practical activity to demonstrate convection currents, provide groups of pupils with cubes of frozen coloured water (the darker the better) and a glass of warm water. Invite them to predict what will happen before adding an ice cube to the warm water and then get them to observe, record and attempt to explain the outcome. Now think about where cool and warm air or water meet like this around the world. Explain that convection currents interconnect. If air or water rises in one place, it leaves a space that has to be filled and this creates a cycle, distributing energy from the sun around the Earth. These global systems are stable because they interact. However, if they are disrupted too much, they are likely to reach a 'tipping point' which causes them to suddenly shift to a new equilibrium.

Climate engineering | *key ideas: futures, technology*

There have been many proposals to solve or mitigate climate change through geo-engineering. Suggestions include carbon capture, fertilizing the ocean with nutrients, positioning mirrors in space to reflect sunlight, and seeding the atmosphere with sulphur dioxide. Divide the pupils into groups and ask them each to research a different climate engineering option. What is proposed, how does it work (scientifically) and is it practical? Pupils should draw up a list of pros and cons. Do they think it is feasible, could it have unexpected consequences, and how long would it take to have a significant impact? This activity could lead into a role play in which pupils pretend to be a scientist arguing for a particular proposal on a 'science programme'. The rest of the class could then judge whether they think it is a good idea.

Climate change debate | *key idea: partnerships*

Ask the pupils to prepare a climate change debate. Invite speakers from local groups and organizations to talk about their work and present their ideas for mitigation and adaptation. The pupils should work together to devise questions they would like to ask. This could either be restricted to the class or become a whole school event. Should it prove difficult to attract external participants, you could invite the headteacher and a couple of other members of staff to form a panel of 'distinguished guests' who will respond to questions instead.

Investigations and fieldwork | *key ideas: community, partnership*

Talk about how different organizations have declared a climate change emergency. Do pupils think these are helpful? If the class were to declare a climate change emergency, what actions would it include? Think in terms of achievable objectives at a range of scales from individual and group action to whole school initiatives. How would any initiatives be organized and who would need to be involved?

Sustainability discussion

What role might technology play in addressing climate change?

Answers might include:

(a) people are ingenious and geo-engineering projects will solve our problems;
(b) technology can address climate change but there will be no 'magic bullet'; and
(c) the most important thing is to reduce our impact on the planet.

A further discussion concerns who should instigate and then pay for any mitigation measures – polluters, fossil fuel companies, wealthy countries, rich people, all of us? Would mobilizing public support be an issue?

Websites

Website 9.1 Weather songs
https://www.youtube.com/watch?v=tfAB4BXSHOA
Website 9.2 Water cycle
https://www.youtube.com/watch?v=ncORPosDrjI
Website 9.3 Convection currents
https://www.youtube.com/watch?v=0mUU69ParFM

References

Cardek, O. (2009) 'Science Students' Misconceptions of the Water Cycle According to their Drawings', *Journal of Applied Sciences* 9: 865–73, available at https://scialert.net/abstract/?doi=jas.2009.865.873

May, T. (1998) 'Children's Ideas About Rivers' in Scoffham, S. (ed.), *Primary Sources*, Sheffield: Geographical Association.

10

Food and Farming

Ingrid Schudel

Food and food production have changed over time as developments have taken place in science, technology, economy and society. Humans started farming around 12,000 years ago. Before this they gathered wild grains and hunted wild animals in hunter-gatherer societies. By changing to actively growing plants and raising animals, humans had greater control of their food supply. This enabled them to settle in one place and gave them greater food security in times of unpredictable climatic events. Evidence of the earliest farming activity has been found in what we now call the Middle East. This area was known at the time for unusually fertile soil, productive freshwater and brackish wetlands, explaining why it was termed the 'Fertile Crescent'.

From early beginnings, different civilizations independently learned how to collect, store, germinate and care for different crops. These included wheat, barley, peas and lentils in the eastern Mediterranean; rice in China; sugar cane and bananas in New Guinea; sorghum in the Sahel in Africa; potatoes in South America; maize in Central America; and yams in Australia. Pigs and sheep were the first animals to be domesticated (in Mesopotamia), followed by cattle in what are now known as Turkey and India. Llamas, alpacas and guinea pigs were domesticated in South America, and camels in the Arabian peninsula.

In the 1950s and 60s, the world underwent an agricultural revolution often called the 'green revolution', which was associated with chemical fertilizers, agrochemicals and controlled water supply (usually involving irrigation), newer methods of cultivation, including mechanization and hybridized and genetically modified crops. This revolution increased production at a time when the world's population was growing fast. However, it gradually became clear that the green revolution was leading to problems of water pollution, land degradation, habitat loss and chemical poisoning, which, alongside increasing greenhouse gas emissions, raised concerns about human health and sustainability.

Food production today varies according to region and is shaped by cultural, political and economic factors. Modern-day agriculture is a complex mix of large-scale industrialized commercial farming, urban farming and traditional farming. The question is how to combine locally and holistically driven farming practices (such as organic farming, permaculture and traditional practices) with

Figure 10.1 When industrial techniques are applied to farming it impacts wildlife and undermines biodiversity. *Photos: Harvesting: Mourice Flesier, Wikimedia Commons Bee: Ingrid Schudel.*

new conceptions of economics and social-ecological relationships to feed the world more sustainably.

Reflection and discussion

- Why do we sometimes consume food that is grown in distant countries?
- How can we resolve the tension between the demand for cheap food and the need to respect nature and diversity?
- What changes could you make to your diet to make it more sustainable?

FOOD FROM THE GARDEN (AGE 3–7)

What is the main focus of this topic?

How growing fruit and vegetables sustainably helps us and our world to stay healthy.

Key ideas	Subject links	SDG links
Balance Diversity Ecosystem Health	Art Science	SDG2 Zero hunger SDG3 Good health and well-being SDG15 Life on land

Background knowledge

Diversity is important in healthy ecological systems. A wide variety of species (high biodiversity) provides resistance to disease or changes in climate. This ensures that, even if one species suffers a setback, others will be able to take over (rather like a family when one person is ill or has other commitments). Holistic farming practices are built around these principles. For example, permaculture (developed by Bill Mollison and David Holmgren) has diversity as one of its core principles, and is underpinned by the understanding that greater diversity leads to greater resistance. Another principle is to 'integrate' – that is to build on the ways in which living things work with each other and the non-living environment which nurtures them. Children can explore diversity in a practical manner both in their own diets and by tending a food garden. This is an ideal way to begin exploring interdependencies. The Machobane farming system in Lesotho in southern Africa is a useful case study which illustrates further benefits. This system ensures that people eat fresh food all the year round to avoid getting sick (Machobane and Berold 2003).

Interesting facts

- In most cases the skin of a fruit or vegetable is more nutritious than the inside.
- Many of the scary-looking creatures in our gardens are our 'friends' – spiders eat mosquitoes, ladybirds eat aphids, and praying mantises eat caterpillars and beetles.
- Ants are 'farmers' just like humans as they work together to harvest the sap from plants.

Misconceptions and research

A conventional way of teaching about insects and other creatures is by labelling them as either helpful or harmful. This anthropocentric perspective may start young learners off in an antagonistic relationship with living creatures. An alternative is to talk about insects and other bugs being 'in the right place at the right time'.

Teaching ideas

Key vocabulary

creatures	health	soil
garden	marigolds	vitamins

Getting started

Discuss what vegetables the children like and do not like, and where they buy or grow them. Make a class list of the most popular ones. What do the children know about vegetable gardens? Does your school have a garden? Can you make a visit to a nearby allotment or community garden? Tell them that they are going to learn about the importance of fresh fruit and vegetables and the life it supports.

Five a day | *key idea: health*

Bring a selection of fruit and vegetables to school for the children to draw on large sheets of paper. Encourage them to look very carefully so their drawings are as accurate as possible. Talk about the difference between fruit and vegetables – basically fruit grows from flowers and contains seeds. Now arrange the drawings in a class display. Each item could be part of a nutritious five-a-day diet. Discuss why a balanced diet, which includes plenty of fresh fruit and vegetables, matters.

Bugs are our friends | *key ideas: diversity, balance*

Print out from the Internet pictures of some of the different insects and creatures that are found in vegetable gardens. Explain that in different ways they help to keep the plants healthy so we should think of them as friends. Make the point that there is usually no need to spray vegetables with poisons as these kill off living things – both 'good' and 'bad'.

Growing marigolds for our garden | *key ideas: diversity, balance*

Marigolds (calendula) are easy to grow and self-seed easily, too. At an age-appropriate level, share information with the children about the reasons for growing calendula (website 10.1). Now plant some seeds with the children and wait for them to germinate before planting them out in a garden or window box. Remind the children how marigolds attract aphids and thus protect other plants in a vegetable garden. This is one example of how we can avoid using poisonous sprays and work with living things to create a healthy food garden.

Making a wormery | *key idea: ecosystem*

Younger learners can make a simple wormery for the kitchen or classroom following written instructions (website 10.2). It's a surprisingly simple process which introduces them to a key ecological process – cycles and decomposition. In this activity you should encourage children to gently handle and come to feel comfortable with earthworms. Also help them to think about what happens to the food waste broken down by the earthworms.

Investigation and fieldwork | *key idea: diversity*

Organize a visit to a community or home garden. Encourage the children to look for insects and other creatures (you might want to loosen some areas of soil). Now give each child a big piece of paper (and a magnifier if possible) to draw a different object or living thing from the garden, filling the whole page even if they have chosen the tiniest of creatures to draw. Use the drawings to reconstruct this garden on returning to school. An alternative would be to visit a local market and take photographs or draw a poster or make a video of all the varieties of fruit, seeds and vegetables available. Remember that there are many different shades of green!

Sustainability discussion

What can we do to keep ourselves, our gardens and our farms healthy?

Answers might include:

(a) we should eat plenty of fresh fruit and vegetables;
(b) we should avoid using chemicals and sprays which kill insects; and
(c) we should make sure that the soil is healthy so that the food that grows in it is healthy, too.

BUSY BEES (AGE 5–11)

What is the main focus of this topic?

Bees are part of the web of life to which we all belong.

Key ideas	Subject links	SDG links
Conservation Co-operation Webs	Drama English (creative writing) Geography Science	SDG2 Zero hunger SDG3 Good health and well-being SDG12 Responsible consumption and production SDG15 Life on land

Background knowledge

Images of humans collecting honey from wild bees date to 10,000 years ago. Bee farming is shown in Egyptian art from around 4,500 years ago, and honey jars were found in the tombs of Egyptian pharaohs such as Tutankhamun. Today, we still use honey as a delicious sweetener (twice as sweet as sugar) in our food. But we rely on bees for other things, too. Bees help pollinate flowers that then reproduce and spread their fruit and seeds. These provide food for many different creatures and contribute to the diversity and resilience of a habitat.

Modern farming has caused a decline in the population of bees and other pollinators. It focuses on a very limited rage of crops and depends on chemicals to kill weeds, pests and fungi. Additionally, many wilderness areas where pollinators might have thrived have been cleared for farmland. Sustainable farming practices seek to re-establish the relationship between insects and food production. Finding out about bees introduces children to some of the key principles of ecology and biodiversity in a way that they can understand.

Interesting facts

- A bee visits about 10,000 flowers to make one drop of honey and generally travels up to 3 kilometres to forage.
- Three out of four fruit and seed crops across the globe depend on pollinators such as bees.
- There is an average of 30,000 bees in a single hive – about the same as the number of people in a small town.

Misconceptions and research

Focusing on the value of plants and animals for humans can create the misconception that they are there only to serve us. A sustainability perspective emphasizes the value of all forms of life and the importance of maintaining ecological balance.

Teaching ideas

Key vocabulary

bee	nectar	seeds
flower	pollen	waggle dance
fruit	pollinators	

Getting started

Bring an assortment of flowers to class – as large as possible. Ask the children if they know what bees are doing when they visit flowers (they are collecting nectar to make honey, pollen to feed their babies, and they are pollinating plants at the same time). Hand out the flowers and ask children to point out the pollen on each one. They can see if they can rub some off on their fingers, remembering to be sensitive to those children who suffer from hay fever. Show them a close-up picture of a bee with pollen in pollen sacks explaining how the bees collect the pollen.

Depending on pollinators | *key idea: webs*

Begin by asking the children to write down ten things they ate the previous day. Now compile a grand list on the board, keeping it in alphabetical order if possible. Investigate which foods are needed by bees or other pollinators by referring to Pollinator Partnership (website 10.3). Explain that pollinators include all the creatures that transport the pollen from flowers – birds, bats, butterflies, moths, flies, beetles, wasps, small mammals, as well as bees. Pollinators are essential in food production, especially fruit, but are not paid for the work they do and are often not valued as a result. With older children you might talk about the notion of ecosystem services.

World Bee Day | *key idea: celebration*

World Bee Day is 20 May. Look at 'Why bees matter' (website 10.4) and talk about all the different ways bees enrich the world. Now challenge the children to write a poem or short prose piece in praise of bees. Kenn Nesbitt's animal poems could provide a useful model for children to emulate.

You might also invite a local beekeeper to come and talk to class – the children will have lots of questions to ask and want to know if they ever get stung!

Waggle dance | *key idea: co-operation*

Bees communicate to each other through what is called a 'waggle dance'. In this dance a bee traces a figure of eight to indicate the direction of pollen-rich flowers. If the flowers are directly in line with the Sun, the bee dances straight upwards; but if the flowers are at angle to the Sun, the dancing bee changes direction accordingly. The duration of the dance indicates distance away from the hive (website 10.5). Encourage the children to make drawings of different imaginary locations (e.g. nearby flowers in line with the Sun, or distant flowers at a 90-degree angle to the left of the Sun). You might also take the children to the playground where they could perform their own waggle dances.

Honeyguide's Revenge | *key idea: interdependence*

Share the story *Honeyguide's Revenge* with the children (website 10.6). The theme of this traditional Zulu folk tale is that the land cares for them and that they should care for the land in return. At points during the story ask the children to predict what will happen. When you have finished, the children can consider if they think the honeyguide was fairly treated? Depending on your circumstances, older children could ask their parents and elders to share stories about indigenous wisdoms from their own cultures and bring these to class.

Investigation and fieldwork | *key idea: conservation*

Depending on the weather and the time of year, take the class outside to the school playground or some other comparable site. Ask the children to find places where they see bees and other insects visiting flowers. Which flowers seem to attract them most? Talk with the children about how they could make the school garden or school site more insect-friendly. They might draw up a short report with a map and proposal for action to take to the school council.

Sustainability discussion

What are some of the threats facing bees and other pollinators?

Answer might include:

    (a) use of pesticides to protect crops;
    (b) large fields all growing the same crops (monoculture);
    (c) clearance of hedges and wilderness areas; and
    (d) climate change and unpredictable weather.

HEALTHY CHOICES (AGE 7–14)

What is the main focus of this topic?

Knowing where your food comes from and how it is produced enables you to make healthier choices.

Key ideas	Subject links	SDG links
Connections Equality Harmony Recycling	Citizenship Design/technology English Geography	SDG3 Good health and well-being SDG 11 Sustainable cities and communities SDG 12 Responsible consumption and production SDG 13 Climate action

Background knowledge

Buying food from a supermarket involves lots of choices. As we learn more about sustainability, we may decide to change our choices or even stop buying certain products altogether. One key issue concerns locally produced food. Much of the cost of food production goes on transporting it from distant places ('food miles'), and on processing, packaging and storage. Growing food yourself, or buying locally grown organic produce, can reduce the use of energy and is better for the environment. Additionally, it is liable to be healthier as nutrients can be lost through travelling long distances and damaged by heat, oxygen and light. The fresher the food, the healthier it is.

Buying food locally has other advantages. It helps to maintain communities, support the local economy and strengthen the link between producers and consumers. Children who understand where their food comes from and how it is produced will be better placed to understand wider environmental issues such as water pollution, soil management and biodiversity. The ideas which they develop at this stage in their education are important for curriculum progression in later years.

Interesting facts

- Vegetables can lose up to half of their vitamin C within a week and spinach can lose 90 per cent within a day after harvesting.
- Mopane worms (edible caterpillars) have been a good source of protein for generations across southern Africa. They can be eaten as a crunchy snack or cooked in stews.
- The UK imports 95 per cent of the fruit we eat and 50 per cent of the vegetables.

Misconceptions and research

Teachers need to help children to be sensitive about food choices but it is important not to be judgemental. There may be farmers' children in your class as well those whose choices are limited by their socio-economic circumstances.

Teaching ideas

Key vocabulary

fair trade   organic   transportation
food miles   packaging

Getting started

Put a single fruit like an orange or an apple on your desk as a prompt. Get the children to think about all the questions they could ask it. Where was it grown? How old is it? How far has it travelled? Is it nutritious? Has it been sprayed? And so forth. Use these questions to help structure your work on this topic.

Food miles | *key idea: connections*

Bring a selection of packaged food items to the classroom. Try to select items you know the children might eat at home and only choose items which contain one product, like a bag of beans. The children can work in pairs to find the country or place where each item originated. Locate these places with the help of an atlas with the pupils marking them on a blank world map. Can they work out how far each item has travelled to reach them? (There are a number of food miles calculators on the Internet.) Is there a reason they can't be grown locally? Pineapples, for example, need a tropical climate. Write a short report about how food miles might be reduced, and the consequent benefits. Are there are any problems that doing this might cause?

Packaging | *key idea: recycling*

Much of the food that we purchase is packaged or wrapped. Encourage the children to collect some examples of packaging from their home shopping to bring to school. Stress that only clean wrappers should be collected and they need to avoid anything sharp. Sort the packaging into materials that can be recycled as opposed to those that will not biodegrade. What will happen to these items? Talk about the slogan 'Reduce, Reuse, Recycle'. Pick out items from the class collection which illustrate each of these three words. Extend the activity by having the children design a poster around this theme which can encourage the whole school to be more packaging-aware.

Fairtrade | *key idea: equality*

Fairtrade agreements are designed to give workers a reasonable wage and help to protect the environment. However, Fairtrade goods can be more expensive, and farmers who are left out of Fairtrade agreements can find their lives become even harder. The children can conduct their own Internet research to find out more about Fairtrade. 'Come On In to Coobana' (website 10.7) tells the story of Fairtrade bananas from a UK perspective. Can you think of reasons why only some goods are produced under Fairtrade agreements?

Organic farming | *key idea: harmony*

Talk with the children about organic farming and organize a group discussion about the advantages and disadvantages of organic produce. It's (1) better for wildlife; (2) more expensive to produce; (3) prone to decay quickly; (4) better for the soil; (5) more nutritious; and (6) less attractive-looking. Divide the pupils into groups of six or seven. Each group throws a dice until all the children have selected one of the roles. Three children will be arguing in favour of organic produce (roles 1, 4 and 5) and three against (roles 2, 3 and 6). The seventh child will be the judge who guides the discussion. Depending on numbers, another child might listen to the arguments and sum them up. Share conclusions around the class and see if they can come to a consensus.

Investigation and fieldwork | *key idea: systems*

Visit a local food market or arrange a farm visit if possible. Ask about how the food is produced and what is involved in getting it to the customer. How much of the money that you spend to buy the food do the farmers get? Consider packaging, transportation, the use of pesticides and so forth. What changes in their practices do the farmers think would make food production more environmentally friendly? What prevents them from taking these steps?

Sustainability discussion

What matters most to you when you buy food?

Answers might include:

  (a) price;
  (b) quality;
  (c) health;

(d) environmental impact; and

(e) all of the above.

Websites

Website 10.1 Reasons to grow calendula
https://www.tenthacrefarm.com/7-reasons-to-grow-calendula/
Website 10.2 How to make a wormery
https://www.youtube.com/watch?v=ordM5TWyFLw
Website 10.3 Pollinated foods
https://www.pollinator.org/pollinated-food
Website 10.4 World Bee Day
http://www.fao.org/3/i9527en/i9527en.pdf
Website 10.5 Waggle dance
https://www.youtube.com/watch?v=12Q8FfyLLso&t=6ss
Website 10.6 Honeyguide's Revenge
https://africanstorybook.org/reader.php?id=2099
Website 10.7 Come On In to Coobana
https://www.youtube.com/watch?v=v0YXIOxmUGw

Children's books

Nesbitt, K. (2009) *My Hippo Has the Hiccups*, Naperville, IL: Sourcebooks Jabberwocky.

References

Holmgren, D. (2020) *Essence of Permaculture*, Melbourne, Australia: Melliodora Publishing.
Machobane, J. J., and Berold, R. (2003) *Drive out hunger: The story of JJ Machobane of Lesotho*, Bellevue, South Africa: Jacana.

Acknowledgement: I would like thank Stephen Scoffham for contributing some of the teaching ideas featured in this chapter.

11

Jobs, Transport and Energy

*Richard Hatwood, Stephen Scoffham
and Steve Rawlinson*

This area of study focuses on three different aspects of economic and social activity – jobs, energy and transport. These are topics which generate considerable public interest and they are usually foregrounded by politicians, especially in election campaigns. They also raise questions about political power, sustainability and the type of society that we want to live in. Seeing that work is directed towards sustainability objectives, reducing the impact of generating energy (Figure 11.1) and finding ways to minimize the environmental damage from travel are key priorities in the quest for more sustainable ways of living (Scott and Vare 2018). If economics is the mindset that creates society, sustainable development is predicated on how that society is organized.

Work, working patterns and types of employment are continually evolving and changing. Before the Industrial Revolution, most people worked on the land and depended on their physical strength and animal power for their survival. Today, service industries dominate the economy, especially in Westernized nations. Technology has amplified our abilities, enabled us to dominate nature and increased our environmental impact beyond all recognition. The advent of artificial intelligence promises to continue this trend and threatens to make many of the jobs that people do today obsolete. What constitutes work is also liable to be reconfigured. Significant numbers of people provide services, especially in relation to child care and welfare services, which are not officially recognized. A national minimum wage is one suggestion for raising the status of unpaid work and might also help to tackle income inequalities.

With respect to transportation, the movement of people and goods has been transformed over the past century, and it is certainly influencing the current climate emergency. Around a quarter of global carbon dioxide emissions are created by transport. Cars are responsible for about half of this, but air travel is particularly damaging because it emits pollution into the upper atmosphere where it has a disproportionate effect. As the world becomes ever more global in terms of trade and business, making transport more sustainable is a high priority. Cutting down on journeys, walking, cycling and using less polluting forms of transport are seen as promising ways forward (Figure 11.1).

Figure 11.1 Although renewables are growing in importance, around two thirds of world electricity is still generated from fossil fuels. *Source: World in Data. Photo: Steve Rawlinson.*

Another significant development is the shift towards using renewable energy sources to generate electricity. Burning fossil fuels such as coal, oil and gas is being phased out in favour of renewable forms of energy in many industrialized nations. Nuclear power continues to generate controversy, however. Some see it as making an important contribution to a sustainability energy mix, while others argue that the pollution from nuclear waste represents an unacceptable hazard. Whatever their merits, these different measures all represent routes towards sustainability, something which Rhodri Morgan, former First Minister of Wales, declared needs to be built into everything that we do.

Reflection and discussion

1 How would you define work to include unpaid activities, e.g. changing nappies, looking after an elderly relative?
2 What do you think are the pros and cons of nuclear power?
3 Are the proposals for a living wage unrealistic and ideological or a fundamental change we must make in our quest for a more cohesive society?

JOBS (AGE 3–7)

What is the main focus of this topic?

By doing different jobs people help to sustain their community.

Key ideas	Subject links	SDG links
Community	Citizenship	SDG 8 Decent work
Futures	Drama	SDG 9 Industry, innovation and infrastructure
Technology	Geography	
Work	Music	

Background knowledge

In the past many communities in the UK and other similar countries were self-sufficient. The baker, barber, blacksmith, vicar and teacher all contributed to the life of the community so that it could be sustained. This meant that the skills and abilities of different individuals complemented each other and everyone benefited. Today we still rely on many people throughout our lives. What is different is that, rather than living in the same place, our community is now much more scattered, linked through electronic communication and modern means of transport. There have also been dramatic developments in technology, with robots replacing people in significant numbers in manufacturing and repetitive services (Maxton and Randers 2016). This topic introduces young children to the world of work and highlights concepts such as co-operation, interaction and community. It is a reminder that sustainability is multifaceted and that the way we relate to each other impacts not only how we think about ourselves but also how we treat the natural environment. Caring for other people and caring for the environment are two sides of the same coin.

Interesting facts

- A postie (mail carrier) sometimes walks 20 kilometres a day delivering letters.
- Working patterns vary around Europe from an average of 44 hours a week in Greece and Iceland to 29 hours in the Netherlands.
- Some people, especially those from disadvantaged groups, end up without any job at all.

Misconceptions and research

Many young children see their mothers, fathers and carers leave them at school and go off to work. They probably understand that this is to earn money, but have little idea what they actually do. Talking with people who help to keep the school running – the caretaker, secretary, cleaners – is one way to develop pupils' understanding of the world of work. You might also arrange for adults to visit the class, bringing the special equipment that they use for their work. Particularly engaging visitors include the firefighter, the guide-dog trainer and the paramedic.

Teaching ideas

Key vocabulary

community	skill	training
job	tools	work

Getting started

The children should think about the different people who have helped them during the day and the jobs that they do. Make a list on the whiteboard. Now discuss the wide array of other jobs they have seen people doing. Do they need any special equipment to do this work? Do they need to be physically strong or have special training?

Role play | *key idea: interaction*

Set up a 'people who help us' themed role play area. Work with the children to determine the main theme of the space. It could be a doctor's surgery, supermarket or garden centre. Once the theme has been determined, the area can be styled to give the children opportunities to explore the skills and qualities required for the different roles that people undertake. Having some suitable items of uniform, such as hats, tabards, etc., will enable the children to get into role and recognize they are part of a team.

Music while you work | *key idea: community*

Sing some of the songs people have invented to make their job easier and to pass the time in physical or demanding work. Sea shanties are a particularly good example. There are also lots of songs like 'The ants go marching one by one' that build solidarity and togetherness. When it comes to traditional songs, 'Heigh-ho, it's off to work we go!' is one of a number of songs which young children often enjoy. Discuss how music at work has been seen to bring communities together – the Welsh male voice choirs, for example.

Dictionary of jobs | *key idea: diversity*

Working with the children, see if they can think of a job for every letter of the alphabet. For example, A is for acrobat, B is for builder, C is for cleaner and so on. Extend the activity by getting the children to act out some of these roles, perhaps working in groups so they can show interaction between the jobs.

Guess the job | *key idea: technology*

Set up a small display of items linked to different types of work. This might include a trowel, screwdriver, onion, bandage, envelope, map and so on. Some items will probably link to quite a number of different roles. Now turn this activity round and talk about the people who might have been involved in creating each of items in the display. This may open up a discussion around the energy, resources and raw materials needed to create products as well as how tools can enhance our abilities.

Investigations and fieldwork | *key idea: community*

Arrange a visit to a place of work in your locality so pupils can see what happens in a workplace and talk to people who work there about their jobs and the importance of what they do. Alternatively, invite workers from the local community to come to talk to the class. Try to choose jobs that are unusual as well as the work done by local government services. Maybe parents can be involved here. Have any parents got unusual jobs? This also helps build a sense of community in the school.

Sustainability discussion

Do you think all jobs are equally important in supporting a community?

Answers might include:

(a) the jobs that require the most skill are the most important;
(b) the jobs that help people most are the most important; and
(c) all jobs contribute to a community in different ways.

TRANSPORT (AGE 5–11)

What is the main focus of this topic?

The amount that we travel and the way that we do it have environmental impacts.

Key ideas	Subject links	SDG links
Conservation	Drama	SDG 7 Clean energy
Pollution	English	SDG 9 Industry, innovation and
Resources	Geography	infrastructure.
Technology	Mathematics	SDG 12 Responsible consumption
	Science	

Background knowledge

People have always wanted to travel, whether to earn a living, to meet people or to explore the world around them. For centuries the fastest way to travel long distances was either by horse or by sea. Many people undertook arduous journeys on foot. However, in the last couple of centuries transport has been revolutionized. Railways, motorways and shipping routes now link major cities around the world and mass air transport moves people and goods quickly from place to place. Apart from electric trains, these newer forms of transport are all powered by fossil fuels such as coal and different forms of refined oil. The result is that transport is a major source of air pollution and, in turn, one of the largest contributors to the climate emergency. Recently the development of electric cars has advanced rapidly and there are plans to phase out petrol and diesel vehicles. Individual cities have also implemented policies to reduce air pollution and promote public transport. New technologies show that it is possible to redesign transport to be more sustainable. The health benefits of walking and cycling are also being increasingly recognized.

Interesting facts

- Transport accounts for around 28 per cent of US greenhouse gas emissions.
- Roads and car parks take up more than a third of the land in many cities.
- The sale of petrol and diesel cars is being banned in the UK from 2030.

Misconceptions and research

Children have little choice about how they travel, so learning about emissions and the damage that they cause can easily make them feel compromised. Car travel and long-haul flights may be undesirable but they are deeply woven into the fabric of modern life. Being sensitive to the contradictions and ambiguities which are liable to arise from this topic will help to make it effective.

Teaching ideas

Key vocabulary

climate emergency   employment   sustainability
development   energy   transport

Getting started

Talk with the children about the journeys they have made in the last few months. Focus especially on everyday journeys to visit shops, family and leisure facilities. Where did the children go and how did they travel? Have any of them been on longer journeys involving trains or aeroplanes? Tell the class that in this topic they are going to find out more about different forms of transport and the impact that they have on the environment.

Travel choices | *key idea: decision making*

How do children in your class travel to school? Get the pupils to write a report. This should contain a sample survey involving just ten respondents and a brief 'interview' with two pupils who use contrasting modes of transport. The aim of the interview is to find out a bit more about the reasons for their different travel choices. The report should conclude with a recommendation or a short comment on any sustainability issues that have arisen. What factors influence the class with respect to their travel choices? For example, the distance they have to travel, the weather conditions and things they need to carry could all be significant.

Pedestrianization plan | *key idea: democracy*

Conduct a debate around a transport issue. In this scenario the local council has decided to pedestrianize the local high street to reduce pollution and improve conditions for shoppers.

Divide the class into small groups, giving each group a role: local business owner, parent of a child who attends the school on the high street, lorry driver, an older person who has accessibility difficulties, an environmental activist, a member of the local council. Give the children time to form their views and decide if their character is in favour of or against the plan, then debate the proposal. You may want to appoint a pupil to act as the chair who calls different witnesses, or you could fulfil this role yourself.

Using less fuel | *key idea: pollution*

Some forms of transport use much less fuel and are more energy-efficient than others. The following figures shows approximately how far different vehicles travel if each person in it contributes a litre of fuel: intercity express, 220 km; double-decker bus, 170 km; local train, 90 km; car (4 people), 50 km; car (1 person), 12km; aeroplane, 8 km. The pupils can draw a bar graph showing these figures, adding a short explanation and commentary about what it shows.

Investigations and fieldwork | *key idea: change*

Get the children to make a traffic survey in different locations in the school locality. Use tally marks to record the number of different vehicles – cars, buses, bicycles, lorries, etc. – over a set period (10 minutes is often suitable). It is a good idea to do the survey twice to make it more representative, and you might decide to repeat it at different times of day. Analyse the findings when you return to school. How do the different streets compare? Can the children show their findings on a map, distinguishing between streets that are (a) busy, (b) average, (c) quiet? What environmental problems do the children think arise from traffic in your locality? Can they think of any immediate solutions?

Sustainability discussion

How can people be encouraged to travel more sustainably?

Answers might include:

    (a) by making new footpaths and cycle routes;
    (b) by making streets safer for pedestrians, scooters and cyclists;
    (c) by providing better public transport; and
    (d) by making it more expensive to travel by car and plane.

ENERGY AND ELECTRICITY (AGE 7–14)

What is the main focus of this topic?

The way that we generate electricity impacts on the environment.

Key ideas	Subject links	SDG links
Conservation Resources Technology	Design English (persuasive writing) Drama Geography	SDG 7 Clean energy SDG 12 Responsible consumption

Background knowledge

We depend on electricity for just about everything we do in modern life. As well as obvious applications such as heating and lighting, even gas-fired boilers and water supply systems are operated by electricity. Traditionally, power stations have generated electricity by burning coal, oil and gas. These fossil fuels ensured a regular and dependable supply of heat to drive big turbines but also created unacceptable levels of pollution. Renewable energy sources such as wind and solar power have the advantage of using natural resources but depend on suitable weather conditions. In some areas, electricity can be generated by hydropower (tides, waves and dams on rivers) or geothermal sources. Nuclear power stations are another option but they pose a safety risk, and disposing of nuclear waste is a serious problem. This topic introduces pupils to just some of the issues surrounding electricity and energy use. From a sustainability perspective, the shift from traditional to renewable sources is fundamental, because generating power is a major source of greenhouse gases. There are encouraging signs. In the UK, for example, coal-fired power stations have now been more or less completely phased out. However, as the demand for electricity continues to increase around the world, the amount of carbon dioxide from generating power is still rising (Helm 2020).

Interesting facts

- Just about all the electricity in Iceland comes from renewable sources – a mix of geothermal and hydropower.
- Seventy per cent of electricity in France comes from nuclear power – the highest proportion of any country in the world.
- There are over 1,000 coal-fired powered stations in China.
- Enough sunlight reaches the Earth's surface each minute to satisfy the world's energy demands for an entire year.

Misconceptions and research

Misconceptions relating to the differences between 'fuel' and 'energy' are common, and many children are unfamiliar with the difference. Fuel is the raw material that contains energy which is 'unlocked' when it is utilized; humans then use this energy to create electricity or heat.

Teaching ideas

Key vocabulary

electricity	geothermal power	renewable
energy	hydropower	wind turbines
fossil fuel	non-renewable	

Getting started

Show the children a photograph of a living room or other room in a house. Talk with them about everything in that room that uses energy, and in turn everything in their life that uses energy. As they recognize how dependent they are on energy in their daily lives, move the discussion to focus on where energy comes from, what are the main energy sources, and what happens when those sources fail?

Saving energy | *key idea: conservation*

Taking readings from smart meters in their home or at school could enable the children to see just how much power different activities use/need, e.g. how much power does a washing machine/dishwasher use, and how much does that cost? Then, working in pairs, encourage the children to identify ways in which they can save energy in their daily lives. Examples might include turning off lights when not in use, switching off machines that are on standby, and turning off taps when cleaning their teeth (website 11.1). Amalgamate the various suggestions into a class list of appropriate strategies. Ask the children to design stickers to promote energy-saving actions, e.g. stickers to go on a fridge door reminding people to shut it properly. Undertaking this activity in a school context can act as a continuous reminder to be careful of energy usage.

Wind turbines | *key idea: technology*

Wind turbines have become a common feature on our landscape. Indeed, some schools have now got their own wind turbine to generate their own electricity. The children could be asked to consider the pros and cons of such a scheme for their school. This will necessitate them undertaking an audit of energy use in the school, looking at the savings that a turbine would bring after paying for its installation, where it could be installed, and the impact it will have around the school in terms of noise and intrusion on the landscape. Presenting the case to the governors of the school would be an excellent focus for an activity engaging the school council, if there is one.

Renewable energy | *key idea: resources*

Working in small groups the children can research ways of producing renewable energy. These include wind turbines, solar panels, tidal barrages, wave power, hydroelectric dams and geothermal systems. Each group should say something about the advantages and disadvantages of their method, and identify a site within their own country or internationally where it has been developed. They should then produce a report on the role they feel their particular energy source could play in their country's energy mix. Understanding that some methods are more suited to certain locations than others, and that countries cannot rely on just one source, will broaden their understanding of energy policy.

Investigations and fieldwork | *key idea: interaction*

In groups encourage the children to devise their own 'green town', or 'green island', where energy use is kept to a minimum. You might set the context by giving details of the climate (tropical, temperate desert or arctic) and the landscape (lowland, mountain, coastal). The challenge for the children is to design a model house which contains energy-efficient devices, a town and road layout which minimizes journey times and is car-free, and energy generation schemes which work in the locality they have imagined. This activity will involve pupils in bringing together knowledge from different sources, so it is one that could be extended over several weeks. The final designs might be assessed by an external judge, such as an architect, environmentalist or town planner.

Sustainability discussion

How can we ensure that we have enough energy yet avoid polluting the planet?

Answers might include:

(a) by using energy more efficiently (e.g. energy efficient houses);
(b) by using renewable energy instead of power from fossil fuels;
(c) by offsetting and carbon capture;
(d) by finding new ways of making electricity (e.g. hydrogen power).

Websites

Website 11.1 Saving energy
https://www.fantastichandyman.co.uk/blog/how-to-save-energy-for-kids/
Website 11.2 Carbon zero schools
https://ashden.org

References

Helm, D. (2020) *Net Zero: How We Can Stop Climate Change*, London: Collins.
Maxton, G., and Randers, J. (2016) *Reinventing Prosperity*, Vancouver: Greystone Books.
Scott, W., and Vare, P. (2018) *The World We'll Leave Behind: Grasping the Sustainability Challenge*, London: Routledge.

12

The Global Village

Natasha Ziebell and Stephen Scoffham

The concept of the 'Global Village' was conceived by Marshall McLuhan (1962) to describe interconnecting information systems in a globalized world. In the past, communication was limited by the speed of the transport system at the time, but innovations, such as Google going live in 1998 and the first iPhone available for purchase in 2007, have drastically changed how we live and work. As technological and engineering advances continue apace, today's world is appearing to 'shrink' even faster than ever. We can only imagine what might be possible in the next ten, twenty or fifty years.

It is against this background that the UN Sustainable Development Goals (SDGs) have set out an agenda to improve the lives of people all over the world. The goals interlink, and global population growth and settlement patterns are factors that impact on them all. Some of the most pressing issues include the urban population with projections showing that, by 2050, around 70 per cent of people will be living in cities (UN 2021). Other issues include providing adequate housing, access to services and increasing energy demands. With the loss of land from use as market gardens and family farming, there are additional food security issues and challenges with global supply chains. The resilience or capacity of modern systems to cope with these dynamic and ever-changing factors ultimately impact sustainability.

So, what does a sustainable future look like for our settlements across the globe (Figure 12.1)? Innovative practices are already emerging that are set to disrupt and challenge current ideas. Some examples include:

- designing settlements that provide safe, comfortable and affordable housing, using innovative and sustainable design;
- using the principles of passive house design (passivhaus) to create ultra energy-efficient buildings;
- urban agricultural innovations such as aerofarms, creating vertical indoor farms on distribution routes and in urban areas;
- sustainable and accessible transport networks, e.g. Hong Kong's transport system, that has been identified as one of the most sustainable in the world.

Figure 12.1 A model village created by children aged 5 and 6. *Photo: Stephen Scoffham.*

Throughout history, humans have shown resilience and remarkable adaptability. Learning about housing, settlements and population connects children with the physical and social environments that are central to community living. Raising awareness about where we live, why settlements exist in certain locations and how this affects our lifestyle, alongside the global challenges we face, provides the motivation for critical reasoning and creative solutions in working towards a sustainable future.

Reflection and discussion

1 What do the terms 'global' and 'village' mean to you, both as separate and collective terms?
2 What changes have you seen to towns and cities within your lifetime? Is there any evidence they are being made more sustainable?

HOUSES AND HOMES (AGE 3–7)

What is the main focus of this topic?

The way we build our houses effects the environment.

Key concepts	Subject links	Global goals
Community Place Resources	Design/technology English (story) Geography	SDG 11 Sustainable cities and communities

Background knowledge

The concept of home means different things to different people. All over the world, people live in diverse permanent, floating and moveable dwellings. Homes are found in different locations such as urban, regional and rural areas. Traditionally, houses were made from local materials such as bricks, rocks, straw, ice and cob (a combination of mud, clay, straw and manure). More modern materials include concrete, steel, glass and plastic. Some materials are better than others; they are chosen because they are accessible and can provide shelter from the heat, cold, wind and rain.

Homes have changed over time because of innovations in engineering. In the past, if you owned a horse, then you would need a stable nearby that would provide shelter for it. Now, if your primary mode of travel is a car, you might park it in a garage/driveway or leave it on the street. Likewise, kitchens and bathrooms would not traditionally have been attached to a dwelling, but with connections to water, electricity and gas, they are now located in many homes. However, many people around the globe still do not have access to these resources and live in homes with no running water, electricity, gas or proper sanitation.

Interesting facts

- Dome-shaped structures are the most energy-efficient and strongest building design.
- The old incandescent light bulbs give out 90 per cent heat and 10 per cent light, while LEDs offer the reverse (and they last 90 per cent longer). However, increasing light pollution is damaging the health of people and animals.
- The Knap of Howar in Scotland is the oldest house in the world that is still standing, dating back to the Neolithic period (3600 BC).

Misconceptions and research

Photographs and picture-book illustrations are good sources of information about houses in distant lands. However, children should also visit buildings in their own locality and study them at first hand if possible. As always when working with young children, it is best not to take anything for granted. In the reception class, for example, some children may not see houses as whole buildings but, being small in stature, perceive them merely as walls and barriers.

Teaching ideas

Key vocabulary

building	environment	resources
community	home	
country	house	

Getting started

Invite children to share their ideas about what is needed to make a home. Talk about the materials that make a home comfortable. What turns a house into a home? Think also about animal homes – dens, burrows, nests and so forth. You might also talk about the features that all homes have in common – always being sensitive to those children who may come from deprived or diverse backgrounds.

The Three Little Pigs | *key idea: resources*

What resources are used to build a house? Read the fairy tale of *The Three Little Pigs* (website 12.1). What did the pigs use to make their homes and where might the materials have come from? How effective were they in keeping the pigs safe, comfortable and warm? Ask the children to create a story about the 'fourth pig'. What did the fourth pig use to build their house? Were the materials strong enough to keep out the bad wolf, withstand a 'strong wind' or other environmental forces? Is it a sustainable house that uses sustainable materials?

Fantasy houses | *key idea: imagination*

Read the children the rhyme about the old woman who lived in a shoe. Discuss how she might have fitted her family into such a small space. Encourage the children to make drawings of the old woman's house showing the windows, chimney, door and front garden. Extend this idea by bringing a range of objects to school such as a wellington boot, flowerpot, teapot and sieve. Ask the children to look at them carefully and do drawings to show how they might be turned into a house. Finally, show the children some pictures of eco-houses using Google Images (many of them are really unusual). Who might *actually* be able to live in their wellington boot, flowerpot and so forth?

Homes worldwide | *key idea: environments*

What different types of homes do people live in? Show images of homes from different environments around the world. Icehouses and underground houses are particularly good examples. Ask pupils to complete a 'See, Think, Wonder' routine using these prompts: What do you see? What do you think about that? What does it make you wonder? (website 12.2). Now give the children long strips of card which they can fold into panels. They should draw a different house on each panel to make a simple concertina book. Older children might add labels saying where such houses might be found. However, it is essential to avoid perpetuating the idea that in any one country all people live in one type of house. (See the discussion on misconceptions on page 172 of Chapter 13.)

Investigations and fieldwork | *key idea: place*

Plan a short community walk to investigate sustainability in the local area. Are there any obvious examples of the ways that people are trying to make their homes environmentally friendly? Look especially for double glazing, solar panels, water butts and recycling bins. Some houses may have electric charging points for cars or places where bicycles are stored. Do the gardens have a range of plants that will attract insects? Are there vegetables growing in the garden? Are there any newly planted trees? The children could take photos of the things they see to use in a class display when they return to school.

Sustainability discussion

In what ways might homes be made more sustainable in future?

Answers might include:

(a) they will be built of materials that can be recycled;
(b) they will only use energy from renewable sources;
(c) all household waste and rubbish will be recycled; and
(d) they will have gardens that attract birds and insects and in which food might be grown.

SUSTAINABLE CITIES (AGE 5–11)

What is the main focus of this topic?

Making settlements, especially cities, more sustainable is a priority for the future.

Key concepts	Subject links	Global goals
Health Interaction Sustainable living	Design/technology Geography	SDG 11 Sustainable cities and communities

Background knowledge

A settlement is a place where people live. Settlements are often categorized according to their size. Villages are the most basic and ancient form of human settlement and arose so people could pool their labour and live together for comfort and protection. Towns serve as centres for surrounding rural areas where people can buy and sell goods and services. Cities are the largest settlements of all and have regional, national or international importance. They act as a seat for local or national government and have specialist facilities such as hospitals, universities and law courts. They are also major transport hubs.

Around the world cities are growing larger. People may be drawn to cities by the prospect of work and a better life, or driven to them as they are displaced from the land by war or disasters. By 2050 it is predicted that three quarters of all people will be living in cities. The most spectacular changes will be in countries with fast economic growth. China, for example, already has over a hundred metropolitan areas, each with over a million people. Seeing that cities are healthy places for people to live and reducing their environmental footprint will be priorities for the future.

Interesting facts

- Nearly half of people in Copenhagen go to work on a bicycle.
- Some cities like Venice have no cars at all.
- Recycled waste water supplies 40 per cent of the water needed in Singapore.

Misconceptions and research

Children have personal knowledge and experience of the places around them and they will have beliefs about what makes them special, fun and safe. Building on this knowledge can help to make the notion of sustainable cities, which is rather abstract, more accessible. It would be easy to dwell on the negative aspects of city life, but thinking in terms of sustainability shifts the focus towards what is possible in the future. Having children investigate and create their city of the future promotes the kind of positive and hopeful mindset which is known to be important in encouraging learning.

Teaching ideas

Key vocabulary

city	green flag	town
eco-friendly	settlement	village

Getting started

Discuss with the pupils the way that settlements are getting larger. Are they aware of any new developments in their own area? How many of the world's largest cities can they name? Where are they? What makes them famous? Would they like to live there?

Healthy environments | *key idea: health*

What are the factors which make a place healthy and sustainable to live in? Working in pairs, ask the children to draw up their list of around eight to ten things that they value about where they live or would value if they lived in a city. For example, they might focus on safety, recreation, transport, housing, air quality, noise, places to meet and open spaces. Assemble results to compile an agreed class list. As an extension, have the pupils draw up a healthy places survey with a range of questions which they ask respondents to rate on a scale of 1–5. This activity, which can be done either within the classroom or as a homework exercise, allows children to see how people sometimes view the same place differently.

Push-pull factors | *key idea: change*

Why do people leave the countryside to come to live in cities and large urban areas? They may be attracted by factors such as jobs, entertainment, personal freedom and the chance to mix with others. They may be driven by negative forces. Working on the land is very hard work, and floods and droughts can easily wipe out crops. Climate change is an issue in some areas, elsewhere wars and conflicts are displacing other communities. Encourage the children to make a push-pull diagram with arrows showing a person/family being pushed on the one side and pulled on the other towards a city. What will be the impacts of migrant people on the communities left behind and the communities they are moving to? You may find that there are pupils in your class with direct experience of these issues. If so, see if they would like to contribute their stories while respecting their sensitivities.

'Green' cities | *key idea: sustainable living*

Encourage the children to investigate 'green' cities around the world. Examples might include Vancouver, Amsterdam, Curitiba in Brazil, Singapore and Cape Town. Ask them to download a photograph(s) of each city and write a few sentences about the features that make it particularly eco-friendly. Display the work around a world map which identifies the location of each of the cities pupils have studied. Look at the various eco-city league tables. What else can children learn about them? Would they like to live in these cities? What do they see as being the advantages and disadvantages?

Investigations and fieldwork | *key idea: sustainable living*

Find out about the 'green flag' award and discuss the aims of the scheme and the judging criteria with the children (website 12.3). Now ask them to think about what they would include in a 'sustainable city' competition. The green flag award focuses especially on biodiversity whereas the new award would be concerned with how cities could be more environmentally friendly for both people and the environment. Challenge the children to design a poster advertising the new scheme and encouraging people to take part. An additional task might be for them to design and build a 'green city' using junk or Lego.

Sustainability discussion

Discuss with the children how they think cities might change in the future and how they can become more environmentally friendly.

Answers might include:

(a) planting trees and flowers along roads to remove fumes;
(b) creating gardens on rooftops;
(c) using recycled materials in new buildings;
(d) saving all the rainwater that goes into drains to make new lakes; and
(e) creating communities where people look after each other.

POPULATION (AGE 7–14)

What is the main focus of this topic?

Learning about world population growth helps us to understand sustainability issues.

Key concepts	Subject links	Global goals
Community Growth Place Resources	Geography History Mathematics	All SDGs, particularly SDG 11 Sustainable cities and communities

Background knowledge

In 2011, world population reached a significant milestone (7 billion people) and projections suggest that the population could reach 8.5 billion by 2030. The number of people our Earth can support depends on many factors including access to and use of resources, population density and distribution, and environmental impact. These are key issues that have been raised concerning global populations and are central to all the Sustainable Development Goals.

Understanding population statistics can form the foundations for exploring the dynamics which shape a society. Critical questions hinge around the demand for resources, the impact on the environment and the quality of life. This topic introduces pupils to the relationship between population and sustainability. When looking at global population statistics, it is important to note that the numbers are estimations. The projections show that, while the population is increasing, the overall rate of growth is slowing down. At some point in the future, it is predicted world population will stop growing completely and stabilize for the first time since farming began 10,000 years ago. This will be a milestone on our journey to regain the balance between people and nature.

Interesting facts

- There are more scientists alive today than ever lived in all of human history.
- Between around 1980 and 2015, China implemented a one-child policy to limit population growth.
- Education, especially of girls, is the most effective way of reducing family size.

Misconceptions and research

Children and adults can have difficulties conceptualizing the magnitude of very large numbers. *How Much Is a Million?* by David Schwartz (2004) can support children in their understanding of the numbers one million, one billion and one trillion (website 12.4). Exploring familiar animal populations such as bees and ants will enable children to begin to understand and visualize large numbers, e.g. there are about 250,000 ants in the average anthill; 300 bees would fill half a cup.

Teaching ideas

Key vocabulary

census	resources	space
environment	society	statistics
population		

Getting started

The children could collect some population statistics about their class. For example, they could record the age, gender, eye colour, hair colour, height (short, medium, tall), number of siblings and so forth. Ask the children to restrict their survey to a sample of just ten pupils. This will help to keep it manageable and will also make it relatively easily to show the data on a bar graph or, with young children, blocks of Lego bricks. Talk about how a census assembles data about the population of a whole country. This information enables statisticians to identify trends, which is invaluable when planning for the future and thinking about sustainability.

Population fact file | *key idea: balance*

Watch the presentation on world population statistics (website 12.5). Suggest that the children might devise a fact file with ten key facts about world population from the video. They will have to make good use of the pause button! What three facts surprise them most and why? Extend the activity by encouraging the children to devise a short 'world in numbers' quiz. For each question in the quiz, those who are answering have to not only come up with the correct number, they also need to say what this means in terms of sustainability.

Timeline | *key idea: change*

The interactive map of the world (website 12.6) links world population with key historical events. With younger children you might want to explore the map as a class activity drawing out a few key points relating to sustainability. Older children can conduct their own investigations and devise a timeline. Alongside the date this should have two columns: (a) world population and (b) significant environmental event. There is plenty of information to choose from; the essence of this activity is to be selective.

The global village | *key idea: community*

The bestselling book by David Smith (2020), *If the World Were a Village*, imagines the world as a village of 100 people (website 12.7). In this village, sixty-one people come from Asia, thirteen from Africa, twelve are from Europe, eight from South and Central America, five are from North America, and one is from Oceania. Give the children some sheets of graph paper and get them to represent this data visually. Label and cut out the shapes to make a display about world population. As an alternative with younger children, make a visual display using Lego or building blocks.

Investigations and fieldwork | *key idea: future*

Suggest the children could devise their own 'census form' for other children to complete. Explain that this will help the school to plan for the future and help it to become more sustainable. The children will need to decide what they want to find out and why; they will also have to make decisions about how to conduct their census, and how to analyse the results. Once they have done so, they could present their findings to the whole school, giving emphasis to what the results show about the school now and what it means for the future, e.g. is there an overwhelming demand for more bicycle sheds as more children want to ride to school?

Sustainability discussion | *key idea: environmental limits*

How are we going to live within planetary means if the population keeps growing?

Answers might include:

(a) reducing consumption;
(b) sharing resources more equally;
(c) having smaller families; and
(d) using technology to find alternatives to current resources.

Websites

Website 12.1 The Three Little Pigs
https://www.youtube.com/watch?v=xGFjzp8wl1E
Website 12.2 Project Zero Thinking Routines
https://pz.harvard.edu/thinking-routines
Website 12.3 Green Flag criteria
https://www.greenflagaward.org/how-it-works/judging-criteria/
Website 12.4 How Much Is a Million?
https://www.youtube.com/watch?v=O7M_DUiX1A8
Website 12.5 Population statistics
https://www.youtube.com/watch?v=PJ_KQBFN6yI
Website 12.6 World population history
https://worldpopulationhistory.org/map/2050/mercator/1/0/25/
Website 12.7 If the World Were a Village
https://www.youtube.com/watch?v=FtYjUv2x65g

Children's books

Schwartz, D. (2004) *How Much Is a Million?*, New York: Lee and Shepherd Books.
Smith, D. (2020) *If the World Were a Village*, London: Bloomsbury.

References

McLuhan, M. (1962, 2011) *The Gutenberg Galaxy: The Making of Typographic Man*, Toronto: University of Toronto Press.
United Nations (2021) *Population*, available at https://www.un.org/en/sections/issues-depth/population/.

13

Special Places

Paula Owens

Place is a complex concept; it is a human construct – a space sometimes clearly, sometimes loosely, defined and imbued with meaning through the lens of human perspective. Environmental psychologists and geographers have pondered and examined the reciprocity of this construct; seeking to understand both the power of certain environments and landscapes to fire the human imagination, and the power of human ideas and thought in shaping and controlling them. Hilltops, woodland groves and lakes are revered in many cultures as sacred spots. The power of certain landscapes to inspire writers, poets, artists and musicians is also widely recognized. Places of particular ecological interest are often designated for scientific research. Meanwhile national and regional parks mark out and protect areas that are acknowledged as having special qualities.

One of the reasons that the idea of 'place' is complex, and often contested, is because places are not value-neutral. Places both stimulate human actions and are shaped by them. Places are valued and become 'special' for reasons that may be either functional, personal and cultural – or through various combinations of these factors. How we feel about, act in, look after (or not), and ultimately how we change, places is very much bound up with how we come to know, understand and value them. Places influence and reflect our sustainable thoughts and deeds. They are the beating heart of the sustainability puzzle.

Research into significant life experiences has explored the relationships between early experiences in places and environments and lasting dispositions towards them. The findings indicate there are persuasive links between these early positive outdoor experiences and our capacity to think and act in pro-environmental ways as adults (Catling et al 2010). Learning about and experiencing places helps us to understand how we might change the world for better or for worse. There is a strong, interdisciplinary, cognitive aspect to this. Having adequate language to identify, name, describe and explain features and processes, and human–environment interactions is vital. However, it is not enough to learn *about* places and environments, we must learn *how* we belong and understand *how* we and others relate to places in different ways, thereby building empathy, respect for difference, and a willingness to view and interpret places through others' eyes. It is only when we fall in love with the Earth that we will really want to care for it (Figure 13.1).

Figure 13.1 Making a map of special places in the school playground. *Photo: Paula Owens.*

Reflection and discussion

1   Are there any places that have been significant in your life? Can you identify why they are significant to you?
2   Can you think of any particular place-related experiences which have made you interested in sustainability?

WHERE I BELONG (AGE 3–7)

What is the main focus of this topic?

We all need a home, a place where we belong in the world.

Key concepts	Subject links	Global goals
Belonging Habitats Special places	Art English (vocabulary) Geography Religious Education	SDG 3 Global health and well-being SDG 11 Sustainable cities and communities

Background knowledge

All forms of life belong to the world in the sense that they are geographically and ecologically rooted. Some species of plants and animals do well across a variety of environments but most are adapted to particular regions. For example, polar bears are found in the Arctic and approximately 90 per cent of all plants and animals found in Madagascar are endemic, which means they are unique to the island. Thinking more broadly, deserts, tropical rainforests and savannas each have a particular range of flora and fauna which are their defining characteristic. Different forms of life belong to these habitats on a fundamental level, and if they are removed from them, they are liable to perish.

Belonging is equally, or perhaps even more, important to human beings. Without support and nurture, young children are unable to survive. Psychologically we derive a sense of our own identity both from those around us and from our physical surroundings (Tanner, 2019). The plasticity of the brain enables human beings to adapt to their surroundings to a remarkable degree. However, it is through the connections that we make both to the past and the future that we are able to understand ourselves and to flourish. This topic explores two aspects of belonging which are particularly relevant for young children – homes and safety. And as they explore how they belong in the world, children will be laying the foundations for a deep understanding of sustainability.

Interesting facts

- The compass termite builds large, wedge-shaped nests arranged in a north–south orientation. Doing this helps them regulate the heat within their homes.
- Caddis flies' larvae protect their developing bodies by making cases, spun from silk and using substances found in their natural environment.
- Honeybees build nests out of secreted wax in which they live out almost all of their lives, rearing their young and producing food within these carefully designed structures.

Misconceptions and research

Children may think about their homes in stereotypical ways. A classical misconception is for English children to have negative views about homes in African countries, believing that people all live in mud huts. There are two misconceptions here: one is an assumption that 'everyone' lives in a certain type of house, and the other is that homes constructed out of mud are deficient in some way, whereas mud can be an extremely efficient, effective and sustainable housing material.

Teaching ideas

Key vocabulary

favourite	place	shelter
home	safe	special

Getting started

Start by showing some pictures of animal homes and ask children to think why animals might need one. Discuss their need for warmth, shelter and safety. Then ask children what home means to them and why they need one. Make a list together of the most important things about a home that makes it special.

Favourite places | *key idea: belonging*

Ask children to think about their favourite place where they feel they belong and feel safe and comfortable. You could suggest some options such as their bedroom, a spot in the garden or a favourite place they like to visit, or maybe it's grandma's house? Children could draw or model this favourite room or place and add in the features that make it special.

My special place in words | *key idea: connections*

Using a word cloud programme such as Word Art or Tagxedo (website 13.1), import all the children's words and ideas about why their homes or favourite places are special. Identify commonly used words and recurring ideas and themes.

Oi! Get off our Train | *key idea: habitats*

Read *Oi! Get off our Train* by John Burningham and discuss where in the world the animals boarding the train have come from, adding them to a world map or using a globe to point out their natural habitats. Discuss with the children why they might live where they do and why their homes are at risk.

Investigations and fieldwork | *key idea: interaction*

Give the children a blank outline map of the school showing the classrooms, corridors, hall, office, playground and so forth. Now ask the children to identify the places where they feel safe, happy and peaceful, colouring them green on the map. If there are any places which they find frightening or where they feel unhappy, colour them red. Use yellow for places about which they have no strong feelings or no particular knowledge. Talk individually with the children about their maps to find out more about their emotional responses to the school environment.

Sustainability discussion

Which is more sustainable – a home built by humans or by animals? And why?

Answers might include:

(a) animal homes, such as nests, are built out of natural material collected locally;

(b) animal homes blend into the landscape; and

(c) no machinery is used to make an animal's home; they create their home using their own energy.

CONNECTING WITH PLACES (AGE 7–11)

What is the main focus of this topic?

Places are an important part of our identity.

Key concepts	Subject links	Global goals
Community Identity Place	Art Citizenship Geography History Religious Education	SDG 3 Global health and well-being SDG 11 Sustainable cities and communities

Background knowledge

Communities are groups of people who live, work and play together or have ideas, values and beliefs in common. Communities contribute to our sense of belonging and identity. We can belong to different types and scales of community from local to global. These may include our families, school and local community, faith communities and networks of recreational clubs. At a more general level we are all part of a national community with its own traditions and customs. In addition, we also have virtual communities that involve social media networks which widen the reach of children and young people but also expose them to wider streams of information and potential fake news.

Ultimately, we all belong to a global community of living things that includes plants and creatures as well as human beings. Recognizing that we are part of nature and depend on it for our survival is one of the fundamental realizations of sustainability education. This topic draws on children's experience of place to help them explore their sense of identity and to develop an inclusive and empathetic perspective. Understanding ourselves and our inner being is an essential counterpart to understanding the world around us and how we may live in harmony with it.

Interesting facts

- The three most popular pastimes throughout the world are reading, travel and fishing.
- The Statue of Liberty in New York City harbour is frequently quoted as the number one landmark in the world.
- The Angel of the North in the UK is next to a motorway and is seen by one person every second - that's 90 thousand people a day.

Misconceptions and research

The memories we make in our transactions with and through place contribute to how we come to know and feel about the world around us and others in it. Place attachment is a key idea in environmental psychology and is neatly encapsulated in the notion of 'biophilia' (literally 'love of life'), a term coined by biologist E. O. Wilson. It is argued that place attachment contributes to our sense of connectedness and emotional regulation, particularly in the early years of life. It also has a significant role in promoting mental health and well-being

Teaching ideas

Key vocabulary

character   identity   meaning
community   landmark   place

Getting started

Discuss the different communities the children belong to. Think about sports teams, recreational clubs and religious groups. To prompt further discussion, look at a map showing where children live. In what way are we all part of a global community?

Meaningful maps | *key idea: place*

Remind the children that maps are pictures or diagrams that show places. Maps sometimes follow agreed rules (e.g. regarding symbols and overhead perspective) but they can also be informal and personal. Invite the children to draw a map of their locality showing places that have a special meaning. These could be hand-drawn or make use of a digital tool such as Digimaps (website 13.2). Encourage them to add notes explaining why they have chosen to show these places. Share the maps as a class and identify features with common significance.

Places in my life | *key idea: identity*

Ask children to create a storyboard sequence of drawings and maps of places which have been significant in their lives. Encourage them to include places visited on holiday, places where they have lived, and places which are important for community activities such as a sports club. Some children may have family living overseas or want to include events such as weddings. The aim is to get them to reflect on the places and experiences which have contributed to shaping their identity.

Place portrait | *key idea: identity*

Find out about some of the places which are special to your region or country. These might include high mountains, dramatic rivers and spectacular coastlines, as well as ancient sites or places where particular events have taken place. The children could work in groups and compile their findings as a 'directory' which will provide a place or country portrait. What image do they think their portrait presents? Would other people have selected different places and told a different story?

Celebrating landscape | *key idea: place*

Share some famous landscape paintings from your culture or location with the children. Examples from a European context might include Constable's 'The Hay Wain', Van Gogh's paintings of southern France or some of David Hockney's more recent works depicting the Yorkshire countryside. You could compare these with the famous seventeenth-century paintings of the Dutch landscape. Now encourage the children to create their own landscape painting of a real or imagined place.

Investigations and fieldwork | *key idea: distinctiveness*

Landmarks signify meaning and are emblematic of beliefs and ideas. Each country has its own range of significant landmarks or wonders: the Pyramids in Egypt; the Taj Mahal in India; the Eiffel Tower in Paris; the Houses of Parliament in London; Uluru (Ayers Rock) in Australia. Get the children to work in small groups to devise a PowerPoint presentation about a landmark of their choice from your own culture or location using six to eight slides. Encourage them to include a map and to say something about the history of their landmark. It could be a building, a natural feature, or a place which is famous for certain events.

Sustainability discussion

Talk with the children about landmarks in and around their district. Which one would they select as a local 'wonder' and why?

Answers might include:

  (a) because it looks beautiful;
  (b) because it is a home for wildlife;
  (c) because everybody likes it;
  (d) because it makes me feel good.

PROTECTING PLACES (AGE 7–14)

What is the main focus of this topic?

People can work to protect places and value nature.

Key concepts	Subject links	Global goals
Change Conservation Development Futures	Design/technology Geography Mathematics	SDG 3 Global health and well-being SDG 11 Sustainable cities and communities

Background knowledge

The physical environment is continually changing. Some places change slowly, over long timescales, while others change far more rapidly. The iconic Grand Canyon, for example, was created by geological forces and subsequent erosion by the Colorado River in a series of complex processes over hundreds of millions of years. At the other end of the scale, a single landslide, earthquake or volcanic eruption can transform a landscape in a matter of minutes.

Human activity also produces dramatic changes. This has been particularly evident in the last couple of centuries as industrialization and the use of fossil fuels has impacted the natural world. Today, human activity continues to grow apace. Increasing consumption rates, the demand for more housing and ever larger cities are seen as part of increasing prosperity and development but the environmental cost is only now starting to be recognized. The notion of sustainable development attempts to square this circle by putting together two different ideas in a single term to guide our activity. A key point is that the future is not given and can take many different forms. As Dave Hicks (2014) points out, we can think about probable, possible and, most of all, about *preferable* futures and work towards them.

Interesting facts

- Italy and China have the largest number of UNESCO world heritage sites in the world – each has fifty-five.
- Saint Michael's Sustainable Community, Costa Rica, and Findhorn Ecovillage, Scotland, are model communities where people live in harmony with nature.
- Mount Kailash in western Tibet is called the Stairway to Heaven. It is believed to be the home of the Hindu god Shiva, and any attempt to climb it is regarded as sacrilegious.

Misconceptions and research

Children can easily be misled by 'fake news' and often pick up on doom-and-gloom stories which then lead to negative attitudes and perceptions about sustainability. While we certainly face some dire challenges, we need to recognize there are many positive things happening in the world. Technology has offered many successes, such as innovative energy solutions and efficient housing. However, on its own, technology is not going to answer all our problems. We also need to work with the solutions nature offers and to think holistically.

Teaching ideas

Key vocabulary

green corridor   land use   sustainable city
heritage site   national park   technology

Getting started

Discuss any changes children have noticed in the local environment and whether they are an improvement or not. Introduce the idea of probable, possible and preferable futures. Talk through a local issue, identifying what a preferable outcome would be.

National parks | *key idea: conservation*

As well as being havens for wildlife, national parks in the UK are used for farming and recreation. Watch Dan Raven Ellison's short video about the different types of land use in the UK's national parks (website 13.3). In this 100-second video, each second of the walk reveals 1 per cent of the land and how it appears from above. Ask pupils to note down the percentage given over to each land-use type and get them to draw a bar chart to show the figures. Discuss how this analysis contributes to their understanding of sustainability and extend the work by finding out about national parks in your country or region (website 13.4).

Sustainable cities | *key idea: futures*

What does a sustainable city look like? Find out about how Alcaldia de Medellin in Colombia has tackled problems of global heating and reduced pollution through the creation of green corridors. At the same time better job prospects have reduced crime (website 13.5). Now find out how Copenhagen could become a model sustainable city of the future (website 13.6) and how roofs in central London might be put to good use (website 13.7). What would the children want to include in their design for a sustainable city?

Good news stories | *key idea: change*

Ask children to find some national and international success stories about conservation and sustainability. These might include stories about how communities have banded together on a project, how government has introduced new laws and regulations, or how technological innovation is helping to solve an environmental problem. Invite the children to share what they have found out with the rest of class and give their story a rating for effectiveness.

Investigations and fieldwork | *key idea: change*

Working in groups, ask children to design a questionnaire to find out what local people think about their neighbourhood and how it might be changed to make it more sustainable. They will need to test out their questionnaire to see how well it works before asking others to complete it. Collate results using a mix of mapping, report writing and graphs.

Sustainability discussion

How can we ensure that special places are not lost for the future? Answers might focus on:

(a) becoming involved in their identification and care;
(b) encouraging others to appreciate them; and
(c) appreciating and understanding the differing views of others.

Websites

Website 13.1 Word art
www.wordart.com
Website 13.2 Digimap for schools
www.digimapforschools.ac.uk
Website 13.3 UK National parks in 100 seconds
https://www.youtube.com/watch?v=Zuzsacn-8aA
Website 13.4 World heritage sites
https://whc.unesco.org/en/list/
Website 13.5 Alcaldia-de-Medellin
https://ashden.org/winners/alcaldia-de-medellin/
Website 13.6 Copenhagen Sustainable City
https://www.youtube.com/watch?v=pUbHGI-kHsU
Website 13.7 Living roofs
https://www.youtube.com/watch?v=PzgmQp-7QuY

Children's books

Burningham, J. (1991) *Oi! Get off our Train*, London: Red Fox.

References

Catling, S., Greenwood, R., Martin, F., and Owens, P. (2010) 'Formative Experiences of Primary Geography Educators', *International Research in Geography and Environmental Education*, 19:4.

Hicks, D. (2014) *Educating for Hope in Troubled Times: Climate Change and the Transition to a Post-Carbon Future*, London: Institute of Education Press.

Tanner, J. (2019) 'Place Attachments: A Sense of Security', *Primary Geography,* 99:8–11.

14

Citizenship and Democracy

Hilde Tørnby

Teachers are often the first adults outside their immediate family that young children encounter on a regular basis. Realizing that we serve as role models and that our presence impacts both ourselves and our community helps pupils grapple with concepts like citizenship, community and democracy. Fostering modes of thought that provide a foundation for these complex concepts, is an essential basis for sustainability education. This chapter uses picture books as points of departure to provide fictional frameworks for a set of activities that will support teachers and pupils in such work (Figure 14.1).

Ideas on how to best govern a society are found in ancient texts such as Plato's *Republic* (375 BC), which has influenced and inspired thinkers and politicians throughout time. Plato reflected on what makes a fair and just society. Political philosophy is a discipline of its own, and is not the focus for this area of study; however, it may function as a backdrop to our comprehension. Citizenship, communities and democracy are interconnected ideas which represent unique qualities of what it entails for a person to live sustainably on this planet.

A sense of belonging is vital in all aspects of life, vital for citizenship, and creates a sense of self-worth. Some children feel very connected to their families and to their school communities, others feel connected only partially to one or none of these domains. A lack of attachment and emotional connectedness may cause loneliness and hopelessness, so there is a risk that those who feel lost, belittled and overlooked may seek social groups where they feel valued. Currently, there is an increase in radicalization in many parts of the world which is impacting children in multiple ways. Despite this, the Covid-19 pandemic shows how democracies can respond to a common challenge (although global inequalities have certainly been highlighted in the process). These events have made it clear to many people that who I am at this particular time in history, how I act and which responsibilities I take on define me and my citizenship, and this shows a possible way to address sustainability issues.

Figure 14.1 Picture books provide fictional frameworks where children can explore complex issues. *Illustration: Hilde Tørnby.*

Reflection and discussion

1 What do you think are the most important aspects of citizenship?
2 Why are healthy communities essential for sustainabiliy?
3 Think of three words that describe the idea of democracy.

ECO-CITIZENS (AGE 3–7)

What is the main focus of this topic?

Developing children's notion of eco-citizenship by studying the life cycle of a butterfly.

Key ideas	Subject links	SDG links
Community	Art	SDG 11 Sustainable cities and communities
Cycles	Drama	
Habitat	English (story)	SDG 15 Life on land
Interaction	Science	

Background knowledge

Young children's presence in this world is often closely connected to observations in nature. There are many questions which immediately elicit a sense of awe and wonder. Who teaches the butterfly to fly? Why do ants exist? Who decided that trees and plants should have green leaves? Engaging with nature is a fundamental basis for sustainability thinking. If you don't love the world, you are never going to want to care for it. Eco-citizenship is a holistic concept where social, cultural, political, economic and environmental dimensions of sustainability are intertwined. This raises questions about how people act in relation to themselves, others and the environment. As Levinas (2005) points out, we exist in the presence of others, and when we harm others we also harm ourselves.

Stories about the natural world are one way to explore these fundamental aspects of citizenship with children in their first years of schooling. This topic is based around *The Very Hungry Caterpillar* by Eric Carle which illustrates the importance of a small insect and its life cycle. Learning about the complexity of insects' lives may foster awareness and eco-citizenship, because studying caterpillars and butterflies will raise children's understanding of how every insect is part of a wider community. This knowledge may bring about a profound understanding of eco-citizenship, namely that balance and harmony, at whatever level, is vital for social and environmental well-being.

Interesting facts

- Butterflies first evolved along with flowering plants 40–50 million years ago.
- Caterpillars can increase their body weight by 1,000 times during their life cycle.
- Monarch butterflies stand out among insects with the longest migration distance, up to 4,000 kilometres.

Misconceptions and research

Eco-citizenship is a complex idea which may seem too abstract for young children. Focusing on just one aspect, the environmental dimension, makes it more accessible. Recent research projects in Norway indicate that children respond to ideas of sustainability through observations in nature and reading literature about nature-related topics (Heggen et. al. 2019). Additionally, it appears that concrete activities and investigations may enhance eco-citizenship and a sense of empowerment.

Teaching ideas

Key vocabulary

butterfly	egg	stomach ache
caterpillar	leaf	Swiss cheese
cocoon	moon	

Getting started

Use the cover or one of the first spreads of *The Very Hungry Caterpillar* as an initial pre-reading activity. Ask the children questions such as: What do you see? What colours do you see? Where is the caterpillar going? What do you think will happen to it? A second option is to find out what the children know about caterpillars. Where do we find them? What do they look like? What are their lives like?

Readers' theatre | *key idea: community*

The Very Hungry Caterpillar is available in different sizes and formats, and there are several online versions including one read by the author Eric Carle (website 14.1). Moreover, there are many postings of school performances which use a 'readers' theatre' approach. In this, the children each read one sentence of the story which in total then becomes the complete text. In many of the recordings a small role play is included. To conduct a readers' theatre within a regular classroom setting is manageable and an excellent way of really engaging the children with the story.

Life cycle diagram | *key idea: cycles*

After reading the book, talk about the life cycle of a butterfly. An egg turns into larva which in due course creates a cocoon from which a butterfly emerges. You can represent this cycle as a diagram on a wall display (there are some excellent images of this sequence on the Internet). You might also connect the life cycle of the butterfly to the life of humans: baby – child – teenager – adult.

Caterpillar food | *key idea: interaction*

Find out about what caterpillars eat outside the fictional world (website 14.2). What does the book say caterpillars eat? Why do you think the author has included all this snack food that the caterpillar feeds on?

Butterfly paintings | *key idea: beauty, pattern*

Look at pictures of different types of butterfly and talk about their names and how these might have originated. Draw attention to the different patterns which they can see – beauty and harmony are important ideas in sustainability. Why are butterflies so colourful? What is the purpose of the patterns they display? Now invite the children to paint a butterfly of their own. Older children might write a short text to accompany their painting. This could say where the butterfly lives, what it eats, what it likes and what makes it happy.

Investigation and fieldwork | *key idea: habitat*

What can we do to help caterpillars and butterflies thrive in our communities? Plant seeds in pots or gardens in the school area that are caterpillar- and butterfly-friendly. Where might be the best place to put these? Depending on the time of year, the children can also look for caterpillars and butterflies in the school grounds and surrounding area. Leaves that are full of holes are often a sign that there are hungry caterpillars about.

Sustainability discussion

What do caterpillars and butterflies need in order to thrive?

Answers might include:

(a) healthy plants with leaves to eat;
(b) places where they can shelter and be safe; and
(c) a community so they can find a mate and lay eggs.

Make the point that all creatures, including humans, depend on each other in different ways and are interconnected in a web of life.

HEALTHY COMMUNITIES (AGE 5–11)

What is the main focus of this topic?

Developing children's understanding of healthy communities and how we can contribute to them.

Key ideas	Subject links	SDG links
Community Diversity Inclusion Well-being	English (creative writing) Religious Education (ethics) Science	SDG 11 Sustainable cities and communities SDG 16 Peace, justice and strong institutions

Background knowledge

Finding ways to live safe and healthy lives within environmental limits is the key challenge facing humanity at the current time. This means that helping children to become eco-citizens who play their part in creating healthy communities is a top priority. In healthy communities there is always a sense of safety, and diversity is not only tolerated but welcomed. Each individual is of value. Hence, without that individual, the community would look different. Supporting every child's uniqueness is fundamental to education.

This topic focuses on human relationships and builds on the earlier topic for 3- to 7-year-olds. *Cicada* by Shaun Tan is a picture book about an insect working in an office together with humans (website 14.3). He is not regarded as being as valuable as the other workers because he is an insect. Human resources do not apply to him. In the end Cicada transforms from a nymph into a flying insect and leaves the office building to return to the forest. This tale can work on many levels. First and foremost, it draws attention to the need for inclusion and diversity. Secondly, it opens up a discussion about healthy communities.

Interesting facts

- Periodical cicadas live underground for 15–17 years as nymphs – one of the longest lifespans of any insect.
- There are 3,000 species of cicada worldwide.
- Although they make a lot of noise, cicadas are not harmful and they do not sting.

Misconceptions and research

New advances in neurobiology are revealing that brain development and the learning that it enables are directly dependent on social-emotional experience (Immordino-Yang et al. 2019). This means that young children tend to flourish if they grow up in a safe and stimulating environment. Conversely, children who experience persistent adversity are more likely to be aggressive and anxious. Creating a healthy community and thinking about its qualities are thus part of the challenge of developing more sustainable ways of living for future generations.

Teaching ideas

Key vocabulary

cicada	co-worker	promotion
clerk	office	sick day

Getting started

Looking for an emotional response to the key themes in the book is a good way to get started on this topic. Talk with the children about when they feel welcome, when they feel included and how they include others. Another option is to explore the issues that arise from one of the double-page spreads – there are numerous versions of the story on the Internet which will enable you to share images (website 14.4).

Bullying | *key idea: inclusion*

In the sixth spread we see that Cicada is being bullied by his co-workers. Look carefully at this spread and let the children analyse it individually or in groups. You could use the following sequence of questions to serve as scaffolding: What do you see? What do you think? What do you notice? What do you feel? Share responses across the class. Discuss positive actions for dealing with bullies and bullying.

Is it fair? | *key idea: equality*

Have the children imagine they are one of the workers in the office. What would they say to Cicada about the way he is being treated? Ask them to write a short note to Cicada asking for forgiveness and suggesting ways in which he might join in with his fellow workers. You could develop this idea as the starting point for creating a new version of the story in which Cicada is treated as an equal.

Similarities and differences | *key idea: diversity*

This story is about Cicada, an insect. But are there instances in our societies where the problems Cicada faces are similar to that of people? Who does Cicada represent in the human world? Think of the different ways in which Cicada is similar to other workers, and the ways in which he is different. You could represent this as an overlapping Venn diagram in a wall display. Some of the issues which underpin this activity include racism, gender, class discrimination and exceptionalism (the idea that humans are different from other creatures).

Investigations and fieldwork | *key idea: well-being*

Suggest the class could create a list of key elements which contribute to creating environments where children feel happy and thrive. In groups of three or four, let children share their points and reflect over these. Share the points across the class to create an agreed list of common elements. How might these ambitions be achieved? What has to happen for them to become reality? Do they think their school could benefit from some of the elements in their list? This might lead to a dialogue with other classes and teachers in which everyone feels valued as citizens.

Sustainability discussion

Why should we care about creating healthy communities?

Answers might include:

(a) because everyone needs to feel accepted;
(b) because healthy communities are vital for a sense of belonging, identity and life skills;
(c) because they nourish creativity and new ideas; and
(d) because they are the basis for sustainable living.

DEMOCRACY (AGE 7–14)

What is the main focus of this topic?

Developing children's understanding of democracy, how it relates to sustainability and how every citizen can help to protect it.

Key ideas	Subject links	SDG links
Change	Citizenship	SDG 11 Sustainable cities and
Decision-making	Drama	communities
Identity	English (discussion)	SDG 16 Peace, justice and strong
Values	Religious Education (ethics)	institutions

Democracy is a fragile institution. History speaks of democracies that have crumbled and died. Realizing how every citizen contributes to and impacts democracy is an important part of education. Sometimes democracy requires us, for the common good, to overcome selfishness and greed. This is especially the case at times of emergency. As we head further into the environment crisis, it seems likely that social disruption and unrest will challenge democratic institutions around the world. Yet it is only by acting collectively that we can address problems that affect us all.

One picture book that addresses the complex relationship between life conditions, sustainability and economy is *The Lorax* by Dr Seuss. Connections between preserving nature, industrialism and making money are vividly woven into this tale. The story illustrates how everything collapses when the fine line between preservation and exploitation is out of order. The book indirectly teaches the complexities of sustainability in a commercial world. Working with this book in a classroom setting may lead to a profound insight into the challenges of sustainability.

Interesting facts

- Democracy dates back to Greece in the fifth century BC.
- The term 'democracy' combines two Greek words, *demos* (people) and *kratos* (power/rule).
- In most countries women only won the right to vote in the twentieth century.

Misconceptions and research

Children often tend to think of problems in very simple, black-and-white terms. *The Lorax*, and the related topics it caters for, may serve as food for thought regarding the complex relationship between people and nature as it points at undemocratic processes. If the Once-ler had understood the complexities of ecosystems and taken in the needs of its inhabitants, a more democratic approach may have saved this world.

Teaching ideas

Key vocabulary

citizenship	protect	thneed (a piece of clothing)
democracy	silk	
greed	smog	

Getting started | *key idea: identity*

Read *The Lorax* with the class or share one of the versions which are available on the Internet (website 14.5). Pay attention to the illustrations as well as the text and make a list of some of the special names and terms which are used. Now talk with the children about some of the characters and features in the story. Who do the Once-ler and the Lorax represent? Can you think of someone who is like them? Why do you think the author included plants and animals which readers will not know?

Business is business | *key idea: values*

The Once-ler is described as greedy and business-minded in the book. When the Lorax comes to speak on behalf of the trees, the bears, the birds and the fish, the Once-ler is more concerned about profit and expansion than making adjustments to protect nature. He says: 'I, the Once-ler, felt sad as I watched them all go. BUT . . . business is business! And business must grow.' The Lorax speaks on behalf of the trees because they have 'no tongues'. Why does the Once-ler not listen to the Lorax? In which ways could the Once-ler have saved the environment? How could he have created what Norwegians call a 'green shift'?

Individualism or the common good | *key idea: decision making*

To consider one of the main ideas in *The Lorax*, individualism versus the common good, an ethical dilemma may serve as a useful gateway. This involves exploring problems where students find arguments for and against different courses of action. The two dilemmas described below are possible starting points; however, they are only meant as examples. So, adaptations or different cases may be more fruitful in your setting.

The football team dilemma You are chosen to play on a new football team, but since you are the best player on your original team, you do not know what to do. (1) You know that your team will suffer, if you leave. (2) You know that if you start playing for the new team, you are one step closer to your dream. Find one argument for leaving your old team and one argument against.

The party dilemma You are invited to a friend's birthday party and would love to bring a gift. However, you do not have any money to buy one. Recently you received an expensive bottle of perfume from your grandmother which is still unopened. Should you give this to your friend? (1) Your friend knows you do not have any money. (2) This perfume means a lot to you since it is from your grandmother. (3) You will feel bad, not bringing a gift for you friend. Find one argument for giving away your perfume and one against.

A difficult choice | *key idea: decision making*

Give the pupils a sheet of A4 paper and get them to fold it so as to create eight panels of equal size. Now ask them to make up a cartoon sequence/storyboard which explores an issue where people have to make a difficult environmental choice. For example, their storyboard could focus on what happens when it is suggested a tree will have to be cut down to make room for a cycle track, or sprayed with poisonous chemicals to protect it from disease. Working in groups, the children could now decide how to act out their stories to the rest of the class. Once they have been refined, they might then be presented to the head teacher or local dignitary acting as an arbiter. Such an activity empowers children to express their views and show they have value.

Investigations and fieldwork | *key idea: change*

Whatever your school environment, there are almost bound to be local issues which people are debating and where opinions differ. Many of these concern new developments and have an environmental dimension – new roads, housing schemes and proposals for recreational facilities are common themes. Find out what is happening in your area and select an issue which interests the children. Encourage them to research the proposal and draw up a list of pros and cons. Give them the opportunity to debate the issue so that they become aware of alternative voices. Recognizing that people have different perspectives and value systems is an essential part of living in a democracy.

Sustainability discussion

Would an elected world government help to promote sustainability?

Answers might include:

(a) it would make it easier for nations to work together; and
(b) it would pass laws that all nations would have to obey.

What difficulties could you foresee in setting it up and allowing it to work?

Websites

Website 14.1 The Very Hungry Caterpillar
https://www.youtube.com/watch?v=vkYmvxP0AJI.
Website 14.2 Caterpillar diet
https://butterfly-conservation.org/news-and-blog/what-do-hungry-caterpillars-really-eat
Website 14.3 Cicada
https://www.youtube.com/watch?v=LBr550M_kpU
Website 14.4 Shuan Tan talking about Cicada
https://www.youtube.com/watch?v=gnIs_mMKfoU
Website 14.5 The Lorax
https://www.youtube.com/watch?v=FLFHdMNin0c

Children's books

Carle, E. (1969, 2002) *The Very Hungry Caterpillar*, London: Puffin.
Taun, S. (2018) *Cicada*, London: Hodder Children's Books.
Zeus, Dr (1971, 2021) *The Lorax*, London: HarperCollins.

References

Heggen, M. P., Sageidet, B. M., Goga, N., Grindheim, L. T., Bergan, V., Krempig, I. M., Utsi, T. A., and Lynngård, A. M. (2019) 'Children as eco-citizens?', *Nordina* 15:4, 387–402.

Immordino-Yang, M., Darling-Hammond, L., and Krone, C. R. (2019) 'Nurturing Nature: How Brain Development is Inherently Social and Emotional, and What This Means For Education', *Educational Psychologist* 54:3, 185–204.

Levinas, E. (2005) *Humanism of the Other.* Urbana and Chicago: University of Illinois Press.

15

Pollution and Resources

Yocheved Yorkovsky and Stephen Scoffham

People, animals and plants all need clean air, water and food coming from the soil and sea for their survival. Human activity since the discovery of fire in the Stone Age, through the Agricultural and Industrial Revolutions, to the development of modern technology has increasingly impacted the environment. However, since the 1950s, the pace of change has increased dramatically. Just about every socio-economic indicator has shown a dramatic surge, as the growth of human numbers, industry, trade and consumption has transformed the world (Figure 15.1). This period, known as the Great Acceleration, is unique in human history. And it has made great demands on the natural environment that can no longer be sustained.

Pollution takes many different forms. Air pollution coming mainly from industry, power plants, transportation and agriculture is creating acid rain and resulting in poor air quality at a regional scale. This is responsible for respiratory diseases and triggers thousands of premature deaths each year, especially in urban areas. Meanwhile, at a global scale, human activity is leading to ever increasing levels of carbon dioxide and potentially irreversible climate change. The introduction of a variety of harmful substances into the natural environment is also damaging the soil and contaminating rivers and seas, and making the oceans more acidic. In summary, pollution is damaging ecological systems and causing biodiversity depletion, climate change and worsening human health and living conditions.

At the moment, the global economic system and international power relations compound these problems. The modern lifestyle in developed countries and in the big cities of less developed countries encourages a culture of overconsumption, while in other parts of the world many people struggle to meet their basic needs. A more just and equitable society is one of the targets adopted by the UN Sustainable Development Goals. At the same time, a shift towards eco-friendly production to ensure good use of natural resources, improved energy efficiency, sustainable infrastructure and better food management is long overdue. Reducing consumption and encouraging recycling and reuse would also help to cut out waste and pollution, as many economists and environmentalists have argued.

This chapter focuses on these complex, interrelated issues. It highlights a few popular school topics which have scope to be extended and developed. One key idea which lies behind all the activities

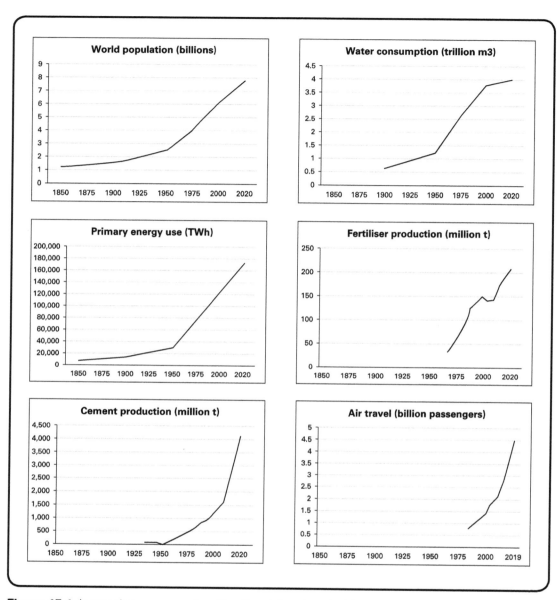

Figure 15.1 Increasing consumption (the Great Acceleration) has endangered the planet within a human lifetime. *Source: World in Data and other sources.*

is the notion of the ecological or environmental footprint. This is a measure of the impact that a person, company or activity has on the environment. Collectively, some nations tread much more heavily on the environment than others. The United States, for example, has a footprint which is around ten times more than many African countries. This means that the average American child consumes ten times more than the average African. Finding ways to communicate this without causing anxiety and guilt is a challenge which was considered earlier in this book (see Chapter 4). As so often with sustainability education, practical activities and action offer a hopeful way forward.

Reflection and discussion

- What lifestyle changes could you make to reduce your impact on the environment?
- What role does technology play in reducing ecological footprints – what are the positive and negative aspects?
- Do countries with large ecological footprints have a moral duty to reduce their footprints? If so, what action could they take?

WASTE AND LITTER (AGE 3–7)

What is the main focus of this topic?

Rubbish, especially plastic waste, needs to be disposed of carefully.

Key ideas	Subject links	SDG links
Care	Art	SDG12 Responsible consumption
Pollution	Geography	
Recycling	Science	

Background knowledge

Waste can be divided into two main categories. Biodegradable waste breaks down over time and provides nutrients for other forms of life. Vegetables, for example, take around a month to decay, wood takes years and metal may take decades, but they all eventually get reused by different forms of life as a part of a cyclical process. Non-biodegradable waste forms a second category of waste which is difficult to dispose of, is virtually indestructible and is sometimes toxic. Sadly, there have been many instances in recent years when toxic waste has been shipped from rich to poor countries where it has poisoned the land and led to outbreaks of diseases such as cancer.

Nowadays, one of the most common forms of waste is plastic. Plastic is the name of a range of synthetic materials which are derived from oil and made into other materials, many of which are only used once before they are thrown away. Plastic debris can come in all shapes, forms (hard or soft) and sizes (microplastics are less than 5mm) and are non-biodegradable. They reach everywhere and may accumulate on land where they contaminate the soil or end up in the sea where they poison fish and birds. Microplastics have been shown to enter the food chain. Over a period of time, ocean currents have carried plastic waste to every part of the Earth. In some places, far from land, the plastic has become caught up in a vortex known as a gyre to create huge areas of waste. These great garbage patches are easy to ignore because they are so remote but they are a reminder that plastic needs to be disposed of carefully, especially the microplastics which are virtually invisible to the naked eye.

Interesting facts

- Microplastics are probably in everything we eat and drink as well as in the air we breathe.
- By 2050 there could be more plastic by weight in the ocean than fish.
- The amount of waste dumped every year would fill a line of lorries round the Earth twenty-four times.

Misconceptions and research

There are good reasons to present this topic in a positive way so children do not become too concerned about the problems caused by waste. Helping children to see that their behaviour makes a difference is a good strategy as it leads to a sense of personal responsibility and agency.

Teaching ideas

Key vocabulary

litter	plastic	rot
ocean	recycle	waste

Getting started

Talk with pupils about the different things they throw away. You could begin by looking in the class litter bin. What things do pupils throw away at home? Do they recycle anything? If so, what?

Explore their ideas about what happens to waste when it is recycled. See if your local council has any information on how waste is recycled and what happens to it after the process.

Does it rot? | *key idea: cycles*

Explain to pupils that there are different types of waste – some things rot, other things do not. You can demonstrate this by watching what happens to a slice of apple over just a few days. Now give the children a list of materials and ask them to identify the things that will rot. If there is a school garden, visit the compost heap to see how it is being used. You might develop this activity by setting up a class wormery (website 15.1).

Waste collage | *key idea: recycling*

Tell the children they are going to create a model or collage from rubbish. Ask them to bring to school small waste items such as sweet wrappers, metal foil, old buttons, food packaging and so on (stress that only clean items are needed and that they must avoid anything sharp or precious). Using these waste materials helps the children to create a collage picture by glueing their rubbish to a cardboard base. Let them choose their own theme – animals are often a popular choice. Think carefully about the textures and colours. Discuss how they have found a way of reusing waste materials.

Ocean garbage | *key idea: pollution*

Enact the way that plastic waste is arriving, collecting and becoming concentrated in ocean gyres. Using the hall or an open outdoor space ask about fifteen pupils (half the class) to spread out and scatter around. Explain that each child represents a piece of plastic waste that has found its way into the ocean. At a given moment the children should start moving slowly in clockwise circles and crowd together to create a gyre. Repeat this activity with the other half of the class. What do they notice about the way they congregate together? Depending on the age range, show the children some photographs of ocean garbage (website 15.2). How does this make them feel? Can they think of ways that this waste might be removed?

Investigations and fieldwork | *key idea: care*

Go for a walk in and around your school to look for waste and litter. If you have tongs and a bag, children can collect what they find. They might also take photographs, and the older children might mark on a map where they find different items. What do they discover about where the litter is found? How did it get there? What might be done to stop people dropping litter?

Sustainability discussion

What could we do to reduce waste and litter pollution?

Answers might include:

    (a) we could reduce consumption and refuse to buy things that are wrapped in plastic;
    (b) we could reuse the rubbish that we throw away;
    (c) we could recycle waste that is biodegradable.

POLLUTION (AGE 5–11)

What is the main focus of this topic?

Pollution can affect air, land or water and is harmful to life.

Key ideas	Subject links	SDG links
Connections	Drama	SDG12 Responsible consumption
Interaction	Geography	
Pollution	History	
	Science	

Background knowledge

When something that is harmful or poisonous is added to the environment, it causes pollution. Smoke or dust in the air is a type of pollution as it is bad for the lungs when we breath it in. Contaminated drinking water is another type of pollution, as the germs and viruses it contains can make people ill. Sometimes chemical spills and effluent poison the land and seep into rivers. Pollution can also be the result of natural events such as volcanic activity. The eruption of Krakatoa in 1883, for example, put so much dust and ash into the atmosphere that it lingered for years, cutting out sunlight, reducing temperatures and causing crops to fail across the northern hemisphere.

Human activity is making pollution problems worse, especially in recent years. Industry, transport, agriculture and urbanization are all contributing to the problem. In cities, poor air quality is a particular issue as it triggers an estimated 7 million premature deaths annually (Greenpeace 2020). Meanwhile, around the world, the gases released from burning fossil fuels are one of the main causes of global warming (Helm 2020). Part of the problem is that often the consequences of pollution only become apparent many years after the event. At the same time, the costs of dealing with pollution problems are very often borne by those who suffer from it rather than those who created it.

> ## Interesting facts
>
> - Over a million seabirds are killed by pollution every year.
> - Electronic waste contains valuable minerals but is very hard to recycle.
> - The rocks and sediments which are being laid down today will contain traces of plastic and other pollutants.

Misconceptions and research

It is easy to confuse global warming and the ozone hole as they are both global-scale air pollution problems. Global warming is caused by a layer of 'greenhouse gases' which are building up around the Earth causing temperatures to rise. The ozone hole describes the loss of ozone which occurs in polar regions in the spring as pollutants that have accumulated in the winter are activated by sunlight, allowing harmful ultraviolet rays to pass through the atmosphere.

Teaching ideas

> ## Key vocabulary
>
> | | | |
> |---|---|---|
> | disaster | pollution | survey |
> | fumes | smog | vandalism |

Getting started

You might begin by reading the children a classic story, such as *Dinosaurs and All That Rubbish* by Michael Foreman. Now see what the children already know about pollution. They may be aware of local examples or have heard about major incidents. Explain that pollution effects all forms of life, not just people. It can also have indirect consequences. Polluted water, for example, may start by killing fish but then poison the birds that feed on them, thereby spreading through the food chain.

The Great Smog | *key ideas: pollution, interaction*

Find out about the Great Smog that hit London in 1952. What caused it? How did the weather make it worse? How did it effect Londoners? How many people died from it? What did people decide to do? Did it ever happen again? As well as photographs of the smog itself, there are videos describing the events which will help pupils understand the impact of the smog and its historical significance (website 15.3).

The plastic ducks | *key idea: connections*

Show the children the video about the plastic ducks which washed off a container ship in 1992 and have now been found in many parts of the world (website 15.4). Now ask them to fold a sheet of paper into six boxes so they can create a storyboard recording the sequence of events. You may want to look at an atlas to find out more about the ducks' journey. Talk with the children about how this relates to sustainability – the bright yellow ducks are more or less indestructible. Extend the activity by helping pupils to find out what they can do to prevent plastic pollution. Kids Against Plastic offers some practical approaches for them to consider (Meek and Meek (2021) and website 15.5).

Pollution mobile | *key idea: pollution*

Make a pollution mobile as part of a class pollution display. Begin by dividing the children into groups and ask them to make a list of different examples of air, water and land pollution. They can sort their lists into categories – air, land or water. The children should now write their words on rectangular pieces of card, selecting just four or five words in each category. Join the words together in a column using string or thread and suspend them from a frame to create a mobile. You can use a coat hanger or garden sticks for the frame. Each of the three columns will need a heading and the words will need to be written on both sides of the card.

Pollution disasters | *key idea: interaction*

Encourage the children to research some major pollution accidents around the world. These could include the gas leak at Bhopal in 1984, the nuclear explosion at Chernobyl in 1986 and the Deepwater Horizon oil spill in 2010. Put the children into groups to discover what happened and the effect it had on people and the environment. Each group can present their findings as a mock news report to the rest of the class. Children could enact different roles: news presenter, local resident, reporter, doctor, politician and so forth.

Investigation and fieldwork | *key idea: pollution*

Working with the children, compile a list of local pollution problems. Examples might include car fumes, traffic noise, litter, dog poo/bags, unpleasant smells, overhead wires, vandalism, aircraft noise, graffiti, polluted water and building waste. Devise a survey sheet using these headings and take the children on a walk in the local area to see what they discover. Use a scoring system such as 0 = No problem at all, 5 = Minor problem, 10 = Major problem. The children can take photographs as they do their survey. You might also devise a second walk to see how it compares. Discuss what might be done to reduce pollution in your area.

Sustainability discussion

What can be done to reduce pollution?

Answers might include:

(a) passing new laws to prevent it happening;
(b) taking better care to stop pollution accidents;
(c) thinking about the consequences of our own behaviour.

NATURAL RESOURCES (AGE 7–14)

What is the main focus of this topic?

People need to use natural resources wisely so they do not become polluted or depleted.

Key ideas	Subject links	SDG links
Conservation	Citizenship	SDG12 Responsible consumption
Resources	English (descriptive writing)	
Sustainable living	Geography	
	History	
	Mathematics	

Background knowledge

Natural resources are defined as those things that people use which come from nature. Some natural resources such as oil, gas and metal ores are non-renewable (finite), which means they will eventually run out. Others such as fish, food crops and wood are renewable, which means they regenerate and can be replaced. Wheat, for example, is resown in the spring after it has been harvested and trees are replanted after they have been felled. Soil, too, is regarded as a renewable resource. However, if soil is overused or polluted, it becomes degraded and may be unable to support plant life or simply blow away.

People depend on Earth's resources in order to survive, and managing them carefully is going to be crucial in the years ahead. Although new sources of minerals are always being discovered, reserves of copper, lead, zinc and phosphorous are becoming increasingly depleted. There are also concerns over the rare earth metals, such as lithium, used in electronic equipment, many of which come from China. A key concept is that of peak production – the point at which production reaches a maximum and after which supplies become increasingly difficult to access. The overconsumption of some renewable resources, such as fish, is also a major problem. This raises questions not only about resource management but also about international co-operation. As so often, sustainability issues are interconnected on multiple levels and not easily resolved.

Misconceptions and research

We use natural resources all the time, so we often take them for granted. However, current levels of consumption and the pollution that it creates cannot be sustained. Global natural systems – especially air, water and land – are losing their resilience and could become unstable with disastrous consequences. Finding practical ways to help children understand these abstract notions is a key challenge in sustainability education.

Interesting facts

- A total of sixty-two different types of metal goes into the average mobile handset.
- The average US citizen uses more than ten times as much water in a day than many Africans.
- Russia and China are especially rich in natural resources.

Teaching ideas

Key vocabulary

conservation	materials	renewable
ecological footprint	non-renewable	resources

Getting started

Talk with the children about how everything around us is made from different resources. Trees are turned into pulp which is made into paper. Iron ore is made into metal which is used in buildings. Wheat is made into flour which is then baked to create bread. Make a list of all the different resources they can think of. Think also about resources like air and sunlight, which don't need to be processed but are freely available. How can we give them value if we don't have to buy them?

Zigzag book | *key idea: resources*

Give the children a long strip of card which they can fold into eight or more panels. Now ask them to select a resource – wood, metal or oil. Using the panels, they should make a drawing or write notes about different things that are made from this resource. Use the first panel for the title and the last one for notes about sustainability.

Whales | *key idea: conservation*

Investigate what is being done to save whales from extinction. Whale hunting started in earnest in the seventeenth century and reached a peak in the 1960s, since when hunting has been reduced and sanctuaries established. You could start with Herman Melville's story, *Moby Dick, or the White Whale*, that was hunted by Captain Ahab (website 15.6). Why did people hunt whales and what were the dangers? Now find out some of the international agreements to protect them. The blue whale displayed at London's Natural History Museum adds another dimension to this story (website 15.7). It has been conserved and renamed Hope to symbolize humanity's ability to shape a sustainable future (website 15.5). The children can be encouraged to write an illustrated account of how whales were once ruthlessly hunted but are now being saved for the future. You might also look at Simon James's charming book *Dear Greenpeace* (2016) about a whale that lives in a pond.

Ecological footprints | *key idea: sustainable living*

The sum total of the resources that we use is known as our ecological footprint. You might like to look at one of the footprint calculators available on the Internet and discuss the questions – these tend to be loaded and are not always easy for children to answer. Now give the children figures for average footprints for ten selected countries (website 15.8) which they can use to create graphs to visually represent the data. What implications can they draw from the figures? Get them to find out about Earth Overshoot Day – the day each year when collectively humanity has consumed its resource allowance.

Investigation and fieldwork | *key idea: resources*

Organize a short walk in your neighbourhood. Encourage the children to note down different examples of the way that resources have been used. Can they find six things that are made of wood, six things that are made of clay (brick and tiles) and six different things made of metal? What other resources, such as stone and plastic, can they find on their walk? Where do they think these different resources might have come from and how long will they last?

Sustainability discussion

Which natural resources do you think are most valuable?

Answers might include:

(a) rare minerals like gold and diamond because they cost the most;
(b) food and water because we need them to survive;
(c) sunlight because all life depends on it; and
(d) all resources are important in different ways.

Websites

Website 15.1 Making a wormery
https://www.youtube.com/watch?v=ordM5TWyFLw
Website 15.2 Ocean garbage
https://www.google.com/search?q=plastic+in+the+ocean+images#x0026;rlz=1C1GCEU_en-GBIL915
IL915#x0026;source=lnms#x0026;tbm=isch#x0026;sa=X#x0026;ved=2ahUKEwjupo_
e6J3wAhVygf0HHd1OBGsQ_AUoAXoECAEQAw#x0026;biw=1097#x0026;bih=535#x0026;d
pr=1.75
Website 15.3 Plastic ducks
https://www.youtube.com/watch?v=-RPUmRmdcjw
Website 15.4 Great Smog
https://www.youtube.com/watch?v=xajjmbJrfEM
Website 15.5 Kids Against Plastic
https://www.kidsagainstplastic.co.uk
Website 15.6 Moby Dick
https://www.youtube.com/watch?v=uVd_LzWJIC8
Website 15.7 The Natural History Museum whale
https://www.nhm.ac.uk/discover/whale-move-conservation-commences.html
Website 15.8 Ecological footprints
https://en.wikipedia.org/wiki/List_of_countries_by_ecological_footprint

Children's books

Foreman, M. (1993) *Dinosaurs and All That Rubbish*, London: Puffin.
James, S. (2016) *Dear Greenpeace*, London: Walker Books.

References

Greenpeace (2020) *2020 Air Quality Report*, available at https://www.greenpeace.org/static/planet4-romania-stateless/2021/03/d8050eab-2020-world_air_quality_report.pdf.

Helm, D. (2020) *Net Zero: How We Can Stop Climate Change*, London: Collins.

Meek, A. and Meek E. (2021) 'The Primary Geography Interview: Kids against plastic', *Primary Geography* 104: 22–23.

16

Unequal World

Ben Ballin

Sustainability can be likened to a 'three-legged stool', supported by environmental, social and economic legs. If one leg is weak, the stool topples over. This chapter particularly considers the social and economic legs, although all three depend on each other. It involves some complicated concepts, which some pupils may find challenging unless they are carefully prepared.

Inequality of all kinds remains widespread and persistent in many parts of the world. It relates not only to disparity of income but also to gender, race and opportunity. Marginalized communities, in particular, often find their entry point to environmental concerns is framed by inequality (Pullido 1996). Inequality is thus the lens through which many people – including children – experience sustainability.

One of the Sustainable Development Goals (SDG 10) focuses on reduced inequality and specifically aims to 'reduce inequality within and between countries'. This includes both economic and social inequalities. In recent years, economic equality within some countries has made 'modest gains' (UN 2021). South Africa and the Comoros archipelago are among the most unequal countries, while Norway and Ukraine are among the most equal.

With respect to social inequality, UN figures from 2014 to 2020 show that almost one in five people report having experienced personal discrimination. This often combines with economic factors in a phenomenon known as 'intersectionality'. For example, Roma children are up to nine times more likely to be excluded from schools in parts of England than their white peers (McIntyre et al. 2021), while their families are much more likely to be out of work and in poor health. Furthermore, gender equality is generally considered to be such a significant intersectional factor that it has a Sustainable Development Goal in its own right (SDG 5). Refugees are at the extreme of exclusion. Worldwide numbers had grown to 24 million by mid-2020, the highest number on record. The climate crisis is expected to displace many millions more as floods, storms, droughts and forest fires become more frequent.

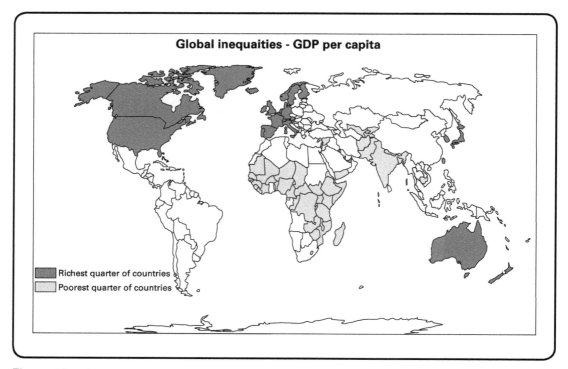

Figure 16.1 Average income in the USA and western Europe is around fifty times greater than in many countries in Africa. *Source: World Bank.*

Acute inequality is intrinsically unsustainable (Figure 16.1). As Haugton (1999) puts it,

> the unjust society is unlikely to be sustainable in environmental or economic terms in the long-run, since the social tensions which are created undermine the need for recognising reciprocal rights and obligations, leading in all manner of ways to environmental degradation and ultimately to political breakdown.

We may already be seeing the early signs of this breakdown in some parts of the world.

Reflection and discussion

- Children have strong feelings about injustice. What issues which relate to this have you found are important to them?
- In the face of entrenched inequality and injustice, how can people be inspired to work against entrenched inequality and injustice for a positive outcome?
- Many children will be directly affected by social and economic inequalities. How can these issues be addressed with due sensitivity?

HOW DARE YOU! (AGE 3–7)

What is the main focus of this topic?

Treating people fairly doesn't always mean they should be treated the same.

Key ideas	Subject links	SDG links
Equality	English (creative writing)	SDG1 No poverty
Diversity	Geography	SDG2 Zero hunger
Inclusion	Mathematics	SDG5 Gender equality
Social justice	Religious Education	SDG10 Reduced Inequality

Background knowledge

Childhood itself often combines with other elements to reinforce inequality. Children are relatively powerless players in the face of the forces that impact their lives. As a result, the worldwide climate and environment crisis is increasingly being framed as a question of justice between the generations. As the student environmental campaigner Greta Thunberg forcefully argues, 'We probably don't even have a future any more. Because that future was sold so that a small amount of people could make unimaginable amounts of money' (Thunberg 2019). Henrietta Fore, executive director of UNICEF, also makes this same point very clearly: 'No-one suffers more from a change in climate than a child' (Fore 2021).

Intergenerational inequality can have an economic dimension. According to the UN (2021), younger people are twice as likely as adults to be working poor. Inequality also impacts diet and health. Henrietta Fore asks,

> How is it in the 21st century that we still have 149 million children under 5 with stunting and almost 50 million with wasting? How is it possible that overweight and obesity in children and young people are continuing to rise, and increasingly among the poor? And why are healthy diets becoming more expensive while unhealthy, non-nutritious diets are becoming cheaper?
>
> Fore 2019:6

Interesting facts

- Niger has the world's youngest average population, with almost half the population aged under 15.
- At the other end of the spectrum, over a quarter of the Japanese population is over 65.
- In the 1950s, three countries had kings who had come to the throne when they were under 4 years old: Egypt, Iraq and Nepal.

Misconceptions and research

It is a commonplace that, from a very young age, children have a strong sense of justice. As Charles Dickens wrote in *Great Expectations*, 'In the little world in which children have their existence, whosoever brings them up, there is nothing so finely perceived and so finely felt as injustice.' This perception is backed up by experiments which show infants aged 19 months have a context-specific sense of fairness (Sloane et al. 2012). One of the implications is that self-reflection is a key element in children's growing understanding of morality and justice. This includes explicit reflection on the intersectional power relations involved: age, gender, race, social class and related factors.

Teaching ideas

Key vocabulary

basic needs	justice	survey
emotion	solution	wants
fairness		

Getting started

Share a few examples of situations with children which raise questions about equity. For instance, is it fair or unfair that an elephant gets more food than a mouse, or that a blind person can bring their guide dog into a building with a 'no dogs' sign on the door? What if it was the other way around (e.g. the mouse got more food and the guide dog not allowed in)? Is being fair always the same as being treated the same? In talk pairs, ask children to think of similar examples from their own experience (e.g. being allowed sweets or taken to the park).

Flipped fairy stories | *key ideas: inclusion, social justice*

Take a familiar fairy story and explore it from the point of view of the villain. How does the 'wicked fairy' feel when she is not allowed to attend the Sleeping Beauty's christening? Has the 'Big Bad Wolf' been misunderstood? Photocopy pictures from these books and ask the children to write (or say) speech and thought bubbles for the characters. Films like the 2019 *Maleficent: Mistress of Evil* and books like *The True Story of the Three Little Pigs* (Jon Scieszka 1991) can be really useful, while *Voices in the Park* (Anthony Browne 1998) allows children to see a simple story from four different perspectives.

Rules of Summer | *key idea: inclusion*

Rules of Summer by Shaun Tan (2013) tells the story of an older/bigger and younger/smaller child. Over most of a surreal summer holiday, the former sets the rules for the latter, but by the last day of the summer they have found a way to do things more equitably. Taking one image from the first part of the book, hot seat a character and invite children to suggest how they might do things differently (model this first, with yourself in role, then invite children to take your place). Moving to an image from the last few pages, ask children to draw themselves on a Post-it note and 'put themselves in the picture'. How does it feel to be there (with all your senses as well as emotionally)?

Wants and needs | *key idea: diversity*

Cut out a selection of advertisements from junk mail or lifestyle magazines. Ask children to group these into things that people want and things that they need (some items might be both: you could use overlapping hoops to show this, forming a Venn diagram). Organize a class discussion. What are people's physical needs (shelter, food, water, etc.)? What about emotional needs? Does everybody need the same things?

Investigation and fieldwork | *key ideas: inclusion, social justice*

Children carry out a playground survey during break- and lunchtimes, using tally charts and simple plan views. Who uses which areas most? Is the space used fairly? What do the school rules say about it? Should anything be changed, and if so, how? To help manage potentially strong feelings, it may be useful for children to be asked to present findings and ideas from perspectives other than their own.

Sustainability discussion

Why does fairness matter?
Answers might include:

(a) because everybody deserves respect;
(b) it helps avoid fights and arguments; and
(c) because we all share the same world.

CHILDREN'S RIGHTS (AGE 5–11)

What is the main focus of this topic?

Everybody in the world, including children, has equal human rights.

Key ideas	Subject links	SDG links
Equality	Art	SDG1 No poverty
Diversity	Citizenship	SDG2 Zero hunger
Inclusion	Design	SDG5 Gender equality
Human rights	Drama	SDG10 Reduced Inequality
Social justice	English	
	Geography	
	Mathematics	

Background knowledge

It is important for children to realize that, like all other people, they have basic human rights and that these are protected in law. The main international framework supporting children's rights is the UN Convention on the Rights of the Child, agreed by all but one of the member states, namely the USA. No one right is more important than any other and they are all important in different ways. The key point is that, whatever their ethnicity, gender, religion, language, abilities or any other status, every child is afforded the same level of protection.

The Convention contains fifty-four articles. Four 'general principles' help explain the others:

- Non-discrimination (article 2);
- Best interest of the child (article 3);
- Right to life, survival and development (article 6);
- Right to be heard (article 12).

Rights are also protected under other agreements, especially the Universal Declaration of Human Rights (UN 1948), as well as national laws. National and international courts help to enforce these rights. However, asserting their rights is not always easy for children or marginalized groups.

Interesting facts

- Article 31 of the UN Convention includes children's right to play.
- We have all heard about climate strikes, but children striking is not new. There were several children's strikes for better education and against strict punishments in England between 1889 and the 1920s.
- In eighteenth-century England, children were seen as their parents' property. If a child was abducted, the crime was considered as theft of the child's clothes!

Misconceptions and research

While the legal issues involved in human rights can be complex, children can start understanding their basic rights from an early age. Research by Davies et al. (2005) found that, while pupils recognized that teachers were wary of engaging with potentially contentious ethical or political questions, they nonetheless 'wanted uncomfortable information, and wanted to know what teachers thought'. Research also suggests that the practice of human rights from an early age matters more than simply learning *about* human rights. This includes but goes beyond the idea of 'pupil voice'. A key recommendation of the Cambridge Primary Review (Alexander 2010) links explicitly to the UN Convention and states that 'children should be actively engaged in decisions which affect their education'.

Teaching ideas

Key vocabulary

article	human rights	responsibilities
citizenship	law	rights
convention	protection	

Getting started

Copy some of the UN Convention articles and share them out among table groups. What do children think they mean (are there any unfamiliar words?). Can they think of examples of when a different article would matter (e.g. from stories, news or personal experience)? Children silently review each other's work, adding comments or questions as appropriate, then discuss ideas as a class. Unicef-UK offers a child-friendly *Pocket Book of Children's Rights*, while illustrator Chris Riddell (2015) has produced a beautiful version of the Human Rights Act, written in simple language. UNICEF's Rights Respecting Schools is another key source (website 16.1).

Dispossession and survival | *key ideas: social justice, inclusion*

Varmints by Helen Ward (2007) is a fictional children's story that explores experiences of dispossession. Show children the YouTube film (website 16.2) and stop it at 8 and then 11 minutes. What is the character writing? Who is it for? What are they thinking and feeling at 16 and then 19 minutes (when they wake up)? What words might they add to the last page of their book? When in this story are the characters really living? Just surviving? Children share ideas and consider historical or present-day examples where people might have felt or written similar things (e.g. during colonization, military occupation or as a result of environmental destruction).

The rights to health and life | *key ideas: equality, human rights*

Some human rights are about our basic needs (e.g. Article 5 of the Universal Declaration). and there is data that indicates how well these rights are being met. Using Worldometers (website 16.3), show the children figures for people with no access to a safe drinking water source. What do they see? What is this number called? What does it tell us? (The figure, in the hundreds of millions, is gradually going down, meaning there is an improvement in absolute terms). Now ask them to look at the figure for world population and ask the same questions. What does it show us when we compare the two figures (i.e. in relative terms)?

Going hungry | *key ideas: social justice, equality*

Why do some children go hungry? Put the children in small groups and get them to write down the following reasons on separate pieces of card.

There are too many people. There is not enough food to go round. Wars stop farmers growing food. Food is not shared out fairly. Farmers do not use new ways to grow crops. People waste food. Farm animals eat food which could feed people. Food costs too much.

Now ask the children to arrange their cards with the most important at the top and the least important at the bottom and discuss the responses around the class. Extend the activity by asking each group to consider how and where they could find out whether the causes they think are most important are actually so.

Investigation and fieldwork | *key idea: inclusion*

Select an environment, such as a local park, and ask the children, in different groups, to investigate how it meets the needs of different social groups, e.g. older people, parents with young babies, young children, teenagers, people with disabilities, religious minorities, different genders. What suggestions for improvement can they make? The children could apply this same activity to their schools and present their findings to the leadership team or school council.

Sustainability discussion

Do responsibilities always come with rights?
Answers might include:

(a) yes, if we want people to respect our rights, then we must respect theirs;
(b) yes, but parents, schools and governments have more responsibility than children; and
(c) not always – you have rights, no matter what you have done or are able to do.

RICH WORLD, POOR WORLD (AGE 7–14)

What is the main focus of this topic?

This section looks at global poverty and global wealth.

Key ideas	Subject links	SDG links
Equality	Citizenship	SDG1 No poverty
Diversity	English	SDG2 Zero hunger
Inclusion	Geography	SDG5 Gender equality
Social justice	History	SDG10 Reduced Inequality

Background knowledge

Sustainable Development Goal 1 aims to 'end poverty in all its forms everywhere'. There is some good news here. The share of the world's workers living in extreme poverty fell from 14 per cent in 2010 to 6.6 per cent in 2019 (UN 2021). However, if we take China out of the extreme poverty equation, the figures look less good as it was responsible for just over 60 per cent of this decrease. Moreover, SDG 1 sets the level of 'absolute poverty' at US $1.25 per day, well below what many people need simply to survive. Even a slightly higher level would make visible the very real poverty of millions more people. All this potentially overlooks the question of overconsumption by the rich, which is fuelling environmental degradation and increasing pollution without bringing tangible benefits. Meanwhile, the global headlines also fail to take account of inequalities within and between countries and disparities within and between communities.

Interesting facts

- Since 2008, the Kingdom of Bhutan has used Gross National Happiness rather than money as its main measure of success.
- Just sixty-two people own as much wealth as half of the world's population.
- A 2010 Princeton University study found that once US citizens earned over US $75,000 a year, having extra money didn't make them any happier.

Misconceptions and research

Be careful about how you frame questions to do with wealth and poverty. Writers such as Adichie (2009) and Wainaina (2005) remind us of the importance of avoiding a single, stereotypical story of the 'Third World'; Andreotti (2013) explores how personal and cultural 'baggage' can distort our perspective; and Ballin (2016) notes that marginalized places and communities are often underrepresented in official data and news reporting. All four writers, however, agree that being aware of these factors (which could be seen as a form of 'unconscious bias') is itself a step towards overcoming them.

Teaching ideas

Key vocabulary

consumerism	migration	relative poverty
distribution	poverty	wealth
inequality	refugee	

Getting started

The Nigerian writer Ben Okri talks about 'different kinds of riches'. Discuss what he might mean by that (e.g. can you be money-poor but rich in other things? Or vice versa?). What does it mean to have 'enough'? Can we put a figure on it? Invite children to draft some 'paradox' statements, such as 'We are rich in goods but poor in the time to enjoy them.'

Travelling on | *key idea: diversity*

People (and other living things) have always migrated between places, in the search for safety, resources and a suitable home. This makes migration an excellent focus for a thematic study in History. Thinking about the UK, for example, why did successive waves of migrants come to the UK from pre-Roman times to the present day? What was the experience of these migrants, and what was their impact and legacy?

The poverty tree | *key ideas: equality, social justice*

Children work in groups to draw a tree shape on a large sheet of paper. Thinking about the local area, they note some of the signs of poverty on its leaves (e.g. food banks). On the branches, they note some of the direct causes of these things (e.g. low pay). Next, they note some of the deeper or indirect causes as roots (e.g. companies using zero hours contracts). As a class, they could then explore what a 'world poverty tree' would look like. What about a 'wealth tree'?

How do we measure poverty and wealth? | *key idea: equality and social justice*

Children research different ways of measuring human development, including poverty and wealth. For example, GDP per capita, the Gini Index, the Human Development Index, the Happy Planet Index. What do they include and what do they leave out? Children compare how their own country is ranked on the different measures. Which measures do they think are most useful and why? Could measuring wealth differently (i.e. in terms of happiness) enable us to understand how to make the world more just and sustainable?

Investigation and fieldwork | *key idea: sustainable living*

Buy Nothing Day usually comes on 27 November, just after the peak shopping day in the United States. It aims to promote environmental awareness and reduce consumerism. As a whole class, children do a feasibility study for a Buy Nothing Day, involving the whole school community. Is this a good idea? How will they get others involved? What do others say about it? Are there any objections? What free activities would be organized? What would success look like? At the end of the study, children either plan a day based on the study or propose an alternative.

Sustainability discussion

Is it a good idea for people everywhere to be provided with enough money to live on (a universal basic income)?
Answers might include:

(a) it is a nice idea, but how would it be paid for?;
(b) it might discourage some people from working;
(c) will this add to the worldwide problem of overconsumption?; and
(d) it would free many people from financial worries and let them focus on other things.

Websites

Website 16.1 Rights Respecting Schools
https://www.unicef.org.uk/rights-respecting-schools/
Website 16.2 Varmints
https://youtu.be/YxD02c2pIsI
Website 16.3 Worldometers
https://www.worldometers.info

Children's books

Browne, A. (1998) *Voices in the Park*, London: Walker Books.

Riddell, C. (illustrator) (2015) *My Little Book of Big Freedoms*, London: Amnesty International UK.

Scieszka, J. (1991) *The True Story of the Three Little Pigs*, London: Puffin.

Tan, S. (2013) *Rules of Summer*, London: Hodder.

Unicef-UK (n.d.) *Pocket Book of Children's Rights*, London: Unicef-UK.

Ward, H. (2007) *Varmints*, London: Templar Publishing.

References

Adichie, C. N. (2009) 'The danger of a single story', *TED Talk*, July 2009, available at https://www.ted.com/talks/chimamanda_ngozi_adichie_the_danger_of_a_single_story.

Alexander, R. (2010) *Children, Their World, Their Education* (Cambridge Primary Review), London: Routledge.

Ballin, B. (2016) *Getting to Know the World*, Cambridge: Cambridge Primary Review Trust, available at https://cprtrust.org.uk/cprt-blog/getting-to-know-the-world/.

Davies, L., Harber, C., and Yamashita, H. (2005) *Key findings from the DFID project, Global Citizenship: The Needs of Teachers and Learners*, Birmingham: Centre for International Education and Research, University of Birmingham.

Fore, H. (2021) 'Climate change is the other planetary crisis that won't wait', available at https://www.unicef.org/reimagine/five-opportunities-children-open-letter Accessed 22.02.2021.

Fore, H. (2019) 'Foreword' in *The State of the World's Children 2019*, New York: UNICEF.

McIntyre, N., Parveen, N., and Thomas, T. (2021) 'Exclusion rates five times higher for black Caribbean pupils in parts of England', in *The Guardian*, 24 March 2021, available at https://www.theguardian.com/education/2021/mar/24/exclusion-rates-black-caribbean-pupils-england.

Pulido, L. (1996) *Environmentalism and Economic Justice*. Tucson: University of Arizona Press.

Sloane, S., Baillargeon, R., and Premack, D. (2019) 'Do Infants Have a Sense of Fairness?', *Psychological Science*, available at https://journals.sagepub.com/doi/full/10.1177/0956797611422072.

Thunberg, G. (2019) *No One Is Too Small to Make a Difference*, London: Penguin.

UN (1948) *Universal Declaration of Human Rights*, available at https://www.un.org/en/about-us/universal-declaration-of-human-rights.

UN (2021) 'Sustainable Development Goals', available at https://sdgs.un.org/goals.

Unicef-UK (1992) 'How we protect children's rights', available at https://www.unicef.org.uk/what-we-do/un-convention-child-rights/.

Wainaina, B. (2005) 'How to write about Africa', *Granta* 92.

17

Sustainable Living

Stephen Scoffham

Forecasting the future is an imperfect process. Looking back to predictions that were made in the past shows how wrong they can be. Some predictions were unnecessarily gloomy and played into doomsday scenarios; other predictions were little more than fantasy or wish fulfilment. Only a few actually hit the mark. Despite these caveats, there is overwhelming evidence that disaster lies ahead. For years scientists have been issuing warnings about the ever-increasing strain on the bio-physical systems which support terrestrial life. These were starkly confirmed in the sixth assessment report from the IPCC (2021) which confirms that major climate changes are now inevitable and irreversible. There is now a mainstream consensus that the next few decades are a last chance to stabilize the climate and restore the balance between people and nature. Up until now, multiple negative feedback loops have masked the impact of human activity, but in future these are liable to turn positive, fuelling runaway effects. By the time a new point of equilibrium is achieved, the planet will be permanently poorer and much less conducive to human life. We will, as David Orr (2014: ix) puts it, have 'evicted ourselves from the only paradise humans have ever known'. The stable and benign geological epoch that has enabled human beings to flourish for the past 12,000 years, which is known as the Holocene, will have come to an end.

There is no single action that will set humanity on the course towards a new kind of sustainable life style or ideal world (Figure 17.1). It will require multiple changes and a deep reappraisal of our values and beliefs to address the challenges that lie ahead. Introducing children to some of the possibilities and providing them with a sense of purpose and hope at a time of great uncertainty is the underlying aim of this area of study and, indeed, the whole of this book. Many commentors agree with Dave Hicks (2014: 3) that the world will change 'dramatically and permanently' during the course of the current century. Educating children for the future and helping them to develop vision and resilience for what lies ahead has never been more important.

Reflection and discussion

- Can you think of any predictions either in your personal or public life which have turned out to be completely wrong?
- What kind of 'dramatic and permanent' changes do you think Dave Hicks might have in mind?

Figure 17.1 Thomas More envisaged an ideal, imaginary island he called *Utopia*. *Photo: Unknown Author, Wikimedia Commons.*

SUSTAINABILITY STORIES (AGE 3–7)

What is the main focus of this topic?

Sustainable living is underpinned by a sense of belonging, identity and care.

Key ideas	Subject links	SDG links
Care	Art	SDG 12 Responsible consumption
Imagination	English (creative writing)	SDG17 Partnerships
Interdependence	Religious Education (ethics)	

Background information

Stories are one of the main ways that people communicate and express ideas. They can encapsulate ambiguities and convey cultural values in a memorable way, and they provide metaphors that help to guide our actions. Stories have a particular appeal for young children as they try to see patterns and make meaning of their own physical and social surroundings. This topic builds on this propensity and highlights a few well-established stories which relate to different aspects of sustainability – social and economic as well as environmental. The illustrations which accompany the text are integral to the image that each story conjures up and the delight which children take in listening to them is testimony to their appeal. Engaging children with sustainability issues in a positive manner is one way to provide firm foundations for future learning.

Interesting facts

- The paintings in the Chauvet cave in France are the oldest known representation of storytelling, dating back 36,000 years. They are believed to tell the story of a volcanic eruption.
- Indigenous people used to create 'journey sticks' to remember different routes and tell about their travels. They made the sticks by tying material they found along the way to a stick in chronological order.
- Researchers have found that people tend to challenge arguments based on fact, while stories can change behaviour by stimulating brain networks associated with empathy.

Misconceptions and research

It is easy to underestimate children's ability to understand sustainability issues and what needs to be done to address them. With respect to education, Jerome Bruner proposed the general principle: 'Any subject can be taught effectively in some intellectually honest form to any child at any stage of development.' Moreover, the ability to think creatively and make unusual links and connections is often acknowledged to one of the gifts of childhood. This means that children of whatever age have something meaningful to contribute.

Teaching ideas

Key vocabulary

care   pollution   sustainability
friendship population
paradise   power

Getting started

All the stories featured in this topic illustrate different aspects of sustainability and there are multiple versions of them, all readily available on the Internet. However, if you are able to obtain print versions to display in a book corner, along with other related titles, that would be a real benefit. Giving children the chance to look at a book at their leisure and ponder the story and illustrations helps to deepen their engagement and understanding.

The Snail and the Whale | *key idea: interdependence*

This story by Julia Donaldson is about a journey to a far-off land, but it is also about the friendship of two unlikely creatures. One of the key points is that, although the snail is very much smaller and less powerful than the whale, it still saved the whale's life. After reading the story, see if the children can think of two other creatures that might team up to help each other. Encourage them to think of scenarios where a seemingly powerful creature is rescued by a weaker one. Make the larger point about how all living things depend on each other, even though this may not be immediately obvious.

Belonging | *key idea: change*

In this engaging story, Jeannie Baker shows how the view through a window gradually changes as a gritty city street is transformed over time into a leafy paradise with trees, grass and flowers. Inspired by the story, invite the children to make their own 'before' and 'after' drawings using the spot the difference formula. To keep this simple, you could get pupils to do an outline drawing of a road and street first, which you could photocopy for them to complete in different ways to show the changes.

The Trouble with Dragons | *key idea: care*

The trouble with dragons, as Debi Gliori explains, is that there are not only too many of them but they also gobble up far too many resources and create far too much waste. This is a story about overpopulation and pollution, but it is also a story about caring, sharing and working together. Introduce children to the story, then reread it slowly, asking the children to listen carefully to (a) the problems that dragons cause and (b) the advice from the other animals. Make a list of these things in two columns. Discuss with the children what they have learnt from this book.

One World | *key idea: care*

In this story by Michael Foreman, two children go to the beach to create a miniature sea world in a bucket and marvel at the plants and creatures that they find. However, they also discover that their miniature world is polluted with a blob of oil. They reflect on what they can do to care for the environment and how we are all part of creation. Read this story to the children and invite them to create their own miniature worlds. Most schools will not have access to the sea, but using moss, pebbles, twigs, leaves and other items, children can create a 'small world' woodland environment, maybe even populating it with a few 'animals' that they have decided to draw.

Investigations and fieldwork | *key idea: imagination*

Introduce the children to some other sustainability picture-book stories. Pupils may want to contribute books that they know about or have at home. There is a good range of stories about animals, the natural environment and pollution, but try to include books on social issues as well if possible. Exploring, where possible, the environments that favourite stories are set in is another way of enabling the children to appreciate what the story is trying to tell them. For example, telling the story of *Winnie the Pooh* while in a wood brings the imaginary world alive.

Sustainability discussion

What have the children learnt about looking after their world and each other from their reading? Answers might include:

(a) they show animals, like people, can live together;
(b) you need to see all sides to a story; and
(c) sometimes the answers to problems are not the most obvious ones.

NEW WAYS OF LIVING (AGE 5–11)

What is the main focus of this topic?

We can develop new ways of using resources and relating to nature.

Key Ideas	Subject links	SDG links
Conservation	Design	SDG 8 Quality education
Resources	Drama	SDG 12 Responsible consumption
Rewilding	Mathematics	

Background information

There is no shortage of ideas about how we might reform our economic and social systems in the light of the sustainability crisis. What is lacking is a consensus about the best action to take and a willingness, at both a political and social level, to put it into action. This topic draws attention to strategies which could make a difference. It focuses particularly on farming and ways to reverse the decline in wildlife because, ultimately, we all depend on biodiversity for survival. Changes in legislation, taxation policy and international agreements will be critical to this process but are hard for children to grasp as they are mostly abstract. The aim here is to present some constructive ideas without getting involved in the complexities which obscure the basic aim of finding new ways of living within planetary boundaries. The need to find new ways of living which respect the environment is something which children of all ages can appreciate and understand.

Interesting facts

- There is nearly five times the amount of farmland in the world today as there was in 1700.
- Vultures, beavers and bison have been reintroduced in parts of Europe through rewilding projects and have a beneficial effect on the ecosystem.
- Recycling just one ton of paper can save over 25,000 litres of water, 2.5 cubic metres of landfill space and seventeen trees.

Misconceptions and research

Actively exploring problems and devising possible solutions empowers children and gives them a sense of agency. The alternative is for children to feel disempowered and position themselves as victims. Sustainability education, pursued in a positive manner, thus provides an opportunity to initiate an upward spiral of engagement and action which can help young people meet the challenges of their future. Giving them the confidence to both ask the difficult questions and make wise judgements is an ambition teachers need to facilitate.

Teaching ideas

Key vocabulary

cycles	recycling	urban farming
economy	rewilding	vegetarian
future		

Getting started

This topic hinges around what David Attenborough argues is the biggest question of our time. How can we create a future in which both people and nature can thrive? By way of introduction, watch the video 'How to Save the Planet' in which David Attenborough sets out four key ways forward (website 17.1).

Rewilding | *key idea: conservation, balance*

Find out about different rewilding projects, especially any that are happening in your area. For example, in southern England, the Knepp Wildlife Project is a particularly well-known example of how intensive farmland can be given back to nature (website 17.2). Invite the children to research an animal which they know has disappeared but is now being considered for reintroduction. What is its natural habitat? When and why did it die out? Is everyone in favour of reintroducing it? Pupils could use their work as the basis for a presentation to another class or for a school assembly. As well as presenting facts and figures, there is scope for enacting small scenes, e.g. a public enquiry.

Thinking about meat | *key idea: connections*

Get the children to think about the food they have eaten recently. How many times have they eaten meat, or are they vegetarian? Now ask them to draw a graph of average annual meat consumption in different parts of the world: USA, 120 kg; Europe, 60–80 kg; Kenya, 16 kg; India, 4 kg or less. Encourage the children to write a few sentences analysing and assessing the data. In which country do people on average eat the most/least meat and what might explain these differences? Consider how eating meat links to sustainability? One of the most notable examples is the clearance of the

Amazonian rainforest for ranching. Why do some people become vegetarian? A class discussion will enable different viewpoints to be aired and appreciated.

Urban farming | *key idea: resilience*

Technology and innovation are changing food production, making it possible to have farms even in built-up areas. Working from the Internet or other sources (website 17.3), the children can investigate an urban farming project of their choice. Examples include roof gardens, vertical farming, aquaculture, hydroponics and city permaculture. (In order to avoid technical language, you may want to devise your own presentation for children to work from, particularly with younger age groups.) When they have conducted their research, invite individual children to say a few words about what they have found out to the rest of the class. Do they think urban farming is practical and could it bring meaningful benefits? What are the downsides to their chosen examples?

Circular economy | *key idea: resources*

The circular economy applies the idea of cycles to the way we use resources. There are two different cycles. Natural cycles involve anything that is biodegradable such as food, wood and clothes made from natural fibres. By contrast metals, plastics and synthetics belong to a technical cycle. In both cycles raw materials become the 'nutrients' for the next part of the cycle and nothing is wasted. Ask the children to draw diagrams showing how the two cycles apply to specific items. For example, in a natural cycle, leaves grow on trees, fall to the ground, rot and enrich the soil helping new trees to grow. In a technical cycle, iron ore is turned into metal which is used to make products such as saucepans which are recycled when they wear out and turned back into metal to make more goods.

Investigations and fieldwork | *key idea: cycles*

Following the journey of a piece of their clothing from the raw material through the manufacturing process to the finished garment enables children to appreciate the many inputs of material, labour, power/energy, technology and innovation that results in what they wear. They should also consider what happens to that garment when it wears out, or is no longer fashionable. Is it recycled and made into something else, given to a charity shop so somebody else can use it, or sent to a landfill site as waste? The children can make flow diagrams to help them understand the linkages in this cycle and the sustainability issues that are involved. If possible, visit a local recycling centre or factory where pupils can learn more about recycling everyday household items.

Sustainability discussion

How could people change their behaviour to reduce their impact on the planet?
Answers might include:

(a) they could try to avoid buying goods with unnecessary and non-recyclable packaging;

(b) they could make careful choices about the food they eat and where it comes from;

(c) they could stop buying things they do not really need; and

(d) they could see that the things they throwaway are reused or recycled whenever possible.

THE FUTURE WE WANT (AGE 7–14)

What is the main focus of this topic?

How we imagine the future influences the choices we make today.

Key Ideas	Subject links	SDG links
Future Humility Vision	English Religious Education	SDG 17 Partnerships

Background information

Trying to come to terms with the environment crisis which is steadily unfolding all around us is no easy matter. Joanna Macy and Chris Johnstone (2012: 1) argue that we are living at a strange moment in history when 'a profound loss of confidence in the future' is the pivotal psychological reality of our times. In order to move forward, they believe we need to bring our fears out into the open so they lose their power to haunt us. Imagining the future that they want draws children into articulating their hopes and fears. It encourages them to reflect on their lives and aspirations while deepening their own sense of identity and purpose. It also raises questions about beliefs and values. One of the threads that runs through this process is the notion of intergenerational equity. Recognizing our responsibility to the future has the potential to shape our behaviour in the present. This is evidenced by the various youth movements that have grown up to campaign for sustainability, and also in the enthusiasm with which children engage with work which explores their futures.

Interesting facts

- Esperanto is a universal second language that was invented in the nineteenth century to bring about world peace but has never really caught on.
- A hundred years ago people thought we would have flying cars by now.
- Today, people wonder if the machines we are inventing will be more intelligent than we are and take over the world.

Misconceptions and research

Whether the focus is on their personal life or planetary issues, children have a strong interest in the future. However, having only lived for a few years, they sometimes find it hard to envisage lengthy time frames. For a 10-year-old, a decade is a life time ahead and fifty years may seem impossibly distant. Introducing children to long-term trends is one way to help them decentre. Working with members of an older generation (e.g. in the school garden), who will talk with them about the past, is another option.

Teaching ideas

Key vocabulary

economy	society	United Nations
environment	Sustainable Development Goal	utopia

Getting started

Talk with the children about a perfect world where there are no conflicts and everyone lived in harmony with each other and the environment. Thomas More's *Utopia* (Figure 17.1) was one attempt to envisage what this would be like. Would a perfect world be rather boring? Could it ever be achieved? What would prevent it happening?

Imagining the future | *key idea: future*

Working in pairs or small groups, ask pupils to share their ideas about the future. They should arrange their ideas under three headings: (a) what they think is probable; (b) what they think is possible; and (c) what they think is preferable. You can give this activity extra depth but asking pupils to think first about their own lives, and secondly about the world in general. You can also sort the responses into those that are positive and those that are negative. In general, are children hopeful or pessimistic about the future that lies before them?

Sustainable Development Goals | *key idea: sustainable living*

Introduce the children to the UN Sustainable Development Goals (website 17.4). Either explain or have them research the background to the goals – they are intended to provide a framework for the future which applies to every nation. Divide the children into small groups and ask them to write each goal on a small piece of card. They should now see if they can sort the cards into groups. The environment, economy and society are useful headings. Conclude by discussing the approach each group has taken. Do pupils think the goals are (a) helpful and (b) realistic? Can they think of anything that is missing that needs to be put in as an extra goal? (The goals include gender equality but not racial equality.)

Letters to the Earth | *key idea: humility, awe and wonder*

Invite the children to write 'letters to the Earth' expressing their gratitude for what it has provided and regret for what has been done to it. They could focus on themes such as (a) love for the world, (b) the mystery of life, (c) hopes for the future, (d) apologies for what has been lost and (e) action to protect the environment. As an extension you might turn this activity round and get pupils to write 'letters from the Earth' in which they imagine the planet as a forgiving parent and share these via social media (website 17.5). You could also look at the various contributions in *Letters to the Earth* (2019), a collection introduced by Emma Thompson.

Definitions of sustainability | *key idea: vision*

In this final activity the children make up a sentence to define the term 'sustainability'. First, working on their own, each child draws round the outline of their outstretched hand. Now, still on their own and in silence, ask them to write five single words (or very short phrases) which they associate with sustainability in each of the digits. Now encourage them to compare what they have written in pairs and threes and agree on a set of terms to write on a new hand outline. The final challenge is to write a sentence which brings all the words/phrases together and only uses the word 'and' once. As an extension the pupils can write their sentences out clearly on a large sheet of paper, to display on a corridor wall as a 'gallery walk'.

Investigations and fieldwork | *key idea: partnership*

Identify an organization in your area that has a sustainability focus – this might be a wildlife group, an environment organization (such as Groundwork), an allotment association, a food bank, a charity, or a business making sustainable products. Invite a representative to come to talk to the children about their work, their sustainability policies and their plans for the future. This will enable the children to understand the practicalities of working in a sustainable way. Encouraging the children to become involved in the activities of the organization would be a way to reinforce their experience and learning.

Sustainability discussion

What would children like to know more about with respect to sustainability and the environment? There are many different themes and topics which pupils might want to consider along with practical action to address specific problems. This discussion could be an interesting small-scale research exercise its own right and has the potential to impact on curriculum planning.

Websites

Website 17.1 How to Save the Planet
https://m.youtube.com/watch?v=0Puv0Pss33M
Website 17.2 Rewilding
https://www.youtube.com/watch?v=PpW8qSpoQj8
Website 17.3 Urban farming
https://www.greenbiz.com/article/how-16-initiatives-are-changing-urban-agriculture-through-tech-and-innovation
Website 17.4 Sustainable Development Goals
https://sdgs.un.org/goals
Website 17.5 Letters to the Earth
https://www.letterstotheearth.com/

Children's books

Baker, J. (2008) *Belonging*, London: Walker Books.
Donaldson, J. (2003) *The Snail and the Whale*, London: Macmillan Children's Books.
Gliori, D. (2009) *The Trouble with Dragons*, London: Bloomsbury.
Foreman, M. (2004) *One World*, London: Andersen Press.
Thompson, E. (ed.) (2019) *Letters to the Earth*, London: Collins.

References

Attenborough, D. (2020) *A Life on Our Planet*, London: Witness Books.
Hicks, D. (2014) *Educating for Hope in Troubled Times*, London: Trentham Books/Institute of Education Press.
IPCC (2021) *Climate Change: The Physical Science Basis*, available at https://www.ipcc.ch/report/ar6/wg1/.
Orr, D. (2014) 'Foreword' in Boring, W. P., and Forbes, W. (eds), *Teaching Sustainability*, Nascogdoches, TX: Stephen F. Austin State University Press.

Part IV

Implementation

As in any area of education, implementing sustainability education involves detailed planning and organization. This final section focuses on practicalities and considers how the topics and areas of study outlined earlier in this book can be integrated with the existing school curriculum. It also addresses progression and includes a detailed summary of learning outcomes for pupils of different ages which are indicative of sustainability literacy. The section concludes with a series of case studies which show how schools in the UK and other parts of world have set about introducing and developing sustainability education. The significance of (a) local circumstances and context and (b) the values and ethos of individual schools emerge as key factors.

Sustainability education is evolving rapidly as circumstances change and the environmental emergency becomes ever more apparent. It lacks the frameworks, procedures and common understandings which give coherence to traditional disciplines, and it represents a new way of thinking about the world and our place within it. This creates uncertainties, but it is precisely because the goalposts are constantly moving that introducing sustainability in classroom settings is such an exciting endeavour.

18

Designing Your Sustainability Curriculum

The school curriculum is a highly complex and contested arena in which political, social, cultural and ideological forces vie with each other to wrest control of children's learning. Teachers and educators have a very significant voice in this debate, not least because of their professional expertise and their duty to implement whatever is specified. It has been argued in this book that, if education is to step up to the mark and play its part in addressing the environmental emergency, then sustainability education needs to be taken much more seriously and teachers need to have more support and guidance on how to introduce it to children. As the evidence of impending crisis gathers momentum, there is every reason why sustainability should be at the core of the curriculum, rather than at the edges.

One of the theorists whose ideas about the curriculum have proved particularly influential is the British educationalist, Lawrence Stenhouse. Stenhouse (1975) argued that the curriculum is much more than a simple list of content or a mere outline of educational objectives. Instead, he saw it as an attempt to communicate the essential principles and features of an educational proposal in a way that is open to criticism and capable of being applied in practice. Seeing the curriculum as a recipe for a dish that teachers prepare helps to unpack this definition. Both education and cookery are to some extent experimental processes which can be varied according to taste. Also, both education and cookery are grounded in tangible activity which causes the ingredients to change and leads to results which are subject to scrutiny. One of the implications of this approach is that it emphasizes learning rather than instruction and it gives teachers an active role in research and curriculum development.

A broad understanding and approach to the curriculum opens up possibilities for creativity, flexibility and innovation (Figure 18.1). It positions teachers as curriculum makers and supports the notion of a curriculum of engagement championed by David Lambert and others (2013). It also acknowledges the professional wisdom and practical expertise which teachers bring to the classroom. As Robin Alexander points out, *how* children learn is every bit as important as *what* they learn (2010: 257). The charts and grids which form the bulk of this chapter are intended to help readers engage in curriculum making as they devise their own 'curriculum recipes' and find different ways of incorporating sustainability perspectives into their practice.

Figure 18.1 Discussing the curriculum with colleagues deepens understanding, supports innovation and helps to build a 'community of practice' (Wenger 1998). *Photo: Steve Rawlinson.*

Topic Chart

This chart provides an overview of the topics outlined in the chapters in Part 3 of this book. The topics have been selected so as to balance the environmental, economic and social dimensions of sustainability education. They are not intended to be comprehensive but offer an introduction to a range of key sustainability issues in an age-appropriate way. All the topics relate to the United Nations SDGs. The topics are distinctive and have a specific knowledge base but also enable overlaps into other areas.

Area of Study	Topics Age 3–7 focus	Topics Age 5–11 focus	Topics Age 7–14 focus
6 Earth in Space	The Earth	Air, Land and Sea	Life on Earth
7 Life on Land	Animals	Life in the Wild	Reconnecting with Nature
8 A Watery Planet	Wonderful Water	Freshwater Stories	Saltwater Stories
9 Weather & Climate	Weather Patterns	The Water Cycle	Climate Change
10 Food & Farming	Food from the Garden	Busy Bees	Healthy Choices

Area of Study	Topics Age 3–7 focus	Topics Age 5–11 focus	Topics Age 7–14 focus
11 Jobs, Transport and Energy	Jobs	Transport	Energy and Electricity
12 The Global Village	Houses and Homes	Sustainable Cities	Population
13 Special Places	Where I Belong	Connecting with Places	Protecting Places
14 Citizenship & Democracy	Eco-citizens	Healthy Communities	Democracy
15 Pollution & Resources	Waste and Litter	Pollution	Natural Resources
16 Unequal World	How Dare You!	Children's Rights	Rich World, Poor World
17 Sustainable Living	Sustainability Stories	New Ways of Living	The Future We Want

Subject Grid

This grid shows how the areas of study relate to traditional areas of learning. Those who are teaching individual subjects may want to use the grid to locate activities that relate to their specific area of the curriculum. Equally, those who are following an integrated topic approach may want to identify activities that support specific themes or subjects. The overall aim, as in any programme of learning, is to ensure that pupils follow a broad and balanced curriculum which is pitched at a level that is appropriate to their interests, needs and understanding.

Subject	Ch 6. Earth in Space	Ch 7. Life on Land	Ch 8. A Wet Planet	Ch 9. Weather & Climate	Ch 10. Food & Farming	Ch 11. Jobs, Transport & Energy	Ch 12. The Global Village	Ch 13. Special Places	Ch 14. Citizenship & Democracy	Ch 15. Pollution & Conservation	Ch 16. Unequal World	Ch 17. Sustainable Living
Art	x	x	x					x		x	x	x
Citizenship				x		x				x	x	
Design/technology		x		x			x	x		x		
Drama	x	x	x		x	x			x	x	x	x
English	x	x	x	x	x	x	x	x	x	x	x	x
Geography	x	x	x	x	x	x	x	x	x	x	x	x
History		x				x	x	x			x	
Mathematics		x			x		x			x	x	x
Music	x			x					x			
Religious Education	x			x					x	x		x
Science	x	x	x	x	x	x	x	x		x	x	

Progression in Sustainability Education

Progression in sustainability education involves a number of different dimensions. It is evidenced in the breadth and depth of pupils' knowledge, the extent of their understanding, and their ability to interpret information and data. It involves comparing arguments and making choices in difficult situations. Key concepts such as interconnections, balance, systems and harmony help to structure sustainability thinking. Personal qualities are important, too. Curiosity, creativity, criticality, empathy and humility are part of an array of dispositions which nurture pupils' learning. At a more fundamental level, it is important to acknowledge that sustainability thinking, like all areas of education, has a moral base. This is not to suggest that it is judgemental or sectarian; rather it is a reminder that developing an ethic of Earth care, justice and moral responsibility is the basis for a lasting commitment to the future of the world that we have inherited from our forebears and are now passing on to the next generation sitting in our classrooms.

Children will engage with sustainability education in a variety of ways, and the links between personal experience, informal learning and structured teaching mean that it is hard to characterize. One of the challenges for schools is to avoid repetition while offering pupils opportunities to revisit and consolidate ideas over considerable periods of time. The notion of the spiral curriculum, first proposed by Jerome Bruner (1960), is helpful here. It also draws attention to the opportunities to develop international perspectives as pupils' knowledge of the world increases during the primary years. The constant interplay between the local and global is a key feature of this approach.

Children's progress in sustainability education is liable to be uneven rather than linear. Observing, talking and listening to children (and intervening with appropriate feedback) are important strategies which teachers can employ to encourage pupils and assess their progress. Asking questions is another approach which can help to bridge gaps in pupils' understanding and lead them to make connections. Group learning and practical activities are often particularly effective but do not appeal to all children, some of whom prefer to work individually. However, catering for different learning styles is often easier in sustainability education than other curriculum areas as it involves a greater degree of affective and spiritual learning.

The learning opportunities outlined in the following three tables aim to provide a portrait of sustainability literacy for pupils of different ages and abilities. They relate directly to the activities set out in the topics and areas of study, making it clear how they relate to each other to create an increasingly comprehensive understanding of sustainability. Reading the grids horizontally identifies the area of knowledge to be addressed, an idea for a practical visit or investigation, and opportunities to develop reflective and critical thinking. Reading the grids vertically draws attention to mutually reinforcing learning opportunities both within and between the age phases. Unlike traditional school subjects, sustainability education has a fluid knowledge base so pupils do not need to engage with every topic or area of study. Rather they need to be able to synthesize thinking from various disciplines to reflect critically and constructively on environmental, social and economic issues and case studies, and take appropriate action.

For further advice on curriculum planning and organization, readers may want to refer to Chapter 5 which takes a broader look at the theoretical and practical issues that impact classroom practice. Meanwhile, specific topics and issues relating to sustainability are listed in the index.

Learning Opportunities Age 3–7

Topic	Knowledge and understanding	Practical activities and investigations	Critical thinking and reflection
The Earth 6. Earth in Space	Know that the Earth is a sphere and one of eight planets that orbit the Sun	Represent the distances between the Sun and planets through physical enactment	Appreciate that the Earth is fragile and needs to be treated with care
Animals 7. Life on Land	Know that there is a great diversity of life on Earth	Investigate the diversity of animals in the school grounds	Consider how animals are important in our lives
Wonderful Water 8. A Watery Planet	Know that water is essential to life	Undertake a local 'water walk'	Appreciate why water is special
Weather Patterns 9. Weather and Climate	Know that the weather effects our lives	Measure and record local weather conditions	Consider why the weather matters in our lives
Food from the Garden 10. Food and Farming	Know that fresh fruit and vegetables help to keep us healthy	Investigate the insects and other creatures in a vegetable garden	Think about how to keep ourselves, our gardens and our farms healthy
Jobs 11. Jobs, Transport and Energy	Know that people need training and equipment for different jobs	Arrange a visit to a place of work	Compare the value of different jobs
Houses and Homes 12. The Global Village	Know that people live in different types of home	Undertake a community walk looking for clues to sustainable living	Consider how homes might be made more sustainable in the future
Where I Belong 13. Special Places	Understand that all creatures need places where they feel protected	Record emotional response to places in and around the school	Compare sustainability of animal and human homes
Eco-citizens 14. Citizenship and Democracy	Know about the life cycle of butterflies and humans	Investigate caterpillars in the local environment	Discuss what makes a healthy community
Waste and Litter 15. Pollution and Resources	Know that some waste rots but that other items are not bio-degradable	Undertake a local litter survey	Consider what we can do to reduce waste and litter
How Dare You! 16. Unequal World	Understand that fairness doesn't mean everyone should be treated equally	Find out if spaces around the school are used fairly	Debate why fairness matters
Sustainability Stories 17. Sustainable Living	Understand that stories help us to explore complex ideas	Compile a collection of picture books that focus on sustainability	Talk about how there are usually at least two sides to a story

Learning Opportunities Age 5–11

Topic	Knowledge and understanding	Practical activities and investigations	Critical thinking and reflection
Air, Land and Sea *6. Earth in Space*	Know that the atmosphere (air), continents (land) and oceans (water) are interconnected	Create a map, model or diagram of an imaginary environment that can support life	Realize that the interaction of air, land and water is constantly changing but always in balance.
Living in the Wild *7. Life on Land*	Know that animals are adapted to their environment	Devise a trail linking a range of local plants and wildlife	Recognize that human activity can damage wildlife
Freshwater Stories *8. A Watery Planet*	Understand that rivers shape the land and influence human activity	Simulate the impact of a flood	Recognize that water can be valued in different ways
The Water Cycle *9. Weather and Climate*	Understand that water is constantly moving around the Earth	Compare different flood prevention measures	Realize that the water cycle is essential to our lives
Busy Bees *10. Food and Farming*	Understand why pollinators are essential in food production	Assess ways of making the school garden or site more insect-friendly	Recognize some of the threats facing bees and other pollinators
Transport *11. Jobs, Transport and Energy*	Know about the environmental impact of different forms of transport	Undertake a local transport survey	Discuss how people can be encouraged to travel more sustainably
Sustainable Cities *12. The Global Village*	Know about some great cities and what makes them distinctive	Devise the criteria for a sustainable city competition	Consider how cities might be designed in years to come
Connecting with Places *13. Special Places*	Understand that places contribute to our sense of identity	Find out about famous landmarks around the world	Think about local landmarks and what makes them special
Healthy Communities *14. Citizenship and Democracy*	Understand why inclusion is important	Investigate how the school creates a supportive environment	Discuss why healthy communities matter
Waste and Litter *15. Pollution and Resources*	Know that pollution effects all forms of life and can have unexpected consequences	Undertake a survey of local pollution problems	Consider what can be done to reduce different types of pollution
Children's Rights *16. Unequal World*	Know that children all over the world have certain basic rights	Compare the needs of different social groups	Discuss if rights always come with responsibilities
New Ways of Living *17. Sustainable Living*	Understand that there are ways that both people and nature thrive together	Trace the life cycle of different manufactured products	Debate how people could change their behaviour to live more sustainably

Learning Opportunities Age 7–14

Topic	Knowledge and understanding	Practical activities and investigations	Critical thinking and reflection
Life on Earth 6. Earth in Space	Understand that life has developed over very long periods of time	Devise a presentation or drama to show that all life is connected	Recognize that life on Earth depends on multiple, interconnected systems
Reconnecting with Nature 7. Life on Land	Understand that all life is connected	Draw up a plan to enhance local wildlife	Appreciate the value of bio-diversity
Saltwater Stories 8. A Watery Planet	Understand that oceans help to maintain Earth's balance and harmony	Create and curate a beach museum	Understand the importance of protecting marine environments
Climate Change 9. Weather and Climate	Understand the role of convection currents in global weather systems	Find out about climate change emergency declarations	Evaluate the role of technology in mitigating climate change
Healthy Choices 10. Food and Farming	Know how food is produced and transported	Find out about food production from a market or farm visit	Recognize the impact of food miles, food packaging and pesticide use
Energy and Electricity 11. Jobs, Transport and Energy	Know about different ways of producing and saving energy	Design a carbon-neutral model house	Evaluate the pros and cons of different ways of generating electricity
Population 12. The Global Village	Know that world population is unevenly distributed and growing	Devise and conduct a class census	Consider the challenge of living within planetary limits as world population continues to grow
Protecting Places 13. Special Places	Know that around the world people are working to conserve nature	Find out about the places people value in the local area	Reflect on if and how special places can be better protected
Democracy 14. Citizenship and Democracy	Understand that people sometimes have to make difficult choices	Explore a local issue where people have different opinions	Discuss if an elected world government would promote sustainability
Natural Resources 15. Pollution and Resources	Understand why we need to use natural resources wisely	Make a survey of how natural resources are used in the local area	Debate which natural resources are most valuable
Rich World, Poor World 16. Unequal World	Understand that people can be rich in different ways	Find out about events which aim to reduce material consumption	Consider the pros and cons of a universal basic income to reduce global inequality
The Future We Want 17. Sustainable Living	Understand that the choices we make help to shape the future	Find out about local environmental organizations	Debate what else pupils want to learn about sustainability and the environment

References

Alexander, R. (ed.) (2010) *Children, Their World, Their Education*, Cambridge: Cambridge University Press.

Bruner, J. (1960) *The Process of Education*, Cambridge, MA: Harvard University Press.

Lambert, D. (2013) 'Subject Teachers in Knowledge-Led Schools' in Young, M., and Lambert, D. (eds), *Knowledge and the Future School*, London: Bloomsbury.

Stenhouse, L. (1975) *An Introduction to Curriculum Research and Development*, London: Heinemann.

Wenger, E. (1998) *Communities of Practice*, Cambridge: Cambridge University Press.

19

Sustainability Education in Action

Schools are responding to the challenge of introducing sustainability into their curriculum in multiple ways. Some schools have decided to emphasize practical activities and outdoor work. Others concentrate on social justice and human relationships. Faith perspectives and a commitment to global citizenship provide an underlying vision in many instances. Much depends on the social, cultural and environmental context in which schools are operating, so the examples given here only indicate some of the possibilities. There is no single approach or right way to set about sustainability education, but with enthusiasm and commitment from teachers and clear leadership and vision from the senior leadership team, it is possible to develop exciting new approaches to education within the requirements of a prescribed curriculum.

Eight case studies from schools around the world are highlighted in this chapter. These are just a small sample from the wide range of inspiring initiatives currently being undertaken in many countries with children of all ages in both formal and informal settings. In different ways they all show how committed pupils and teachers can put sustainability education into action and make a difference to pupils' lives. Whole school approaches based on clearly articulated principles are often particularly effective and have an impact which reaches into the wider community and creates grassroots support for sustainability and environmental action. As with all social change, there is often no direct link between cause and effect, and results are often hard to predict. Equipping children with the resilience and vision to face uncertain change with confidence opens the door to a brighter future. After all, as Jane Whittle (2016: 4) enthusiastically reminds us, the pupils in our classrooms today are the very people who have the potential to 'bring about world peace, manage global economies, fight disease, invent new technologies, campaign for community rights or unite cultures'. As well as taking action ourselves, we can help them to develop the capacity to make this a reality.

Outdoor Learning in Australia

Karen Rogers, Grade 1/2 Class Teacher, Ringwood Heights Primary School, Melbourne, Australia

Figure 19.1 *(a)* Talking about pond life and plant species *(b)* Observing the impact of erosion. *Photos: Karen Rogers.*

Imagine a school where you are greeted every morning by the smell of dewy eucalyptus trees and the sound of laughing kookaburras. At Ringwood Heights Primary, in the eastern suburbs of Melbourne, we appreciate our outdoor environment and the opportunities for cross-curricular links that it provides. An example of the advantage afforded by these links, particularly in the area of sustainability, was witnessed through a Grade 3/4 investigation into the big question, 'Is this is a healthy habitat?'

The enquiry focused especially on geographical knowledge of environments and vegetation and science as a human endeavour. A park ranger-led visit to a local bushland area supported us to see the impact of human actions on the local plant and animal habitats, as well as the steps being taken to develop a sustainable plan for the area. As one example, students were able to see first-hand the impact of land clearing and observe how soil washed into a pond was detrimental to the animal and plant species living there. Steps were being taken by local volunteer groups to regenerate the natural vegetation, and students were encouraged to volunteer to help with the replanting.

Returning to school we undertook an audit of our school outdoor habitats to determine how 'healthy' they were. Drawing on the critical and creative thinking curriculum, students were supported to identify areas for improvement. This resulted in student-led changes to sustainability practices including school-wide education about ways to reduce waste, improvements to the existing compost programme, the creation of barriers to reduce soil erosion and compaction, and research to determine the most appropriate planting for a new garden bed within the school. The learning was led by the Grade 3/4 students and implemented across the whole school. Evidence of the strength of the learning was observed as students across the school continued to be aware of their impact on the outdoor environment long after the investigation had 'finished'.

Steiner Schools in Norway

Hilde Tørnby, Oslo Metropolitan University, Norway

Figure 19.2 Circles or spirals are a recurring theme in Steiner pedagogy, emphasizing circles of life and ecological processes. In December our children celebrate Advent through light, songs and smells. They are guided by an angel (adult) to place a burning candle held in a red apple inside a spiral made of pine twigs. There is always music – sometimes from a harp or a violin, at other times there is singing. The ceremony is very quiet and beautiful and sacred. It takes place in a dark room where the only light comes from the Circle of Advent candles. (School Principal) *Photo: Ås Steiner School.*

There are thirty-two Steiner schools in Norway spread across the country. Steiner schools are founded on Steiner pedagogy and are privately run. To be eligible for private-school status in Norway, a school needs an alternative pedagogy, international profile or a more profound Christian footing than their public school counterparts. Private schools are granted the freedom to design their own curricula, but are not limited to it. While Norwegian Steiner schools design their own curricula based on the educational philosophy of Rudolph Steiner (1861–1925), all other schools follow the curricula from the Department of Education.

A main principle in Steiner pedagogy is to view education as holistic, which means that every part of human life is considered in teaching contexts. Rather than dividing knowledge into clear-cut subjects, cross-curricular projects provide an organizing structure. For early years pupils, the difficulty young children have sitting still and paying attention is given careful consideration. This is reflected in the school's curricula as well as in the organization of teaching. Thus, teaching sequences are designed so that children are given opportunities to explore, play and learn through their senses. Furthermore, the idea that people are spiritual beings is vital. In the practicalities of a school setting, the spiritual is given space through daily sessions of movement and restitution. Also implementing artistic ways of expression in all subjects including mathematics and science underscores the idea that human beings are more than just intellectual.

Ås Steiner School is located on the outskirts of Oslo. The school's webpage uses art and photographs to depict pupils in creative projects and close to nature, emphasizing three core principles: freedom, play, arts and nature. Ås Steiner School's vision is to provide an holistic pedagogy which assists children in their development and learning. Realizing that all parts of a child's being are important, not only the intellect, offers valuable entryways to learning. Closeness to nature both in location and in teaching is essential. The school has its own vegetable garden where children plant, weed and harvest. Moreover, complete school days in nature are embedded in the learning aims and form part of the school's organization and rhythm. Learning about ecosystems creates a sensitivity to life's sacredness and plants the idea that we need to protect and care for nature rather than exploiting it.

An International School in Singapore

Martin Stevens, Head of Humanities Junior School, Tanglin Trust School, Singapore

Figure 19.3 Infant children explore the newly created Forest School part of the Tanglin School campus. *Photo: Tanglin School.*

Located on a leafy avenue yet surrounded by high-tech companies, innovative buildings and a testing ground for the next generation of driverless, electric cars, Tanglin Trust School nestles in a hub of forward-thinking companies that have sustainability as a core value. Students, staff and visitors cannot be anything but impressed by the unique setting and the way in which the school fits into the ethos created in just the last fifteen years of development.

Within the Junior School alone, Tanglin encourages pupils to think in terms of sustainability through the carefully picked topic areas. Taking advantage of our location in Singapore, Year 4 children compare two off-lying islands, one of which is developed extensively for fun and adventure tourism, while the other stands as one of the few surviving rainforest habitats in Singapore, untouched by high-rise developments or mass transportation systems. In our Pristine Planet topic, students choose to investigate areas of unique natural beauty and the sustainability issues facing them, a topic inspired by Antarctic adventurer and advocate, Robert Swan. Rainforests and deforestation in Borneo provide the focus for students at the top of the Junior School. In all these topics, a cross-curricular approach inspires students' responses from debates to expressive artwork.

Tanglin has a cross-school team of professionals on the 'Our World' focus group, which provides a means for planning participation in national enterprises and exhibitions such as the School Green Awards. It also plans activities and approaches for Eco Week and Earth Day, as well as being a platform for introducing initiatives such as Forest Schools and creating a Forest School area on campus. Like many of the larger international schools in Singapore, having the full range of pupils from nursery to sixth form enables cross-school partnerships of teachers and students from Infants, Juniors and Seniors. Members of the Head Student team and other senior pupils lead their younger peers, accompany them on trips and provide support at the sustainability exhibitions and events we attend.

As Robert Swan said to our students, 'The greatest threat to our planet is the belief that someone else will save it.' We try to do our part to help our students appreciate that they can be part of the solution.

Leading Change through an Eco Committee

School Eco Committee and Sarah Dukes (Teacher and Sustainability Co-ordinator)
The Chase School, Malvern, UK

Figure 19.4 Sharing and developing ideas in a co-operative setting. *Photo: Allison Shelley/The Verbatim Agency for American Education: Images of Teachers and Students in Action, Creative Commons*

At the Chase School, in Malvern in the UK, the Eco Committee raises awareness of climate change, reduces the school's carbon footprint, and leads the way in action. Established in September 2018 thanks to the resolve of an individual pupil (Phoebe Thomas), we started by implementing simple sustainable changes to school routines. In May 2019, after a wave of climate emergency declarations by councils across the UK, we were particularly disappointed when the local county council rejected a motion to make the authority carbon-neutral by 2030. Undeterred, the Eco Committee persuaded the head teacher with impassioned speeches, a moving video and scientific facts that the school needed to declare its own climate emergency.

With the help the business manager, we have now started to turn our ambitious priorities into achievable actions. As well as increasing knowledge and understanding of climate change, we have improved recycling facilities, expanded drinking water facilities (to reduce the use of plastic water bottles) and encouraged sustainable transport to school. The Eco Committee writes and delivers assemblies, and devises and leads activities. These range from innovative bake sales (secretly vegan or baking with bugs), litter picking, running up a repair club and organizing environmental campaigns. We run in-house 'climate strikes' by pausing usual lessons to deliver climate-themed activities, and host sessions during our annual 'activities week'. We aim to involve and empower pupils as widely as possible, and our actions have led to behaviour change in both students and staff.

Our next steps involve an audit (and increase) of explicit environmentalism within lessons across the curriculum; encouraging a love of nature through reading, drawing and writing clubs; getting a dedicated sustainability section on our school website; achieving Green Flag status; hosting more solidarity 'climate strike' afternoons; planting more trees; and continually reviewing and updating our action cards.

Framing Learning around Harmony Principles

Emilie Martin, The Harmony Project, Bristol, UK

What happens when we learn to learn from nature?

Figure 19.5 This representation of the Cosmati Pavement in Westminster Abbey, London, was recreated by 9-year old pupils in partnership with the Prince's Foundation School of Traditional Arts. The pavement's intricate, geometric design conveys a sense of the harmony and order of the universe. *Photo: Richard Dunne.*

The UK primary school curriculum provides a wealth of opportunities to learn *about* the natural world, and an established body of research recognizes the many benefits of learning *in* natural settings. But what opportunities do we offer students to learn *from* Nature?

The recognition that Nature is a powerful teacher, one that can help us learn to live in healthier, more sustainable ways, underpins the work of The Harmony Project and the Harmony approach to teaching and learning. This approach puts natural principles – such as cycles, diversity and interdependence – at the heart of education. In doing so, students are supported in developing a deep connection with, and understanding of, the natural world. It is an approach that is informing the development of Harmony-inspired curricula in a growing network of schools across the UK and beyond, one of which is South Farnborough Infant School in Hampshire.

Through enquiry-based, cross-curricular learning, children at the school explore and respond to big questions such as: 'Why is water precious to life on Earth?' and 'How can I help look after the Earth?' In Year 2, the children explore the question, 'Why are oceans important?' They investigate in Science how hot and cold water moves in different ways and relate this to ocean currents, use atlases in Geography to locate their nearest beaches, and in Literacy create information texts about rock pools. The learning is closely linked to Nature's principles of Harmony, and the children are encouraged to discuss, for example, the significance of the diversity of living things we find on a beach and the role of the oceans in the water cycle. They reflect on how we can relate this understanding to our own lives and actions.

The children engage with environmental challenges as part of their learning, but the school also fosters in them a strong sense of their own agency through a range of child-led initiatives. These range from pen recycling to measuring and monitoring food waste at lunchtime and identifying ways to minimize it. The impact of this approach has been significant. As one teacher at the school put it, 'Harmony learning opens children's eyes to the real wonders of the world and helps them see that they can be agents of change.'

Forest Schools

Stephen Pickering, Petroc College, Barnstaple, UK, and the University of Worcester, UK

Figure 19.6 Balancing challenge with confidence in a woodland setting. *Photo: Seattle Municipal Archives, Wikimedia Commons*

Forest School is a child-centred approach to learning that reaches back to Scandinavian open-air culture which many schools are now adopting. With Forest Schools the learning comes from a child's relationship with the environment. Indeed, the environment is the teacher while the teacher merely facilitates opportunities for the children to learn. Because all subject areas of a typical school curriculum can be covered through Forest School, there is a danger that Forest School is viewed as a way to teach. Rather it should be thought of as a forum from which to learn.

At St Wulston's Forest School, Worcestershire, UK, I worked in the woods with a group of 6-year-olds. There was a boy there who lacked self-confidence and constantly asked for help – even for the smallest of things. At one point he decided he wanted to climb up into a tree and hang from a branch that was just out of reach, and asked me for help. I suggested he should try by himself first and I moved away to watch from a distance. After a great deal of head scratching and trial and error he managed to roll one of the logs from the friendship circle, climb up onto it (I was actually pleased to see him keep trying even though he fell off a few times) and finally grab hold of the branch. By this time some of his friends had gathered and he proceeded to show them how to grab the branch, too. Before leaving for something else to do, he went to great effort to return the log.

This simple activity – one of many thousands that take place in Forest School around the world each week – demonstrates a lot more than a child's ability to solve a problem, or develop resilience and a growth mindset. Learning in Forest School is not just about cognition, although that is clearly there; it is about learning through the whole body. The epitome of hand, heart and head is actively engaging with a natural object, like the log and branch described above, developing an emotional reaction; in this case determination, and then thinking about the problem and how to solve it. But the hand, heart and head is not only about a child learning a skill, or mastering an activity: in deep engagement with the natural world each child is also learning respect for the environment, appreciation, wonder and trust in nature, and importantly their place as custodians of the natural world.

Using Eight-way Thinking

Steve Rawlinson, Geography Consultant, UK

Eight-way thinking was developed by Ian Gilbert (2014) to study places and is based on the theory of multiple intelligences first proposed by Howard Gardner (1970). It provides a valuable framework which can be used in sustainability education as it encourages children to reflect on their own perceptions and enables them to share their ideas and recognize that the same place or issue may be viewed in multiple ways. This is a key step in developing the empathy and problem-solving skills that are essential in addressing the current environment crisis.

The framework can be used with learners of all ages and applied both in the real world via fieldwork and in the virtual world via electronic media. Users are asked to devise questions or share thoughts using a sequence of eight prompts which invite them to describe, analyse, compare or speculate. To show how this works in practice, eight-way thinking is here applied to the Angel of the North, an iconic sculpture by Antony Gormley

Sights	What can you see from here? What can the Angel see?
People	Who comes to this place? Why would people come here?
Numbers	How tall/wide is the Angel? How many people see it each year?
Sounds	Is it peaceful, despite the traffic? What does an angel sound like?
Nature	What plants grow here? Is this a good use for an old mine?
Feelings	How does the Angel make you feel? Does the weather change your ideas?
Actions	Who decided to put a sculpture here? Who made it?
Words	What three words describe the Angel? What is its name? Rusty Rita?

Figure 19.7 Some of the questions and thoughts that arise when eight-way thinking is applied to a sculpture. *Photo: Steve Rawlinson.*

which has come to symbolize north-east England (Figure 19.7). (For further examples visit the companion website.)

Eight-way thinking has advantages in that it is a different and effective way of developing a sense of place and understanding about an issue. Also, it enables the children's voice to be heard as they have control over their questions and observations, which imparts ownership to their learning. This makes it an integrated and enjoyable approach to outdoor learning that can be applied in different contexts. The opportunities to work with the local community on issues that arise is a further benefit which consolidates its role as a sustainability pedagogy.

Developing the Curriculum around Social Action and the SDGs

Naheeda Maharasingam, Head Teacher, Rathfern Primary School, London, UK.

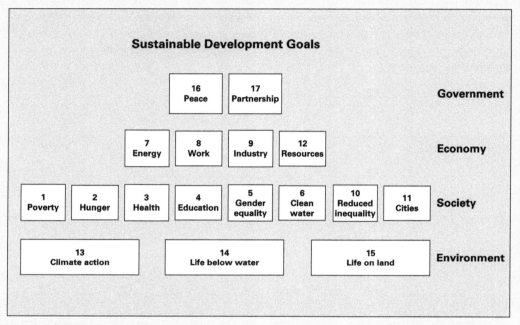

Figure 19.8 The SDGs can be grouped in many different ways. This arrangement emphasizes how human activity depends on the environment and the role that people can play in bringing about changes.

At Rathfern Primary School, London, we place the goals of social and environmental justice at the centre of our curriculum. Our commitment to social action is driven by moral purpose and a deep awareness of the injustices in our community, both locally and globally. Along with Freire (1970), we see education as a way of thinking beyond the confines of immediate experience to imagine a future that doesn't merely reproduce the present. We aim to envision, educate and interrupt.

We were attracted to the SDGs because they provide a framework for transformative change that pivots around social action. We have identified key moral questions linked to every curriculum topic for pupils to consider and discuss. These are refined and reframed in an iterative process that enables teachers to challenge children's ideas and promote the development of new perspectives and alternative ways of thinking.

Understanding the SDGs through a local, national and global approach enables our pupils to connect tangibly with inequalities. Our pupils have been inspired to set up and run our own school food bank. Pupil participation in decision making is integral as it empowers both themselves and others. This means children are involved in the evaluation, planning and control of local decisions, e.g. how to support the homeless, where to plant trees, how to address the idling of cars. We hold democratic elections where pupils become 'leading citizens' at weekly meetings to reflect on action linked to core values and responsibility. These give pupils real scope to steer what happens in our school.

Our approach supports the shaping of individual and collective knowledge, skills, values and attitudes to enable our learning community to move along pathways towards sustainable development, and become a catalyst for development itself.

We aim to develop a community committed to social action and motivated to interrupt unsustainable and unjust development. As an educator with over twenty-five years' experience, pursuing the goals of social and environmental justice feels utopian at times but it is nevertheless compelling.

References

Freire, P. (1970, 2007) *Pedagogy of the Oppressed*, London and New York: Continuum.
Gardner, H. (1993) *Frames of Mind: The Theory of Multiple Intelligences*, London: Fontana.
Gilbert, I. (2014) *Independent Thinking*, Carmarthen: Independent Thinking Press.
Whittle, J. (2016) 'Editorial', *Primary Geography* 90.

Glossary

Anthropocene A controversial term for a new geological epoch representing the period in which humans have had a lasting and potentially irreversible impact on the Earth.

Biomimicry A way of thinking that learns from and mimics the strategies and systems of the natural world to find solutions to complex human problems that are both effective and sustainable.

Biophilia A term attributed to E. O. Wilson and Aldo Leopold which describes the feeling of being drawn towards nature and having an innate connection with other forms of life.

Biosphere The air, land, water, flora and fauna which surround the Earth and which provide our life support systems.

Black swan event An unpredictable event outside the norm which has profound consequences but is often said, with hindsight, to have been predictable. The rise of the Internet and personal computers are both examples.

Chaos theory The idea that a minor difference at the beginning of a process can result in a significant alteration to its outcome over time. Unpredictable weather patterns are often cited as an example.

Citizenship Citizenship carries three dimensions: (a) legal status, (b) political agency and (c) a sense of self-identity. Interpretations vary across the globe, but the ways laws assist and protect people is a common denominator for a healthy society. The other side of the coin is how a citizen behaves.

Community of practice A group of people with common aims/interests/passions who work together by pooling their knowledge or expertise. Communities of practice can arise in any social setting from the workplace to electronic platforms.

Confirmation bias The tendency to seek and remember information to support existing beliefs or values, ignoring alternative views.

Copernican revolution The shift in thinking that accompanied the theory, advanced by Polish astronomer Copernicus, that the Earth orbits the Sun. Earlier theories regarded the Earth as a stationary body at the centre of the universe.

Cycles Cycles are circular processes of growth, decay and regeneration that operate at different scales and timeframes in both human and natural contexts.

Doughnut economics A theory of economics, devised by Kate Raworth, which sets out parameters for sustainable living. It uses a ring doughnut as a visual metaphor to depict a safe space for humanity, bounded by ecological overshoot on the one side and social deprivation on the other.

Earth Charter An international declaration of fundamental values and principles agreed in 2000 that provides an inclusive, integrated ethical framework to guide the transition to a more just, sustainable and peaceful future.

Earth Overshoot Day The day in any given year when humanity's demand for ecological resources and services starts to exceed Earth's capacity to provide them. In 2021, Earth Overshoot Day fell on 29 July.

Ecosystem services   The free services provided by ecosystems from which people derive many benefits. Examples include provisions (food, wood and other resources), environmental regulation (water purification, soil protection) and cultural services (mental well-being and spiritual regeneration).

Emergent properties   The principle of self-organization means that the interaction of the different parts of a complex system can give rise to new or emergent properties which were not present in the components. Particularly evident in the bio-physical world, emergence and novelty are also features of human organizations where groups of people come together to generate innovation.

Environmental/ecological footprint   The effect that a person, company or activity has on the environment. It is a quantitative measure that seeks to consider multiple impacts and is expressed as the area of land needed to support a particular way of living. Some countries, such as the USA, have very large environmental footprints while many African countries tread much more lightly on the Earth.

Extinction Rebellion   Established in 2018, this international movement aims to use non-violent civil disobedience to compel government action to avoid tipping points in the climate system, biodiversity loss and social and ecological collapse.

Extrinsic values   Visible measures of success or achievement such as wealth, public image and social power.

Feedback loops   Feedback describes the way an activity or event can amplify and correct itself. For example, within a population of rabbits, more adults lead to more babies which further increases the population which is ultimately brought under control by diminishing food supply. Positive feedback loops provide re-enforcement while negative feedback is self-correcting.

Gaia theory   First proposed by James Lovelock in the 1960s and named after Gaia, the earth goddess of Greek mythology. Its central tenet is that the Earth and its natural cycles can be considered as a self-regulating living organism.

Gross Domestic Product   The total value of all the goods and services produced over a period time and is often measured on a national basis. GDP is an important indicator of economic performance but fails to take account of unpaid work, social welfare or personal happiness. Alternative indicators which include education, health, equality and personal happiness have been proposed but have yet to be widely adopted.

Great Acceleration   The rapid changes that have occurred in environmental and socio-economic processes as a result of human activity since the 1950s. (See Anthropocene)

Global commons (Tragedy of)   A term devised by Garret Hardin to describe unregulated natural resources such as air, water and land. The way these resources are depleted (e.g. through overfishing and deforestation) is to everyone's detriment and hence tragic.

Green consumerism   A green consumer is said to be someone who understands the need to protect the environment and consequently seeks to purchase environmentally friendly products or services.

Green shift   The transition to producing goods and services in such a way as to significantly reduce negative consequences for the climate and the environment.

Greenhouse gases   Greenhouse gases trap solar radiation and have the effect of creating a 'blanket' around the world which is resulting in global warming. Human activity has dramatically increased levels of carbon dioxide, methane and nitrous oxide, all of which are important greenhouse gases.

Gyre   A circular pattern of currents in an ocean basin. There are five major gyres, such as the North Atlantic gyre, which have a significant impact on the oceans and currents. Growing quantities of marine debris have now become trapped in gyres, leading to vast garbage patches far from land.

Holocene   The geological epoch covering the last 11,500 years of Earth's history from the end of the last Ice Age. The stable climate during this period corresponds with the rapid growth of human numbers and is sometimes described as a 'Goldilocks period'.

Human exceptionalism   The notion that human beings are essentially different to all other organisms and superior to them. The idea that all problems can be solved by human ingenuity and technology is another example of exceptionalism.

Integrated reporting   Integrated reporting explains how an organization creates value over time with respect to different types of capital – natural, human, social, manufactured and financial. This provides a much broader understanding of business activity than a simple profit and loss account.

Interdependence   Interdependence can take a variety of forms. It can benefit both parties, it can benefit neither party, or one party can benefit at the expense of another.

Intrinsic value   The value that something such as a plant or a tree has in its own right, irrespective of its utility. Intrinsic values often underpin social and environmental concern and are central to many moral judgements.

Jevons paradox   Somewhat surprisingly, technological innovation or government support can reduce production costs which stimulates consumption and increases the use of resources. This is known as the Jevons paradox.

Metropolitan area   A very large built-up area with a nucleus or core that is closely integrated with adjacent communities. New York City, for example, is at the core of a metropolitan area that includes towns and cities in neighbouring states.

Moore's law   The observation that the speed and capability of a computer doubles roughly every couple of years, even as components become cheaper. There is no agreement on exactly when this trend will cease.

Nature deficit disorder   The alienation from nature that results when people, especially children, spend increasing amounts of time indoors (Louv 2005). This makes them more susceptible to disorders such as negative moods, reduced attention span and obesity, but also highlights the value of greater exposure to natural settings, including those in urban places. Nature deficit disorder is a useful phrase to describe a common problem but is not a recognized medical condition.

Neoliberalism   A political approach that sees competition as the defining characteristic of human relations. It favours free markets and minimal government intervention in the economy. In terms of education, it promotes marketization policies and transferring services into private ownership rather than government control.

Paradigm   A way of looking at the world involving a distinct set of concepts, ideas or perspectives. Changing the paradigm changes the way you think about something.

Paris Agreement   The Paris Agreement is a legally binding international treaty on climate change adopted in Paris in 2015. By substantially reducing global greenhouse gas emissions, it aims to keep global temperature rise below 2° C and preferably to 1.5° C.

Peak production   Generally applied to the oil industry, the Hubbert peak theory states that oil production follows a bell-shaped curve because the amount of oil under the ground in any region is finite. Peak production therefore marks a maximum which is then followed by steady decline (resource depletion).

Planetary boundaries   Scientists have identified nine planetary support systems which are essential for human survival. A healthy system can absorb a certain amount of disruption but pollution and other forms of disruption can cause it to become destabilized. The point at which this happens represents a planetary boundary. (See Tipping point)

Precautionary principle   The precautionary principle emphasizes that innovations need to be approached with caution as they may have unexpected and harmful impacts on both human and environmental health. The principle suggests that, rather than waiting for something unwelcome to happen, we need to guard against creating the conditions in which it could occur in the first place.

Regenerative design   Regenerative design is a way of designing goods so that resources are recycled and revitalized rather than wasted. Inspired by examples from the natural world, it is sometimes called a 'cradle to cradle' approach as it considers the entire life cycle of a product. An eco-friendly house that is heated by renewable energy, recycles water and is built of natural materials is an example of a complex product that incorporates regenerative design principles. (See Biomimicry)

Resilience   Resilience stems from the diversity and overlaps in a system which enable it to absorb shocks and unexpected events that would otherwise knock it off balance.

Rewilding   The process of restoring and expanding habitats which have been degraded in order to reverse biodiversity loss and to create more sustainable environments.

Shifting baseline syndrome   The tendency for ideas about what is normal or natural to shift from one generation to the next. This is particularly evident with respect to biodiversity where young people, who have never experienced the abundance of life seen by their grandparents, assume it is normal for woodlands and meadows to be degraded.

Soul wound   An idea from traditional North American culture which describes the trauma that can occur when people are alienated from the natural world.

Spaceship Earth   The idea that the Earth is like a spaceship in which the crew need to work together for the common good was popularized in the 1960s by Buckmaster Fuller. It suggests that, if only we can discover the operating manual, we will be able to control our direction of travel.

Stewardship   An ethic that embodies taking care and being responsible for something (or somebody) you have been entrusted to look after. It is a term which is often applied to the relations between humans and the environment but has paternalistic overtones.

Sustainable development   Initially defined as development that meets the needs of the present without compromising the ability of future generations to meet their own needs, today it has a broader meaning, and encompasses economic growth, environmental stewardship and social welfare.

Sustainable Development Goals   The UN Sustainable Development Goals (SDGs) are a universal call to action to end poverty, protect the planet and ensure that all people enjoy peace and prosperity by 2030. Adopted by all the United Nations member states in 2015, there are seventeen different goals, along with supporting targets and indicators, that form an interlinked policy framework.

Systems thinking   Pioneered by biologists over the last century, systems thinking sees living organisms as integrated wholes rather than a disparate collection of parts. It emphasizes complexity, networks and organizational patterns, and offers a novel way of thinking about life which focuses on interrelationships and resists reductionism.

Taxonomy   A scientific system of classifying things, especially plants and creatures, which have common characteristics. The term is derived from two Greek words, *taxis* (arrangement) and *nomia* (distribution).

Tipping point   A tipping point occurs when a system becomes destabilized and suddenly shifts to a new point of balance. The monsoon in South Asia is an example of a weather system that is triggered by regional tipping points.

Triple bottom line   The triple bottom line accounting framework incorporates three dimensions of performance: social, environmental and financial. It is an example of one of a number of mechanisms that can help an organization move towards more regenerative practices and sustainable operations.

Values   Desirable goals that motivate action in both our personal and professional lives. Some values relate to our individual survival needs and self-enhancement (e.g. security, power and achievement); others (e.g. concern and co-operation) apply to communal welfare. Sustainability issues often hinge around values conflict.

Wicked problem   A complex social or cultural issue that is difficult to explain and impossible to solve because it is incomplete, contradictory and ambiguous. Many environmental issues have 'wicked' characteristics.

Zero emissions   Governments, companies and communities around the world are adopting targets to ensure that the pollution from different forms of economic activity is completely eliminated over a given time. Zero emissions are especially associated with transport, agriculture and energy production, which are major sources of greenhouse gases.

Bibliography

(Not including children's books)

Adichie, C. N. (2009) 'The danger of a single story', *TED talk*, July 2009, available at https://www.ted.com/talks/chimamanda_ngozi_adichie_the_danger_of_a_single_story.

Alexander, R. (ed.) (2010) *Children, Their World, Their Education*, Cambridge: Cambridge University Press.

Artis, S., Cohen, A. M., Juguzny, I., and Kieras, K. (2020) 'This is Zero Hour' in Armon, J., Scoffham, S., and Armon, C. (eds), *Prioritizing Sustainability Education*, London: Routledge.

Assadourian, E. (2017) 'EarthEd: Rethinking Education on a Changing Planet', in *EarthEd: Rethinking Education on a Changing Planet*, Washington, DC: Island Press.

Attenborough, D. (2020) *A Life on Our Planet*, London: Witness Books.

Ballin, B. (2016) *Getting to Know the World*, Cambridge: Cambridge Primary Review Trust, available at https://cprtrust.org.uk/cprt-blog/getting-to-know-the-world/ https://www.washingtonpost.com/news/wonk/wp/2015/03/24/how-china-used-more-cement-in-3-years-than-the-u-s-did-in-the-entire-20th-century/.

Barnes, J. (2015) *Cross-Curricular Learning 3–14* (3rd edn), London: Sage.

Barnes, J., and Scoffham, S. (2017) 'The Humanities in English Primary Schools: Struggling to Survive', *Education 3–13*, 45:3, 298–308.

BBC (2001) *Blue Planet*, available at https://www.bbcearth.com/shows/blue-planet.

Berry, T. (2006) *Evening Thoughts*, San Francisco: Sierra Club Books.

Biesta, G. (2015) 'The Duty to Resist: Redefining the Basics for Today's Schools', *Research on Steiner Education* 6: 1–11.

Biesta, G. (2016) *The Beautiful Risk of Education*, London: Routledge.

Bonnet, M. (2013) 'Sustainable Development, Environmental Education and the Significance of Being in Place', *The Curriculum Journal*, 24:2, 250–71, available at DOI: 10.1080/09585176.2013.792672

Brandt, W. (1980) *North-South: A Programme for Survival*, London: The Brandt Commission, Pan Books.

Bruner, J. (1960) *The Process of Education*, Cambridge, MA: Harvard University Press.

Capra, F. (1997) *The Web of Life*, London: Flamingo.

Capra, F., and Luisi, P. (2014) *The Systems View of Life: A Unifying Vision*, Cambridge: Cambridge University Press.

Cardek, O. (2009). 'Science Students' Misconceptions of the Water Cycle According to their Drawings', *Journal of Applied Sciences* 9: 865–73, available at https://scialert.net/abstract/?doi=jas.2009.865.873.

Carson, R. (1962) *Silent Spring*, New York: Fawcett Crest.

Catling, S., Greenwood, R., Martin, F., and Owens, P. (2010) 'Formative Experiences of Primary Geography Educators', *International Research in Geography and Environmental Education*, 19:4.

Clift, R., Sim, S., King, H., Chenoweth, J., Christie, I., Clavreul, J., Mueller, C., Posthuma, L., Boulay, A.-M., Chaplin-Kramer, R., et al. (2017) 'The Challenges of Applying Planetary Boundaries as a Basis for Strategic Decision-Making in Companies with Global Supply Chains', *Sustainability* 9:2, 279, available at https://doi.org/10.3390/su9020279.

Cremin, T., Barnes, J., and Scoffham, S. (2009) *Creative Teaching for Tomorrow: Fostering a Creative State of Mind*, Deal: Future Creative.

Daly, H. E. (2008) 'A Steady State Economy', *The Ecologist*, available at https://theecologist.org/2008/apr/01/steady-state-economy.

Dasgupta, P. (2021) *The Economics of Biodiversity: The Dasgupta Review, Abridged Version*. London: HM Treasury, available at https://assets.publishing.service.gov.uk/government/uploads/system/uploads/attachment_data/file/957292/Dasgupta_Review_-_Abridged_Version.pdf.

Davies, L., Harber, C., and Yamashita, H. (2005) *Key findings from the DFID project, Global Citizenship: The Needs of Teachers and Learners*, Birmingham: Centre for International Education and Research, University of Birmingham.

Dolan, A. M. (2022) *Teaching Climate Change in Primary Schools*, London: Routledge.

Earth Charter (2000) available at https://earthcharter.org/library/the-earth-charter-text/.

Eaude, T. (2017) 'Humanities in the Primary School – Philosophical Considerations', *Education 3–13* 45:3, 343–53.

Ehrlich, P. (1968) *The Population Bomb*, New York: Buccaneer Books.

Fischer, M. B. E. (2009) 'Building a Scientific Groundwork for Learning and Teaching' in Christodoulou et al. (eds) *Usable Knowledge*.

Fore, H. (2019) 'Foreword' in *The State of the World's Children 2019*, New York: UNICEF.

Fore, H. (2021) 'Climate change is the other planetary crisis that won't wait', available at https://www.unicef.org/reimagine/five-opportunities-children-open-letter Accessed 22.02.2021.

Frandy, T. (2018) 'Indigenizing Sustainabilities, Sustaining Indigeneities: Decolonization, Sustainability, and Education', *Journal of Sustainability Education* 18, available at http://www.journalofsustainabilityeducation.org/.

Fredrickson, B. (2000) 'The Broaden-and-Build Theory of Positive Emotions', *Philosophical Transactions of the Royal Society* 359 no. 1449: 1367–77.

Freire, P. (1970, 2007) *Pedagogy of the Oppressed*, New York: Continuum.

Freire, P. (2004) *Pedagogy of Hope*, London: Continuum.

Gardner, H. (1993) *Frames of Mind: The Theory of Multiple Intelligences*, London: Fontana.

Gilbert, I. (2014) *Independent Thinking*, Carmarthen: Independent Thinking Press.

Gorman, A. (2021) *Earthrise*, available at https://www.youtube.com/watch?v=xwOvBv8RLmo.

Harari. Y. N. (2015) *Sapiens: A Brief History of Humankind*, London: Vintage.

Haraway, D. (2016) *Staying with the Trouble: Making Kin in the Chthulucene* (Experimental Futures). Durham, NC: Duke University Press.

Heggen, M. P., Sageidet, B. M., Goga, N., Grindheim, L. T., Bergan, V., Krempig, I. M., Utsi, T. A., and Lynngård, A. M. (2019) 'Children as eco-citizens?', *Nordina* 15:4, 387–402.

Helm, D. (2020) *Net Zero: How We Can Stop Climate Change*, London: Collins.

Hicks, D. (2006) *Lessons for the Future*, Victoria, BC and Oxford: Trafford.

Hicks, D. (2014) *Educating for Hope in Troubled Times: Climate Change and the Transition to a Post-Carbon Future*. London: Institute of Education Press.

Holmgren, D. (2020) *Essence of Permaculture*. Melbourne: Melliodora Publishing.

Horvath, J. (2016) *Educating Young Children Through Natural Water*, London: Routledge.

Howard-Jones, P., Sands, D., Dillon, J., and Fenton-Jones, F. (2021) 'The Views of Teachers in England on an Action-Orientated Climate Change Curriculum', *Environmental Education Research* 1–37, available at DOI: 10.1080/13504622.2021.1937576

Hulme, M. (2014) *Can Science Fix Climate Change?*, Cambridge: Polity Press.

Immordino-Yang, M., and Damasio, A. (2007) 'We Feel Therefore We Learn: The Relevance of Affective and Social Neuroscience to Education', *Mind, Brain and Education* 1, 3–10.

Immordino-Yang, M., Dorling-Hammond, L., and Krone, C. R. (2018) *The Brain Basis for Integrated Social, Emotional and Academic Development*, Washington, DC: Aspen Institute, available at https://www.aspeninstitute.org/wp-content/uploads/2018/09/Aspen_research_FINAL_web.pdf

Immordino-Yang, M., Darling-Hammond, L., and Krone, C. R. (2019) 'Nurturing Nature: How Brain Development is Inherently Social and Emotional, and What This Means For Education', *Educational Psychologist* 54:3, 185–204.

Ingold, T. (2011) *Being Alive: Essays on Movement, Knowledge and Description*, London: Routledge.

IPCC (2021) *Climate Change: The Physical Science Basis*, available at https://www.ipcc.ch/report/ar6/wg1/.

Jackson, T. (2017) *Prosperity Without Growth* (2nd edn), London: Routledge.

Jensen, J. (2014) 'Learning Opportunities for Sustainability in the Humanities' in Boring, W. P., and Forbes, W. (eds), *Teaching Sustainability*, Nacogdoches, TX: Stephen F. Austin State University Press.

Kellert, S. R. (2012) *Birthright: People and Nature in the Modern World*, New Haven and London: Yale University Press.

Kemp, N., and Scoffham, S. (2022) 'The Paradox Model: Towards a Conceptual Framework for Engaging with Sustainability in Higher Education', *International Journal of Sustainability in Higher Education* 23:1.

Kingsnorth, P., and Hine, D. (2009) *Uncivilization: The Dark Mountain Manifesto*.

Klein, N. (2014) *This Changes Everything*, London: Penguin.

Kollmuss, A., and Aygeman, J. (2002) 'Mind the Gap: Why do people act environmentally and what are the barriers to pro-environmental behaviour?', *Environmental Education Research*, 8:3, 241–59.

Kuhn, T. (1962) *The Structure of Scientific Revolutions*, Chicago: The University of Chicago Press.

Kumar, S. (2009) 'Grounded Economic Awareness' in Stibbe, A. (ed.), *The Handbook of Sustainability Literacy*, Totnes: Green Books.

Kumar, S. (2021) 'The Primary Geography Interview', *Primary Geography* 106: 16–18.

Lambert, D. (2013) 'Subject Teachers in Knowledge-Led Schools' in Young, M., and Lambert, D. (eds), *Knowledge and the Future School*, London: Bloomsbury.

Lander, L. (2017) 'Education for Sustainability: A Wisdom Model' in Leal Filho, W., Mifsud, M., Shiel, C., and Pretorius, R. (eds), *Handbook of Theory and Practice of Sustainability in Higher Education 3*, New York: Springer.

Lent, J. (2017) *The Patterning Instinct: A Cultural History of Humanity's Search for Meaning*, Amherst, NY: Prometheus Books.

Leopold, L. B. (ed.) (1993) *Round River: From the Journals of Aldo Leopold*, Oxford: Oxford University Press.

Levinas, E. (2005). *Humanism of the Other*, Urbana and Chicago: University of Illinois Press.

Locke, J. (1693, 1970), *Some Thoughts Concerning Education*, London: Scholar Press.

Lovelock, J. (2000) *Gaia: A New Look at Life on Earth*, Oxford: Oxford University Press.

Machobane, J. J., and Berold, R. (2003). *Drive out hunger: The story of JJ Machobane of Lesotho*, Bellevue, South Africa: Jacana.

Mackintosh, M. (2004) 'Children's Understanding of Rivers' in Catling, S., and Martin, F. (eds), *Researching Primary Geography*, London: Register of Research in Primary Geography.

Macy, J., and Johnstone, C. (2012) *Active Hope*, Novato, CA: New World Library.

Markinowski, T., and Reid, A. (2019) 'Reviews of Research on the Attitude–Behavior Relationship and Their Implications for Future Environmental Education Research', *Environmental Education Research* 25:4, 459–71.

Marshall, G. (2015) *Don't Even Think About It*, London: Bloomsbury.

Maxton, G., and Randers, J. (2016) *Reinventing Prosperity*, Vancouver: Greystone Books.

May, T. (1998) 'Children's Ideas About Rivers' in Scoffham, S. (ed.), *Primary Sources*, Sheffield: Geographical Association.

McIntyre, N., Parveen, N., and Thomas, T. (2021) 'Exclusion rates five times higher for black Caribbean pupils in parts of England', *The Guardian*, 24 March 2021, available at https://www.theguardian.com/education/2021/mar/24/exclusion-rates-black-caribbean-pupils-england.

McLuhan, M. (1962, 2011) *The Gutenberg Galaxy: The Making of Typographic Man,* Toronto: University of Toronto Press.

Meadows, D. H., Meadows, D. L., Randers, J., and Behrens, W. W. III (1972) *The Limits to Growth*, New York: Universe Books.

Mezirow, J. (1985) 'A Critical Theory of Self-Directed Learning', *New Directions for Adult and Continuing Education* 25: 17–30.

Monbiot, G. (2016) 'Neo-liberalism – the ideology at the root of all our problems', *The Guardian*, 15 April 2016, available at https://www.theguardian.com/books/2016/apr/15/neoliberalism-ideology-problem-george-monbiot.

Monbiot, G. (2017) *Out of the Wreckage*, London: Verso.

Moss, A., Jensen, E., and Gusset, M. (2016) 'Probing the Link Between Biodiversity-Related Knowledge and Self-Reported Proconservation Behaviour in a Global Survey of Zoo Visitors', *Conservation Letters* 10:1, 33–40.

Neimanis, A. (2017) *Bodies of Water*, London: Bloomsbury.

Orr, D. (1994) *Earth in Mind: On Education, the Environment and the Human Project*, Washington, DC: Island Press.

Orr, D. (2014) 'Foreword' in Boring, W. P., and Forbes, W. (eds), *Teaching Sustainability*, Nascogdoches, TX: Stephen F. Austin State University Press.

Otto, R. (1923) *The Idea of the Holy*, Oxford: Oxford University Press.

Owens, P., Scoffham, S., Vujakovic, P., and Bass, A. (2020) 'Meaningful Maps', *Primary Geography* 102, 15–17.

Palmer, J. (1998) 'Environmental Cognition in Young Children' in Scoffham, S. (ed.), *Primary Sources*, Sheffield: Geographical Association.

Parkin, S. (2010) *The Positive Deviant: Sustainability Leadership in a Perverse World*, London: Routledge.

Piaget, J. (1928) *The Child's Conception of the World*, London: Routledge & Kegan Paul.

Porritt, J. (2013) *The World We Made*, London: Phaidon.

Pulido, L. (1996) *Environmentalism and Economic Justice*, Tucson: University of Arizona Press.

Raworth, K. (2017) *Doughnut Economics: Seven Ways to Think Like a 21st-Century Economist*, London: Random House.

Read, R., and Alexander, S. (2018) *This Civilization is Finished*, Melbourne: Simplicity Institute.

Readman, J. (2006) *George Saves the World By Lunchtime*, London: Penguin.

Rees, W. (2021) 'Climate Change Isn't the Problem So What Is?', keynote lecture delivered at Tel Aviv University, 28 January, available at https://www.youtube.com/watch?v=9oVTHKzC7TM&feature=youtu.be.

Rittel, H. W. J., and Webber, M. M. (1973) 'Dilemmas in General Theory of Planning', *Policy Sciences* 4:2, 155–69.

Rockström, J. (2020) 'Ten years to transform the future of humanity – or destabilize the planet', *TED talk*, available at https://www.ted.com/talks/johan_rockstrom_10_years_to_transform_the_future_of_humanity_or_destabilize_the_planet?language=en#t-44.

Rockström, J., and Klum, M. (2015) *Big World Small Planet*, Stockholm: Max Ström Publishing.

Schudel, I. J. (2017) 'Modelling dialectical processes in environmental learning: An elaboration of Roy Bhaskar's onto-axiological chain', *Journal of Critical Realism* 16:2, 163–83, available at di://dx.doi.org/10.1080/14767430.2017.12880.

Schwartz, S. H. (1992), 'Universals in the Content and Structure of Values: Theoretical Advances and Empirical Tests in 20 Countries', *Advances in Experimental Social Psychology* 25, 1–65.

Schwartz, S. H. (2012) 'An Overview of the Schwartz Theory of Basic Values', *Online Readings in Psychology and Culture* 2:1, available at https://doi.org/10.9707/2307-0919.1116.

Scoffham, S. (1980) *Using the School Surroundings*, London: Ward Lock Educational.

Scoffham, S. (2013) 'A Question of Research', *Primary Geography* 80, 16–17.

Scoffham, S. (2015) Should Children be Learning About Climate Change?' in Sangster, M. (ed.), *Challenging Perceptions in Primary Education*, London: Bloomsbury.

Scoffham, S., and Barnes, J. (2011) 'Happiness Matters: Towards a Pedagogy of Happiness and Well-being', *The Curriculum Journal* 22:4, 535–48.

Scott, W., and Vare, P. (2018) *The World We'll Leave Behind: Grasping the Sustainability Challenge*, London: Routledge.

Scott, W., and Vare, P. (2021) *Learning, Environment and Sustainable Development*, London: Routledge.

Sheldrake, M. (2020) *Entangled Life*, London: Bodley Head.

Sloane, S., Baillargeon, R., and Premack, D. (2019) 'Do Infants Have a Sense of Fairness?', *Psychological Science*, available at https://journals.sagepub.com/doi/full/10.1177/0956797611422072.

Sobel, D. (2008) *Childhood and Nature: Design Principles for Educators*, Portsmouth, NH: Stenhouse Publishers.

Speth, J. G. (2008) *The Bridge at the Edge of the World*, New Haven and London: Yale University Press.

Stenhouse, L. (1975) *An Introduction to Curriculum Research and Development*, London: Heinemann.

Sterling, S. (2001) *Sustainable Education: Revisioning Learning and Change*, Dartington: Green Books.

Sterling, S. (2019) 'Planetary Primacy and the Necessity of Positive Dis-Illusion', *Sustainability* 12:2, 60–6.

Stern, N. (2006) *The Economics of Climate Change: The Stern Review*, London: HM Treasury, available at https://webarchive.nationalarchives.gov.uk/+/http://www.hmtreasury.gov.uk/media/4/3/executive_summary.pdf.

Sustainable Solutions Development Network (2020) *Accelerating Education for the SDGs in Universities*, available at https://resources.unsdsn.org/accelerating-education-for-the-sdgs-in-universities-a-guide-for-universities-colleges-and-tertiary-and-higher-education-institutions?mc_cid=57cd628037&mc_eid=726fdf3cb.

Swanson, A. (2015) 'How China used more cement in 3 years than the U.S. did in the entire 20th Century', *The Washington Post*, 24 March 2015, available at https://www.washingtonpost.com/news/

wonk/wp/2015/03/24/how-china-used-more-cement-in-3-years-than-the-u-s-did-in-the-entire-20th-century/.

Thunberg, G. (2019) *No One Is Too Small to Make a Difference*, London: Penguin.

Thunberg, G. (2019) Speech to the United Nations Climate Action Summit, New York, 23 September, available at https://www.nbcnews.com/news/world/read-greta-thunberg-s-full-speech-united-nations-climate-action-n1057861.

UN (1948) *Universal declaration of Human Rights*, available at https://www.un.org/en/about-us/universal-declaration-of-human-rights.

UN (2021) *Population*, available at https://www.un.org/en/sections/issues-depth/population/.

UN (2021) *Sustainable Development Goals*, available at https://sdgs.un.org/goals.

UNESCO (2017) *Education for Sustainable Development: Learning Goals*, available at https://unesdoc.unesco.org/ark:/48223/pf0000247444.

UNESCO (2019) *What is Education for Sustainable Development?*, available at https://en.unesco.org/themes/education-sustainable-development/what-is-esd.

Unicef-UK (1992) 'How we protect children's rights', available at https://www.unicef.org.uk/what-we-do/un-conv-tio'n-child-rights/.

Vane-Wright, R. J. (2009) 'Planetary Awareness, World Views and the Conservation of Biodiversity' in Kellert, S. R., and Speth, J. (eds), *The Coming Transition*, New Haven: Yale School of Forestry and Environmental Studies.

Wainaina, B. (2005) 'How to write about Africa', *Granta* 92.

Wenger, E. (1998) *Communities of Practice: Learning, Meaning and Identity*, New York: Cambridge University Press.

Wheelan, B. (1995) 'Riverdance' from *Riverdance (Music from The Show)*, track 8, Dublin: Celtic Heartbeat.

Whittle, J. (2016) 'Editorial', *Primary Geography* 90.

Wildlife Trust (2017) *The River Otter Beaver Trial Science and Evidence Report*, available at https://www.exeter.ac.uk/creww/research/beavertrial/.

Wilkinson, R., and Pickett, J. (2018) *The Inner Level*, London: Penguin.

Witt, S., & Clarke, H. (2016) 'Rescuing the earth through small world play', in Winograd, K. (ed.), *Education in Times of Environmental Crises: Teaching Children to Be Agents of Change*, London: Routledge, 219–33.

World Commission for Environment and Development (1987) *Our Common Future*, Oxford: Oxford University Press.

WWF (2018) *Living Planet Report 2018: Aiming Higher*, Grooten, M., and Almond, R. E. A. (eds), Gland, Switzerland: WWF, available at https://www.worldwildlife.org/publications/living-planet-report-2018.

WWF (2020) *Living Planet Report 2020 – Bending the Curve of Biodiversity Loss*, Almond, R. E. A., Grooten, M., and Petersen, T. (eds), Gland, Switzerland: WWF, available at https://c402277.ssl.cf1.rackcdn.com/publications/1371/files/original/ENGLISH-FULL.pdf?1599693362.

Index

www.ingramcontent.com/pod-product-compliance
Ingram Content Group UK Ltd.
Pitfield, Milton Keynes, MK11 3LW, UK
UKHW010024280225
455688UK00006B/266